Betty Crocker

ANNUAL RECIPES

Betty Crocker, Betty Crocker Original Supreme, Betty Crocker Potato Buds, Betty Crocker Rich & Creamy, Betty Crocker SuperMoist, Betty Crocker Supreme, Bisquick, Cheerios, Chex, Cocoa Puffs, Country Corn Flakes, Green Giant, Green Giant LeSueur, Green Giant Mexicorn, Green Giant Niblets, Green Giant Select, Gold Medal, Gold Medal Better for Bread, Gold Medal Wondra, Golden Grahams, Old El Paso, Pasta Accents, Yoplait, are registered trademarks of General Mills, Inc.

This edition published by arrangement with Wiley Publishing, Inc.

General Mills, Inc.
Betty Crocker Kitchens
Director, Book and Online Publishing: Kim Walter
Manager, Publishing: Lois Tlusty
Recipe Development and Testing: Betty Crocker Kitchens
Food Stylists: Betty Crocker Kitchens
Photography: General Mills Photo Studio

Editor: Kimberly Tweed
Book Designer: Tracey J. Hambleton

For consistent baking results, the Betty Crocker Kitchens recommend Gold Medal Flour.

ISBN-13 978–1–60529–715–6 hardcover

Printed in the United States of America

2   4   6   8   10   9   7   5   3   1   hardcover

Cover: White Silk Raspberry Tart (page 260)

For more great ideas, visit www.bettycrocker.com

C O N T E N T S

Chili with Corn Dumplings (page 99)

Introduction

Here it is, the latest edition of *Betty Crocker Annual Recipes*, and once again we've taken your favorite recipes from *Betty Crocker* magazine and compiled them into one convenient collection. Among these more than 240 delicious recipes, you are sure to find something to please every friend or family member—whether they enjoy sweet treats like gooey Caramel Brownies or savory meals like Creamy Chicken Lasagna—it's all inside.

Start any morning off right by serving mouthwatering dishes like Cheese-Stuffed Hash Browns, Stuffed French Toast Strata with Orange Syrup and Roasted-Vegetable Egg Bake. Pull together delicious lunches with Dill Shrimp and Egg Salad Wraps, Ham and Cheese Tortilla Roll-Ups or Baked Turkey, Cheddar and Bacon Sandwiches.

Impress your friends and neighbors at your next get-together by serving up beautiful and delicious appetizers such as Gorgonzola- and Hazelnut-Stuffed Mushrooms, Brie and Cherry Pastry Cups and Dried Fruit and Cream Cheese Roulade. And be the hit of any bake sale by whipping up Cookies 'n Creme Brownies, Chocolate Chunk Blondies or Raspberry Cheesecake Bars.

Besides hundreds of tasty recipes, you'll also find pages of new information, such as fun ways to spice up your soups, salads and sandwiches and incredible tips to bake a perfect cake every time. We've also given you 15 innovative menu plans to help make every meal extraordinary—from game days and slumber parties to New Year's Eve and special dinners for just the two of you.

You'll also find "Quick" labels on all the recipes that can be prepared in less than 30 minutes—still allowing you to create a fantastic meal even when you're short on time. Imagine things like Bow-Tie Pasta with Beef and Tomatoes, Creamy Salmon with Gemelli and Vegetables and Southwest Chicken and Couscous on your table in no time flat.

For those looking for delicious food with little fat, we provide the "Low Fat" label on any dish that has 6 grams or less of fat per serving—side dishes and desserts have 3 grams or less. With fantastic choices like Chicken Breasts with Cucumber Peach Salsa, Honey-Orange Ham, Grilled Caramel Apples and Graham and Fruit Bars, you'll never feel deprived again while watching your weight.

And to help you sort through this year's collection of recipes, we've again included a list of recipes arranged by season, allowing you to choose the perfect dish, no matter what the weather. And of course, there is also a beautiful full-color photo for each recipe to help you see how wonderful your finished meals will look on the table.

We hope you enjoy this edition of *Betty Crocker Annual Recipes*. Thanks for joining us once again!

Betty Crocker

Inspired Entertaining

MENU IDEAS TO MAKE EVERY OCCASION SPECIAL

Time spent with friends and family is even more special when you can share delicious meals that you've prepared yourself. Try one of these innovative menus to put together an entire meal that will surely make your special guests feel warm and welcome no matter what the occasion. Whether you have a crowd gathered on a snowy day to watch the game, you're entertaining kids at a slumber party or you're grilling in the backyard to welcome summer, you'll find great ways to combine recipes to prepare a delicious meal from start to finish.

To Chase the Chills

Pepper Jack Cheese Quick Bread (page 12)

Chili with Corn Dumplings (page 99)

Two-Berry Crisp with Pecan Streusel Topping (page 269)

Hot Cocoa or Cider

The Big Game

Appetizer Beer-Cheese Fondue (page 29)

Chipotle Chicken Drummettes (page 40)

London Broil Sandwiches with Lemon Mayonnaise (page 72)

Easy Macaroni and Cheese (page 130)

Peanut Butter Swirl Brownies (page 237)

Assorted Beer and Soda

Family Night

California BLT Salad (page 117)

Creamy Chicken Lasagna (page 165)

Chocolate Strawberry Shortcakes (page 264)

Milk and Juice

Dinner for Two

Raspberry-Poppy Seed Salad (page 103)

Chicken Breasts with Cucumber Peach Salsa (page 159)

Green Beans with Browned Butter (page 220)

White Silk Raspberry Tart (page 260)

Wine

Sunday Brunch

Scrambled Eggs Alfredo Bake (page 6)

Stuffed French Toast Strata with Orange Syrup (page 2)

Cheese-Stuffed Hash Browns (page 10)

Mixed Fruit Salad (page 8)

Coffee and Tea

Mimosas

Assorted Juices

Spring Supper

Tropical Fruit and Spinach Salad (page 113)

Shrimp Pilaf Florentine (page 133)

Berry Angel Delight (page 262)

Iced Tea

Welcome the Neighbors

Caramelized-Onion Bruschetta (page 43)

Spring Ravioli with Pesto Cream (page 130)

Tropical Fruit Dip for Cookies and Fruit (page 246)

Iced Tea, Coffee and Tea

Ladies' Luncheon

Basil- and Crabmeat-Topped Cucumbers (page 38)

Apple-Pear Salad (page 103)

Dill Shrimp and Egg Salad Wraps (page 55)

Caramel-Carrot Cake (page 279)

Iced Tea, Coffee and Tea

Friday Night Slumber Party

Pool-Side Supper

Grilled to Perfection

July 4th Celebration

Fall Feast

Holiday Hoopla

Ring in the New Year

Seasonal Selections

Looking for something special to make that suits the season perfectly? Take your pick from this helpful list of recipes, grouped by season, to select just the right dish—any time of year.

Spring

Winter

Anytime

Breakfasts and Breads

Great for Morning or Anytime

Bacon and Egg Enchiladas (page 3)

Popovers (page 21)

Stuffed French Toast Strata with Orange Syrup

Prep: 15 min Refrigerate: 6 hr Bake: 45 min

12   slices raisin-cinnamon bread
$^1/_2$ cup pineapple cream cheese spread (from 8-ounce container)
$^1/_2$ cup orange marmalade
2   tablespoons butter or margarine, softened
4   eggs
$1^1/_2$ cups milk
1   teaspoon vanilla extract
     Orange Syrup (below)

1. Spray rectangular baking dish, 13 × 9 × 2 inches, with cooking spray. Toast 6 slices of the bread; place in pan. Spread each slice of toast evenly with cream cheese and marmalade. Butter remaining bread slices; place butter sides up on toast.

2. Beat eggs, milk and vanilla in medium bowl with wire whisk until blended. Pour over bread. Cover with aluminum foil and refrigerate at least 6 hours or overnight.

3. Heat oven to 350°. Uncover and bake 35 to 45 minutes or until deep golden brown and slightly puffed. Cut between bread slices. Serve with Orange Syrup.

6 servings.

Orange Syrup
$^3/_4$ cup light corn syrup
$^1/_4$ cup frozen orange juice concentrate

Mix ingredients in small microwavable bowl. Microwave uncovered on High about 1 minute or until heated.

1 Serving: Calories 535 (Calories from Fat 155); Fat 17g (Saturated 9g); Cholesterol 180mg; Sodium 490mg; Carbohydrate 84g (Dietary Fiber 2g); Protein 12g
% Daily Value: Vitamin A 14%; Vitamin C 16%; Calcium 16%; Iron 14%
Exchanges: 4 Starch, $1^1/_2$ Other Carbohydrate, 3 Fat
Carbohydrate Choices: $5^1/_2$

BETTY'S TIPS

⊕ **Health Twist**
For 500 calories and 14 grams of fat per serving, substitute 1 cup of fat-free cholesterol-free egg product for the 4 eggs.

⊕ **Variation**
For a sweet treat, try the Orange Syrup poured over vanilla ice cream.

⊕ **Do-Ahead**
This is a perfect dish for a company brunch. The work is done the night before, and the strata bakes while you set the table and prepare the rest of the meal.

Stuffed French Toast Strata with Orange Syrup

Bacon and Egg Enchiladas

Prep: 20 min Bake: 20 min
(Photo on page 1)

12   slices bacon

10   eggs

$^1/_2$ cup milk

$^1/_2$ teaspoon onion powder

$^1/_2$ teaspoon ground cumin

2   cans (10 ounces each) Old El Paso® red or green enchilada sauce

10   flour tortillas (8 inches in diameter)

2   cups shredded Mexican cheese blend (8 ounces)

Sour cream, if desired

Taco sauce, if desired

1. Heat oven to 350°. Spray rectangular baking dish, 13 × 9 × 2 inches, with cooking spray. Cook bacon in 10-inch skillet over medium heat, turning occasionally, until very crisp. Remove bacon from skillet, reserving 1 tablespoon drippings in skillet. Drain bacon on paper towels; crumble bacon and set aside.

2. Beat eggs, milk, onion powder and cumin in medium bowl with wire whisk until well blended. Pour into skillet with bacon drippings. As mixture begins to set at bottom and side, gently lift cooked portions with metal spatula so that thin, uncooked portion can flow to bottom. Avoid constant stirring. Cook 5 to 7 minutes or until eggs are thickened throughout but still moist. Do not overcook.

3. Pour $^1/_2$ can enchilada sauce over bottom of baking dish. Fill each tortilla with about $^1/_3$ cup eggs, 1 tablespoon bacon and 2 tablespoons cheese; roll up. Place seam side down on enchilada sauce in dish. Pour remaining $1^1/_2$ cans enchilada sauce over filled tortillas. Top with remaining cheese and bacon.

4. Bake uncovered about 20 minutes or until thoroughly heated and bubbly. Serve with sour cream and taco sauce.

10 servings.
1 Serving: Calories 370 (Calories from Fat 180); Fat 20g (Saturated 9g); Cholesterol 245mg; Sodium 820mg; Carbohydrate 29g (Dietary Fiber 2g); Protein 19g
% Daily Value: Vitamin A 20%; Vitamin C 6%; Calcium 22%; Iron 16%
Exchanges: 2 Starch, 3 Medium-Fat Meat, $1^1/_2$ Fat
Carbohydrate Choices: 2

BETTY'S TIPS

❂ **Time-Saver**
Packages or jars of cooked bacon pieces are available in the refrigerated meat section and salad dressing section of the grocery store. They can be used instead of the freshly cooked bacon. Substitute 1 tablespoon oil for the bacon drippings.

❂ **Do-Ahead**
Assemble this quick brunch dish up to 4 hours ahead, cover and refrigerate. Bake uncovered for 30 minutes. You may find that the tortillas will be a little softer than if the dish were baked immediately, but the flavor will be just as delicious.

❂ **Did You Know?**
Green enchilada sauce is made with mild green chiles and is milder than red enchilada sauce. Take your pick—both are equally good in this recipe.

Rancher's Egg Bake

Prep: 10 Min Cool: 30 min Bake: 1 hr 28 min Stand: 10 min

1²/₃ cups Original Bisquick® mix

1 tablespoon Old El Paso taco seasoning mix (from 1.25-ounce package)

¹/₃ cup milk

8 eggs, slightly beaten

3 cups milk

¹/₂ cup chopped drained roasted red bell peppers (from 7-ounce jar)

1 can (4.5 ounces) Old El Paso chopped green chiles, drained

1 cup shredded Mexican 4-cheese blend (4 ounces)

1. Heat oven to 450°. Generously grease bottom and sides of rectangular baking dish, 13 × 9 × 2 inches, with shortening. Stir Bisquick mix, taco seasoning mix and ¹/₃ cup milk until soft dough forms. Pat dough on bottom of baking dish. Bake 8 minutes. Cool 30 minutes.

2. Heat oven to 350°. Beat eggs, 3 cups milk, bell peppers and chiles in medium bowl with wire whisk or fork until blended. Pour over crust.

3. Cover and bake 30 minutes. Uncover and bake 40 to 50 minutes longer or until knife inserted in center comes out clean. Sprinkle with cheese. Let stand 10 minutes before cutting.

8 servings.
1 Serving: Calories 290 (Calories from Fat 135); Fat 15g (Saturated 6g); Cholesterol 235mg; Sodium 680mg; Carbohydrate 24g (Dietary Fiber 1g); Protein 15g
% Daily Value: Vitamin A 28%; Vitamin C 22%; Calcium 28%; Iron 10%
Exchanges: 1 Starch, 1 High-Fat Meat, ¹/₂ Milk, 1¹/₂ Fat
Carbohydrate Choices: 1¹/₂

BETTY'S TIPS

⚙ **Special Touch**
Garnish this cheesy southwestern-style egg bake with sour cream, cherry tomato quarters and avocado slices, then sprinkle a little taco seasoning mix over the sour cream.

Rancher's Egg Bake

Quick

Ham and Corn Frittata

Prep: 10 min Cook: 17 min

8 eggs

½ cup diced provolone or mozzarella cheese (2 ounces)

½ cup fresh corn kernels or Green Giant® Niblets frozen corn

2 tablespoons chopped fresh chives

2 tablespoons chopped parsley

¼ teaspoon salt

¼ teaspoon pepper

½ cup diced fully cooked ham (2 ounces)

1 tablespoon butter or margarine

1. Beat all ingredients except ham and butter in medium bowl with fork or wire whisk until well mixed. Stir in ham.

2. Melt butter in 10-inch nonstick skillet over medium-low heat. Pour mixture into skillet. Cover and cook 14 to 17 minutes or until eggs are set in center and light brown on the bottom. Turn upside down onto serving plate.

6 servings.
1 Serving: Calories 185 (Calories from Fat 115); Fat 13g (Saturated 6g); Cholesterol 300mg; Sodium 380mg; Carbohydrate 3g (Dietary Fiber 0g); Protein 13g
% Daily Value: Vitamin A 14%; Vitamin C 2%; Calcium 10%; Iron 6%
Exchanges: 2 Medium-Fat Meat, 1 Fat
Carbohydrate Choices: 0

BETTY'S TIPS

☻ **Substitution**
You can use any of your favorite semihard cheeses in this egg dish. Cheddar, Monterey Jack and Swiss are all good choices.

☻ **Time-Saver**
Look for packaged diced cooked ham in the meat department of the grocery store. You may want to cut the ham into smaller pieces if some of them are too big.

☻ **Serve-With**
Warm corn muffins, fresh fruit and sherbet are terrific accompaniments to this quick egg dish.

Ham and Corn Frittata

Scrambled Eggs Alfredo Bake

Prep: 20 min Bake: 15 min

- 1 cup Original Bisquick mix
- ¼ teaspoon Italian seasoning
- 6 tablespoons firm butter or margarine
- 1 egg
- ¼ cup chopped onion
- ¼ cup chopped green bell pepper
- 1 jar (4.5 ounces) Green Giant sliced mushrooms, drained
- 12 eggs, beaten
- ⅓ cup crumbled precooked bacon
- ¾ cup Alfredo pasta sauce

1. Heat oven to 400°. Spray square baking dish, 8 × 8 × 2 inches, with cooking spray. Mix Bisquick mix, Italian seasoning and 4 tablespoons of butter in small bowl with fork or pastry blender until crumbly. Gently stir in egg; set aside.

2. Melt remaining 2 tablespoons butter in 12-inch nonstick skillet over medium heat. Cook onion, bell pepper and mushrooms in butter 3 to 5 minutes, stirring occasionally, until vegetables are crisp-tender. Add eggs to vegetable mixture. Cook, stirring occasionally, until eggs are set; remove from heat. Gently stir in bacon and Alfredo sauce. Spread into baking dish. Sprinkle Bisquick mixture over eggs.

3. Bake uncovered about 15 minutes until topping is golden brown.

6 servings.
1 Serving: Calories 485 (Calories from Fat 340); Fat 38g (Saturated 18g); Cholesterol 520mg; Sodium 770mg; Carbohydrate 17g (Dietary Fiber 1g); Protein 19g
% Daily Value: Vitamin A 28%; Vitamin C 4%; Calcium 18%; Iron 12%
Exchanges: 1 Starch, 2½ High-Fat Meat, 3 Fat
Carbohydrate Choices: 1

BETTY'S TIPS

⚙ **Success Hint**
Part of the quick and easy preparation is using pre-cooked bacon slices. Look for packages of these convenient bacon strips in the section with the regular bacon.

⚙ **Serve-With**
This casserole can be served with a bowl of fresh berries or melon and warm breadsticks.

Scrambled Eggs Alfredo Bake

Roasted-Vegetable Egg Bake

Prep: 15 min Bake: 30 min

1 tablespoon olive or vegetable oil

1 large onion, chopped (1 cup)

1 bag (1 pound 10 ounces) Green Giant Create
a Meal!® frozen oven roasted Parmesan herb
meal starter

1 cup Original Bisquick mix

1 1/2 cups milk

4 eggs

1 cup shredded colby, Monterey Jack or
mozzarella cheese (4 ounces)

1. Heat oven to 400°. Spray rectangular baking dish,
13 × 9 × 2 inches, with cooking spray. Heat oil in
12-inch nonstick skillet over medium heat. Cook
onion and frozen vegetables in oil 8 to 10 minutes,
stirring occasionally, until vegetables are heated
through and crisp-tender. Sprinkle vegetables with
contents of seasoning packet from vegetables; stir
gently to coat. Spread in baking dish.

2. Stir Bisquick mix, milk and eggs until blended. Pour
over vegetables in baking dish.

3. Bake uncovered about 25 minutes or until knife
inserted in center comes out clean. Sprinkle with
cheese. Bake about 5 minutes or until cheese is
melted.

8 servings.
1 Serving: Calories 280 (Calories from Fat 115); Fat 13g (Saturated 6g);
Cholesterol 130mg; Sodium 980mg; Carbohydrate 27g (Dietary Fiber
2g); Protein 14g
% Daily Value: Vitamin A 22%; Vitamin C 8%; Calcium 24%; Iron 8%
Exchanges: 2 Starch, 1 Medium-Fat Meat, 1 Fat
Carbohydrate Choices: 2

BETTY'S TIPS

⊕ **Substitution**
There are other Create a Meal! frozen oven roasted vegetable blends available with slightly different vegetable
combinations and seasonings. Any of them can be used
in this recipe.

⊕ **Variation**
If you'd like, you can add 1 cup chopped cooked chicken
or turkey with the seasoning packet from the frozen
vegetables.

Roasted-Vegetable Egg Bake

Mixed Fruit Salad

Prep: 10 min

1 cup vanilla yogurt

1 tablespoon mayonnaise or salad dressing

$1/4$ teaspoon grated orange peel

2 tablespoons orange juice

6 cups cut-up assorted fresh fruit (melon, berries, grapes)

1. Mix yogurt, mayonnaise, orange peel and orange juice in large bowl.

2. Gently stir in fruit. Store covered in refrigerator.

12 servings ($1/2$ cup each).
1 Serving: Calories 75 (Calories from Fat 20); Fat 2g (Saturated 1g); Cholesterol 0mg; Sodium 25mg; Carbohydrate 13g (Dietary Fiber 2g); Protein 2g
% Daily Value: Vitamin A 8%; Vitamin C 60%; Calcium 4%; Iron 2%
Exchanges: 1 Fruit, $1/2$ Fat
Carbohydrate Choices: 1

BETTY'S TIPS

⚙ **Substitution**
Grated lime peel and lime juice can be used instead of orange.

⚙ **Health Twist**
For 1 gram of fat and 60 calories per serving, use vanilla fat-free yogurt and reduced-fat mayonnaise.

⚙ **Variation**
Instead of combining the fruit and yogurt mixture, serve the yogurt mixture separately with the fruit for dipping.

Sour Cream and Onion Scalloped Hash Browns with Ham

Prep: 10 min Cook: 6 hr

2 packages (5.2 ounces each) Betty Crocker® hash brown potatoes

2 tablespoons butter or margarine, melted

2 cups water

1 can ($10^3/_4$ ounces) condensed reduced-sodium cream of mushroom soup

1 can (11 ounces) Green Giant Mexicorn® whole kernel corn, red and green peppers, undrained

1 container (12 ounces) chive-and-onion sour cream potato topper

$1^1/_2$ cups shredded Cheddar and American cheese blend (6 ounces)

$1/2$ pound fully cooked ham, diced

1. Toss dry potatoes and butter in $3^1/_2$- to 4-quart slow cooker. Stir in remaining ingredients just until blended.

2. Cover and cook on low heat setting 5 to 6 hours.

6 servings ($1^1/_3$ cups each).
1 Serving: Calories 465 (Calories from Fat 245); Fat 27g (Saturated 15g); Cholesterol 80mg; Sodium 1,650mg; Carbohydrate 34g (Dietary Fiber 3g); Protein 21g
% Daily Value: Vitamin A 16%; Vitamin C 10%; Calcium 24%; Iron 8%
Exchanges: 2 Starch, 2 Medium-Fat Meat, $3^1/_2$ Fat
Carbohydrate Choices: 2

BETTY'S TIPS

⚙ **Success Hint**
Tossing the dry potatoes with melted butter preserves their shape during the long, slow cook time.

⚙ **Variation**
Add a can of Old El Paso chopped green chiles for a zippy flavor.

⚙ **Special Touch**
Sprinkle canned French-fried onions on top of the finished casserole for added crunch and flavor.

Mixed Fruit Salad

Sour Cream and Onion Scalloped Hash Browns with Ham

Cheese-Stuffed Hash Browns

Prep: 10 min Cook: 25 min

5 cups frozen shredded hash brown potatoes, thawed
3 medium green onions, thinly sliced
1/2 teaspoon salt
1/4 teaspoon pepper
2 tablespoons olive or vegetable oil
1 1/2 cups shredded Cheddar cheese (6 ounces)

1. Mix potatoes, onions, salt and pepper in large bowl. Coat 10-inch nonstick skillet with slanted side with 1 tablespoon of the oil; heat over medium heat. Spread 2 1/2 cups potato mixture evenly over bottom of skillet; press down with back of broad spatula. Top with cheese to within 1 inch of edge. Spread remaining potatoes over cheese; press down with back of broad spatula.

2. Cook over medium heat about 15 minutes or until potatoes are well browned and crisp. Loosen edge of potatoes with spatula. Place heatproof plate upside down over skillet; carefully turn skillet upside down over plate to remove potatoes.

3. Heat remaining 1 tablespoon oil in skillet over medium heat. Slide potatoes from plate into skillet so uncooked side is down. Cook about 10 minutes or until potatoes are well browned and tender. Slide onto serving plate. Cut into wedges.

6 servings.
1 Serving: Calories 305 (Calories from Fat 125); Fat 14g (Saturated 7g); Cholesterol 30mg; Sodium 840mg; Carbohydrate 35g (Dietary Fiber 3g); Protein 10g
% Daily Value: Vitamin A 6%; Vitamin C 10%; Calcium 16%; Iron 4%
Exchanges: 2 Starch, 1/2 High-Fat Meat, 2 Fat
Carbohydrate Choices: 2

BETTY'S TIPS

✿ **Success Hint**
Using a skillet with a slanted side, such as an omelet pan, helps you easily slide the potatoes back into the skillet. These inexpensive nonstick pans are available in most discount or kitchen stores.

✿ **Serve-With**
A platter of fresh fruit and a basket of warm muffins or scones turn this savory side dish into a breakfast favorite.

✿ **Special Touch**
A dollop of sour cream and a sprinkle of fresh parsley add flavor and color to this yummy potato side dish.

Cheese-Stuffed Hash Browns

Pepper Jack Cheese Quick Bread

Prep: 10 min Bake: 45 min Cool: 35 min

2 cups Gold Medal® all-purpose flour

1 cup shredded Monterey Jack cheese with jalapeño peppers (4 ounces)

1 teaspoon sugar

1 teaspoon baking powder

$^{1}/_{2}$ teaspoon baking soda

$^{1}/_{2}$ teaspoon salt

1 cup buttermilk

$^{1}/_{4}$ cup butter or margarine, melted

2 eggs, slightly beaten

1. Heat oven to 350°. Lightly grease bottom only of loaf pan, 9 × 5 × 3 or 8$^{1}/_{2}$ × 4$^{1}/_{2}$ × 2$^{1}/_{2}$ inches with shortening, or spray bottom with cooking spray.

2. Stir together flour, cheese, sugar, baking powder, baking soda and salt in medium bowl. Stir in remaining ingredients just until moistened (batter will be lumpy). Spread in pan.

3. Bake 35 to 45 minutes or until golden brown and toothpick inserted in center comes out clean. Cool 5 minutes; run knife around edges of pan to loosen. Remove from pan to wire rack. Cool 30 minutes before slicing.

1 loaf (16 slices).
1 Slice: Calories 125 (Calories from Fat 55); Fat 6g (Saturated 4g); Cholesterol 40mg; Sodium 220mg; Carbohydrate 13g (Dietary Fiber 0g); Protein 5g
% Daily Value: Vitamin A 4%; Vitamin C 0%; Calcium 8%; Iron 4%
Exchanges: 1 Starch, 1 Fat
Carbohydrate Choices: 1

BETTY'S TIPS

✿ **Substitution**
If you don't have buttermilk on hand, use 1 tablespoon lemon juice or white vinegar plus enough milk to equal 1 cup.

✿ **Success Hint**
The great thing about quick breads is that they are so quick to fix. They don't need a lot of mixing, just enough so the wet and dry ingredients are combined. Even though the batter may look lumpy, when it's baked, the bread will be light and tender.

✿ **Serve-With**
This zippy bread goes well with Chipotle Pork Chili (page 98) and a fresh fruit salad.

Pepper Jack Cheese Quick Bread

Caesar–Mozzarella French Bread

Prep: 5 min Bake: 12 min

$^1/_2$ loaf (8 ounces) French bread, cut horizontally in half

$^1/_4$ cup creamy Caesar dressing

  8 ounces sliced mozzarella cheese

1. Heat oven to 450°. Place bread on ungreased cookie sheet.

2. Spread dressing on cut sides of bread. Top with cheese.

3. Bake 10 to 12 minutes or until cheese is melted and edges begin to brown. Cut into slices. Serve immediately.

12 slices.
1 Slice: Calories 120 (Calories from Fat 55); Fat 6g (Saturated 3g); Cholesterol 10mg; Sodium 260mg; Carbohydrate 10g (Dietary Fiber 1g); Protein 7g
% Daily Value: Vitamin A 2%; Vitamin C 0%; Calcium 16%; Iron 2%
Exchanges: $^1/_2$ Starch, 1 Medium-Fat Meat
Carbohydrate Choices: $^1/_2$

BETTY'S TIPS

❂ **Health Twist**
"Lite" creamy Caesar dressing will reduce the fat but not the flavor in this recipe. Also try all-skim mozzarella cheese to reduce the fat and calories even more.

❂ **Serve-With**
A bowl of piping-hot Minestrone with Italian Sausage (page 82) and a loaf of this cheesy bread make mealtime a snap.

❂ **Special Touch**
A quick way to add a boost of flavor and color is to sprinkle the hot cheese with chopped fresh basil or parsley just before serving.

Caesar-Mozzarella French Bread

Corn Bread with Chiles

Prep: 10 min Bake: 25 min

1¼ cups Gold Medal all-purpose flour
¾ cup yellow cornmeal
¼ cup sugar
2 teaspoons baking powder
1 teaspoon baking soda
1 teaspoon salt
1 cup buttermilk
¼ cup butter or margarine, melted
1 egg, slightly beaten
1 can (4.5 ounces) Old El Paso chopped green chiles, undrained

1. Heat oven to 400°. Lightly grease bottom and sides of square pan, 8 × 8 × 2 or 9 × 9 × 2 inches, with shortening or spray with cooking spray.

2. Stir together flour, cornmeal, sugar, baking powder, baking soda and salt in large bowl. Stir in remaining ingredients just until moistened (batter will be lumpy). Spread in pan.

3. Bake 20 to 25 minutes or until light golden brown and toothpick inserted in center comes out clean. Serve warm or cool.

9 servings.
1 Serving: Calories 205 (Calories from Fat 65); Fat 7g (Saturated 4g); Cholesterol 40mg; Sodium 760mg; Carbohydrate 30g (Dietary Fiber 2g); Protein 5g
% Daily Value: Vitamin A 8%; Vitamin C 0%; Calcium 6%; Iron 10%
Exchanges: 2 Starch, 1 Fat
Carbohydrate Choices: 2

Corn Bread with Chiles

BETTY'S TIPS

⚙ **Serve-With**
Some foods, like corn bread and chili, are just meant to be together. Serve up a mixed-greens salad with apple slices and Cheddar cheese, and you'll have created a great Saturday night supper.

⚙ **Variation**
If you're not a fan of green chiles, go ahead and leave them out. Instead use 2 teaspoons of your favorite dried herb.

⚙ **Special Touch**
For a fun new way to eat corn bread, bake the batter in corn bread stick pans. Grease the pan with shortening, or spray with cooking spray. Bake at 400° for 14 to 20 minutes or until light golden brown.

Low Fat

Bread Machine Potato-Rosemary Bread

Prep: 5 min Bake: 3 hr

1¹⁄₂-pound loaf (12 slices):

1¹⁄₄	cups water
2	tablespoons butter or margarine, softened
3	cups Gold Medal® Better for Bread™ flour
¹⁄₂	cup Betty Crocker Potato Buds® mashed potatoes (dry)
1	tablespoon dried rosemary leaves, crumbled
1	tablespoon sugar
1¹⁄₂	teaspoons salt
2	teaspoons bread machine yeast

2-pound loaf (16 slices):

1²⁄₃	cups water
2	tablespoons butter or margarine, softened
4	cups Gold Medal Better for Bread flour
²⁄₃	cup Betty Crocker Potato Buds mashed potatoes (dry)
1¹⁄₂	tablespoons dried rosemary leaves, crumbled
1	tablespoon sugar
1¹⁄₂	teaspoons salt
1¹⁄₂	teaspoons bread machine yeast

1. Make 1¹⁄₂-pound recipe with bread machine that uses 3 cups flour, or make 2-pound recipe with bread machine that uses 4 cups flour.

2. Measure carefully, placing all ingredients in bread machine pan in the order recommended by the manufacturer.

3. Select Basic/White cycle. Use Medium or Light crust color. Remove baked bread from pan; cool on wire rack. Serve warm or cooled.

1 Slice: Calories 150 (Calories from Fat 20); Fat 2g (Saturated 1g); Cholesterol 0mg; Sodium 310mg; Carbohydrate 29g (Dietary Fiber 1g); Protein 4g
% Daily Value: Vitamin A 0%; Vitamin C 0%; Calcium 0%; Iron 10%
Exchanges: 2 Starch
Carbohydrate Choices: 2

BETTY'S TIPS

⊙ **Success Hint**

No, it's not a mistake. Slightly less yeast is needed in the 2-pound loaf than is needed in the 1¹⁄₂-pound loaf. Don't forget to crumble the dried rosemary leaves before adding them so you don't end up with larger, sharp pieces of rosemary in the bread.

⊙ **Serve-With**

Layer some sliced turkey, lettuce and tomato between thick slices of this rosemary-studded bread for a great sandwich. Serve with a bowl of creamy Wild Rice Soup (page 84) and a comforting cup of steaming tea.

Bread Machine Potato-Rosemary Bread

Herb Focaccia

Prep: 15 min Rise: 1 hr Bake: 17 min

$3/4$ cup warm water (105° to 115°)

1 package quick active dry yeast

$2^3/4$ cups Original Bisquick mix

1 teaspoon chopped fresh oregano leaves

$1/3$ cup finely chopped red onion

4 teaspoons olive or vegetable oil

1. Stir together water, yeast, Bisquick mix, oregano, $1/4$ cup onion and 3 teaspoons oil in medium bowl (dough will be soft). Place dough on surface sprinkled with Bisquick mix; roll to coat. Knead gently about 20 times, adding a small amount of Bisquick mix if dough sticks to surface, until smooth.

2. Lightly grease cookie sheet with shortening or spray with cooking spray. Pat dough on cookie sheet into 10-inch round. Sprinkle remaining onion over dough. Brush remaining 1 teaspoon oil over onion and dough. Cover and let rise in warm place about 1 hour or until double.

3. Heat oven to 400°. Bake 14 to 17 minutes or until light golden brown. Immediately remove from cookie sheet to wire rack. Serve warm or cooled.

1 loaf (12 wedges).
1 Wedge: Calories 125 (Calories from Fat 45); Fat 5g (Saturated 1g); Cholesterol 0mg; Sodium 390mg; Carbohydrate 18g (Dietary Fiber 1g); Protein 2g
% Daily Value: Vitamin A 0%; Vitamin C 0%; Calcium 4%; Iron 6%
Exchanges: 1 Starch, 1 Fat
Carbohydrate Choices: 1

BETTY'S TIPS

✪ **Substitution**
Out of oregano? You can substitute $1/2$ teaspoon dried oregano leaves for the fresh oregano.

✪ **Serve-With**
Enjoy this easy version of focaccia with your favorite soup. Or help yourself to a slice for an easy grab-and-go snack.

✪ **Variation**
Try chopped fresh rosemary or thyme leaves instead of the oregano for a simple twist to this quick-to-make flatbread.

Herb Focaccia

Low Fat

Bread Machine Sun-Dried Tomato Rolls

Prep: 20 min Rest: 10 min Rise: 45 min Bake: 16 min

$^3/_4$ cup warm milk (105° to 115°)

2 cups Gold Medal Better for Bread flour

$^1/_4$ cup chopped sun-dried tomatoes in oil, drained and 1 tablespoon oil reserved

1 tablespoon sugar

1 teaspoon salt

$1^1/_2$ teaspoons bread machine yeast

1. Measure carefully, placing all ingredients in bread machine pan in the order recommended by the manufacturer.

2. Select Dough/Manual cycle. Do not use Delay cycle.

3. Remove dough from pan; place on lightly floured surface. Cover and let rest 10 minutes.

4. Lightly grease cookie sheet with shortening or spray with cooking spray. Gently push fist into dough to deflate. Divide dough into 12 equal pieces. Shape each piece into a ball. Place 2 inches apart on cookie sheet. Cover and let rise in warm place 30 to 45 minutes or until almost double.

5. Heat oven to 350°. Bake 12 to 16 minutes or until golden brown. Remove from cookie sheet to wire rack. Serve warm or cooled.

12 rolls.
1 Roll: Calories 100 (Calories from Fat 20); Fat 2g (Saturated 0g); Cholesterol 0mg; Sodium 210mg; Carbohydrate 20g (Dietary Fiber 1g); Protein 3g
% Daily Value: Vitamin A 0%; Vitamin C 2%; Calcium 2%; Iron 6%
Exchanges: 1 Starch, $^1/_2$ Fat
Carbohydrate Choices: 1

Bread Machine Sun-Dried Tomato Rolls

BETTY'S TIPS

✿ **Success Hint**
If you like rolls that are golden brown on top but have soft sides, place the rolls closer together on the cookie sheet so they will rise and bake together.

✿ **Serve-With**
Rolled up in rich tomato flavor, these savory rolls pair well with a big bowlful of Continental Pork Stew (page 90).

✿ **Did You Know?**
The intense flavor of sun-dried tomatoes can bring out the best in soups, stews and breads. You'll find these flavor-packed gems sold either packed in oil, which keeps them a little softer, or dry packed in cellophane. The dry tomatoes need to be soaked before using to make them softer.

Parmesan–Black Pepper Breadsticks

Prep: 20 min Bake: 12 min

2 cups Original Bisquick mix
1/2 cup cold water
1/2 teaspoon fresh cracked pepper
1/3 cup shredded Parmesan cheese
1 tablespoon butter or margarine, melted
Additional fresh cracked pepper, if desired

1. Heat oven to 450°. Lightly grease large cookie sheet with shortening or spray with cooking spray. Stir together Bisquick mix, water, 1/2 teaspoon pepper and 2 tablespoons cheese in medium bowl until soft dough forms.

2. Place dough on surface sprinkled with Bisquick mix; roll to coat. Roll into 10 × 8-inch rectangle. Brush with butter. Sprinkle with remaining cheese; press in gently. Cut crosswise into 12 strips. Gently twist each strip. Place 1/2 inch apart on cookie sheet. Sprinkle with additional pepper.

3. Bake 10 to 12 minutes until light golden brown. Serve warm.

12 breadsticks.
1 Breadstick: Calories 105 (Calories from Fat 45); Fat 5g (Saturated 2g); Cholesterol 5mg; Sodium 340mg; Carbohydrate 12g (Dietary Fiber 0g); Protein 3g
% Daily Value: Vitamin A 0%; Vitamin C 0%; Calcium 6%; Iron 4%
Exchanges: 1 Starch, 1/2 Fat
Carbohydrate Choices: 1

BETTY'S TIPS

✿ **Success Hint**
Don't be afraid of the dough when pulling and twisting. Each breadstick will be slightly different in shape and length, but try to keep them as close to the same size as possible, so they'll bake evenly.

✿ **Serve With**
These soft, tasty breadsticks make a great party appetizer or a quick snack.

✿ **Variation**
If you like spicy food, try adding a touch of ground red pepper (cayenne) to these cheesy breadsticks. You'll need only about 1/8 teaspoon, unless you really want to spice it up. Sprinkle it on with the Parmesan cheese.

Parmesan–Black Pepper Breadsticks

Easy Bread Bowls

Prep: 20 min Rise: 20 min Bake: 20 min Cool: 5 min

1 loaf (1 pound) frozen bread dough, thawed
1 tablespoon olive or vegetable oil
1 teaspoon dried basil leaves
$^1/_2$ teaspoon garlic salt

6 servings.
1 Serving: Calories 220 (Calories from Fat 45); Fat 5g (Saturated 1g); Cholesterol 0mg; Sodium 490mg; Carbohydrate 38g (Dietary Fiber 2g); Protein 6g
% Daily Value: Vitamin A 0%; Vitamin C 0%; Calcium 8%; Iron 14%
Exchanges: 2 Starch, $^1/_2$ Carbohydrate, 1 Fat
Carbohydrate Choices: $2^1/_2$

1. Lightly grease outsides of six 10-ounce custard cups with shortening (do not use cooking spray). Place cups upside down on large cookie sheet.

2. Divide dough into 6 equal pieces. Shape each piece into a ball, then pat into 6-inch round. Place rounds over bottoms of custard cups. Brush dough with oil. Sprinkle with basil and garlic salt. Cover and let rise in warm place 20 minutes.

3. Heat oven to 350°. Bake 16 to 20 minutes or until golden brown. Cool 5 minutes; remove from cups and place right side up on wire rack. (Interiors of bread bowls may be slightly moist.)

4. To serve, place warm or cooled bread bowls in individual shallow soup or pasta bowls. Spoon soup, stew or chili into bread bowls.

BETTY'S TIPS

⊛ **Success Hint**
To make handling bread dough as easy as can be, make sure the dough has thawed but has not started to rise. You may also need to reshape the dough rounds after a few minutes on the cups by gently pushing the dough down and shaping as needed.

⊛ **Serve-With**
A thick and chunky chili or stew, such as Vegetable and Bean Chili (page 100) is perfect for these edible bowls.

⊛ **Variation**
Instead of basil, you may want to experiment with other dried herbs, such as thyme, rosemary or oregano. Or try chili powder for an extra burst of flavor with your favorite chili.

Easy Bread Bowls

Low Fat

Popovers

Prep: 10 min Bake: 40 min

1 cup milk
2 eggs
1 cup Gold Medal all-purpose flour
$\frac{1}{2}$ teaspoon salt

1. Heat oven to 450°. Generously grease 6-cup popover pan with shortening. Place pan in oven 5 minutes to heat.

2. Meanwhile, place milk in 1-cup microwavable measuring cup. Microwave uncovered on High 40 to 50 seconds or until warm. Beat eggs slightly in medium bowl with fork or wire whisk. Stir in flour, milk and salt with fork or wire whisk just until smooth (do not overbeat). Fill popover pan cups half full. Bake 20 minutes.

3. Reduce oven temperature to 350°. Bake 15 to 20 minutes longer or until deep golden brown. Immediately remove from pan. Serve warm.

6 popovers.
1 Popover: Calories 125 (Calories from Fat 25); Fat 3g (Saturated 1g); Cholesterol 75mg; Sodium 230mg; Carbohydrate 18g (Dietary Fiber 1g); Protein 6g
% Daily Value: Vitamin A 4%; Vitamin C 0%; Calcium 6%; Iron 6%
Exchanges: 1 Starch, 1 Fat
Carbohydrate Choices: 1

BETTY'S TIPS

✿ **Time-Saver**
Prepare a double batch of popovers when you bake, and freeze the extras. Pierce each freshly baked popover with the point of a knife to let out the steam. Cool them on a wire rack, then wrap tightly and freeze. To reheat thawed popovers, cover loosely with aluminum foil and bake at 375° for about 15 minutes or until warm.

✿ **Variation**
Try a delicious flavor twist in your next batch of popovers. Add $\frac{1}{2}$ teaspoon ground cinnamon and $\frac{1}{4}$ cup finely chopped nuts to the batter.

Popovers

Provolone and Olive Biscuits

Prep: 20 min Bake: 15 min

2 cups Gold Medal all-purpose flour

2 teaspoons baking powder

$1/2$ teaspoon salt

$2/3$ cup butter or margarine

$1/2$ cup shredded provolone cheese (2 ounces)

$1/4$ cup Kalamata or ripe olives, well drained and chopped

$3/4$ cup buttermilk

1. Heat oven to 425°. Stir together flour, baking powder and salt in large bowl. Cut in butter and cheese, using pastry blender or crisscrossing 2 knives, until mixture looks like coarse crumbs. Stir in olives and buttermilk just until moistened and soft dough forms.

2. Place dough on lightly floured surface. Knead 5 or 6 times. Roll or pat dough to $1/2$-inch thickness. Cut with $2^1/2$-inch biscuit cutter. Place 1 inch apart on ungreased cookie sheet.

3. Bake 13 to 15 minutes or until light golden brown. Serve warm.

10 biscuits.
1 Biscuit: Calories 235 (Calories from Fat 135); Fat 15g (Saturated 9g); Cholesterol 40mg; Sodium 390mg; Carbohydrate 20g (Dietary Fiber 1g); Protein 5g
% Daily Value: Vitamin A 10%; Vitamin C 0%; Calcium 12%; Iron 8%
Exchanges: 1 Starch, 3 Fat
Carbohydrate Choices: 1

BETTY'S TIPS

❂ **Success Hint**
A round glass that's $2^1/2$ inches in diameter makes a good stand-in for a biscuit cutter.

❂ **Variation**
Crazy about Cheddar? Try it instead of the provolone in these irresistible biscuits.

Provolone and Olive Biscuits

Appetizers

Appetizers

Start the Evening with Something Special

Ham and Swiss Appetizer Cheesecake (page 32)

Fresh Fruit with Ginger Dip (page 24)

Fresh Fruit with Ginger Dip

Prep: 25 min
(Photo on page 23)

1 cup sour cream
¼ cup apricot preserves
2 tablespoons finely chopped crystallized ginger
1 tablespoon chopped fresh cilantro
24 fresh strawberries
24 (1-inch) cantaloupe balls
24 (1-inch) honeydew melon balls

1. Mix sour cream, preserves and ginger until well blended. Stir in cilantro. Place in small serving bowl.

2. Arrange strawberries and melon balls on platter. Serve with dip.

24 servings (3 fruit pieces and 1½ tablespoons dip each).
1 Serving: Calories 40 (Calories from Fat 20); Fat 2g (Saturated 1g); Cholesterol 5mg; Sodium 10mg; Carbohydrate 7g (Dietary Fiber 1g); Protein 1g
% Daily Value: Vitamin A 8%; Vitamin C 26%; Calcium 0%; Iron 0%
Exchanges: ½ Fruit
Carbohydrate Choices: ½

BETTY'S TIPS

✪ **Substitution**
Instead of the apricot preserves, why not try peach or strawberry?

✪ **Special Touch**
Dress up the fruit plate with sprigs of fresh cilantro. If you like, add some kiwifruit slices, watermelon or fresh pineapple to the platter. Serve the fruit with frilly toothpicks or cocktail forks.

✪ **Did You Know?**
Crystallized, or candied, ginger has been cooked in a sugar syrup, then coated with coarse sugar. It adds a wonderful peppery-sweet flavor to the dip in this recipe.

Cheese and Fruit Kabobs with Cranberry Dip

Prep: 40 min

12 (¹/₂-inch) cubes Gouda cheese (about 6 ounces)

12 (¹/₂-inch) cubes Fontina cheese (about 6 ounces)

12 (¹/₂-inch) cubes Cheddar cheese (about 6 ounces)

12 small strawberries or 6 large strawberries, cut in half

2 kiwifruit, peeled and cut into 12 pieces

12 fresh or canned pineapple cubes
Cranberry Dip (below)

1. Thread cheese and fruit alternately on each of twelve 6-inch wooden skewers.

2. Serve with Cranberry Dip.

12 servings.

Cranberry Dip

²/₃ cup strawberry cream cheese spread (from 8-ounce container)

¹/₄ cup frozen (thawed) cranberry-orange relish (from 10-ounce container)

¹/₄ cup frozen (thawed) whipped topping

Beat together cream cheese and cranberry relish with electric mixer on medium speed and spoon into small bowl. Fold in whipped topping.

1 Serving: Calories 225 (Calories from Fat 145); Fat 16g (Saturated 10g); Cholesterol 55mg; Sodium 340mg; Carbohydrate 8g (Dietary Fiber 1g); Protein 12g
% Daily Value: Vitamin A 10%; Vitamin C 30%; Calcium 26%; Iron 2%
Exchanges: ¹/₂ Fruit, 2 Medium-Fat Meat, 1 Fat
Carbohydrate Choices: ¹/₂

BETTY'S TIPS

❂ **Serve-With**
These colorful kabobs are a perfect addition to a holiday wine and cheese party.

❂ **Do-Ahead**
Prepare the dip a day ahead; cover and refrigerate. Cut the cheese and fruit the day ahead. Store them all separately in plastic bags in the refrigerator. Assemble the kabobs up to 2 hours before serving; then cover and refrigerate.

❂ **Special Touch**
Decorate this fruity dip with a sprig of fresh mint and sparkly fresh cranberries. To make sugared cranberries, brush them with a little corn syrup, then roll them in sugar and let dry.

Cheese and Fruit Kabobs with Cranberry Dip

Quick

Asiago and Sun-Dried Tomato Dip

Prep: 15 min

⅓ cup sun-dried tomatoes (not in oil)

1 cup boiling water

1 package (8 ounces) cream cheese, softened

1 cup finely shredded Asiago cheese (4 ounces)

8 medium green onions, thinly sliced (½ cup)

1 cup chopped mushrooms (3 ounces)

1½ cups sour cream

13 dozen assorted crackers

1. Mix tomatoes and water; let stand 10 minutes. Drain thoroughly and chop.

2. Heat chopped tomatoes and remaining ingredients except crackers in 2-quart saucepan over medium-low heat, stirring frequently, until cream cheese is melted.

3. Spray inside of 1½-quart slow cooker with cooking spray. Transfer tomato mixture to slow cooker. Serve dip with crackers. Dip will hold on Low heat setting up to 2 hours. Scrape down sides of cooker with rubber spatula occasionally to help prevent edge of dip from scorching.

40 servings (4 crackers and 2 tablespoons dip each).
1 Serving: Calories 120 (Calories from Fat 70); Fat 8g (Saturated 4g); Cholesterol 15mg; Sodium 190mg; Carbohydrate 9g (Dietary Fiber 0g); Protein 3g
% Daily Value: Vitamin A 4%; Vitamin C 0%; Calcium 4%; Iron 4%
Exchanges: ½ Starch, 2 Fat
Carbohydrate Choices: ½

BETTY'S TIPS

⊙ **Substitution**
Instead of crackers, serve with assorted raw vegetables such as Belgian endive, cherry tomatoes and snap pea pods.

⊙ **Success Hint**
Because of the richness of the cheeses, the dip may start to separate, and little puddles could appear on the surface. Just stir the dip occasionally to keep it looking fresh and appealing!

⊙ **Did You Know?**
Asiago is a semi-firm Italian cheese with a rich, nutty flavor. It's made from whole or part-skim milk and comes in small wheels with glossy rinds. You can purchase it in wrapped precut wedges or preshredded.

Asiago and Sun-Dried Tomato Dip

Quick

Tex-Mex Layered Dip

Prep: 15 min

1 can (15 ounces) black beans, rinsed and drained
2 tablespoons Old El Paso Thick 'n Chunky salsa
1 1/2 cups sour cream
1 cup guacamole
1 cup shredded Cheddar cheese (4 ounces)
1 small tomato, seeded and chopped (1/2 cup)
2 medium green onions, chopped (2 tablespoons)
Tortilla chips, if desired

1. Mix black beans and salsa in small bowl. Spoon into 10-inch circle on 12- or 13-inch serving plate.

2. Spoon sour cream over beans, leaving about 1-inch border of beans around edge. Spread guacamole over sour cream, leaving border of sour cream showing.

3. Sprinkle cheese, tomato and onions over guacamole. Serve immediately, or cover with plastic wrap and refrigerate up to 6 hours. Serve with tortilla chips.

16 servings.
1 Serving: Calories 130 (Calories from Fat 70); Fat 8g (Saturated 4g); Cholesterol 20mg; Sodium 240mg; Carbohydrate 10g (Dietary Fiber 3g); Protein 5g
% Daily Value: Vitamin A 6%; Vitamin C 14%; Calcium 8%; Iron 4%
Exchanges: 1/2 Starch, 1/2 High-Fat Meat
Carbohydrate Choices: 1/2

BETTY'S TIPS

⊗ **Substitution**
You can use a can of refried beans instead of the black beans. If you're out of salsa, feel free to use ketchup or chili sauce instead.

⊗ **Success Hint**
Go ahead and make this layered dip, cover with plastic wrap and tote to the party. When you arrive, just uncover and serve.

⊗ **Special Touch**
Line the serving plate with shredded lettuce and top with the layered dip. Sprinkle the top with sliced ripe olives or chopped fresh cilantro, then add some cilantro sprigs.

Tex-Mex Layered Dip

Appetizer Beer-Cheese Fondue

Smoked Salmon Spread

Appetizer Beer–Cheese Fondue

Prep: 35 min

1 loaf (1 pound) French bread

1 package (16 ounces) process cheese spread loaf, cubed

1 1/2 cups frozen chopped broccoli (from 1-pound bag), cooked and drained

1/4 cup regular or nonalcoholic beer

1 jar (2 ounces) diced pimientos, drained

1 teaspoon ground mustard

1. Heat oven to 350°. Cut bread into 1-inch cubes. Place bread pieces in ungreased jelly roll pan, 15 1/2 × 10 1/2 × 1 inch. Bake about 10 minutes, stirring twice, until lightly toasted. Transfer to serving bowl or basket.

2. Meanwhile, melt cheese in 2-quart saucepan over medium heat, stirring occasionally. Stir in broccoli, beer, pimientos and mustard. Cook, stirring occasionally, until hot. Pour cheese mixture into ceramic fondue pot over Low heat or into 1 1/2-quart slow cooker at Low heat setting.

3. To serve, skewer toasted bread pieces with fondue forks or wooden skewers and dip into cheese mixture. Cheese mixture will hold in slow cooker on Low heat setting up to 2 hours.

16 servings (1/2 cup bread cubes and 2 tablespoons fondue each).
1 Serving: Calories 200 (Calories from Fat 90); Fat 10g (Saturated 6g); Cholesterol 25mg; Sodium 580mg; Carbohydrate 17g (Dietary Fiber 2g); Protein 10g
% Daily Value: Vitamin A 24%; Vitamin C 20%; Calcium 16%; Iron 8%
Exchanges: 1 Starch, 1 High-Fat Meat, 1/2 Fat
Carbohydrate Choices: 1

BETTY'S TIPS

✪ **Substitution**
Although French bread is delicious with the fondue, you could use another hearty white bread instead. Sourdough, Vienna and Italian bread would all work in this recipe.

✪ **Did You Know?**
In French, the word fondue means "melted." Popular in the 1970s, fondue is making a comeback, particularly for relaxed entertaining.

Quick
Smoked Salmon Spread

Prep: 15 min

12 ounces smoked salmon or trout, skinned and boned

1 package (8 ounces) cream cheese, softened

4 teaspoons prepared horseradish

4 teaspoons finely chopped green onions
Crackers, if desired

1. Place salmon, cream cheese and horseradish in food processor. Cover and process 30 to 60 seconds or until smooth. Stir in green onions.

2. Spoon salmon mixture into serving bowl; serve with crackers. Serve immediately, or cover and refrigerate up to 3 days.

16 servings (2 tablespoons each).
1 Serving: Calories 80 (Calories from Fat 55); Fat 6g (Saturated 3g); Cholesterol 20mg; Sodium 210mg; Carbohydrate 1g (Dietary Fiber 0g); Protein 5g
% Daily Value: Vitamin A 4%; Vitamin C 0%; Calcium 0%; Iron 2%
Exchanges: 1 Medium-Fat Meat
Carbohydrate Choices: 0

BETTY'S TIPS

✪ **Special Touch**
Garnish with chopped green onions or fresh herbs. This spread is also great served on sliced cucumbers or in Belgian endive leaves.

Nutty Cheese Spread with Fruit Chutney

Prep: 20 min Refrigerate: 1 hr Bake: 7 min

$^3/_4$ cup diced dried fruit and raisin mixture (from 7-ounce package)

$^1/_4$ cup sweetened dried cranberries

$^1/_2$ cup apple cider

1 tablespoon cider vinegar

$^1/_4$ teaspoon ground ginger

$^1/_4$ teaspoon ground cinnamon

$^1/_4$ cup chopped walnuts

1 package (8 ounces) cream cheese, softened
Crackers, if desired

1. Mix all ingredients except walnuts, cream cheese and crackers in 2-quart saucepan. Cook over medium heat about 5 minutes, stirring frequently, until fruit is plump and mixture is thick. Cover and refrigerate about 1 hour or until completely cooled.

2. Meanwhile, heat oven to 350°. Spread walnuts on cookie sheet. Bake 5 to 7 minutes, stirring twice, until light golden brown; cool.

3. Mix walnuts and cream cheese in medium bowl. Spread cream cheese mixture in $^1/_2$-inch-thick layer on serving plate. Top with chutney. Serve with crackers.

16 servings.
1 Serving: Calories 90 (Calories from Fat 55); Fat 6g (Saturated 3g); Cholesterol 15mg; Sodium 45mg; Carbohydrate 7g (Dietary Fiber 1g); Protein 2g
% Daily Value: Vitamin A 6%; Vitamin C 0%; Calcium 2%; Iron 2%
Exchanges: $^1/_2$ Fruit, $^1/_2$ High-Fat Meat
Carbohydrate Choices: $^1/_2$

BETTY'S TIPS

✿ **Do-Ahead**
This spiced fruit chutney can be made several days ahead. Be sure to keep it covered in the refrigerator.

✿ **Special Touch**
Make extra chutney, package it in a pretty jar and give it as a hostess gift. It is delicious served with turkey or ham.

✿ **Did You Know?**
Toasting nuts brings out their subtle flavor and also makes them more crunchy.

Nutty Cheese Spread with Fruit Chutney

Betty Crocker
MAKES IT EASY

Dried Fruit and Cream Cheese Roulade

Prep: 15 min Refrigerate: 2 hr

1	package (8 ounces) cream cheese
1	tablespoon red currant or apple jelly
¼	cup dried calimyrna figs
¼	cup chopped dried apricots
2	ounces crumbled chèvre (goat) cheese
¼	cup chopped walnuts
1	tablespoon chopped fresh chives
40	assorted crackers

1. Place cream cheese between 2 sheets of plastic wrap. Roll into 9 × 6-inch rectangle with rolling pin. Remove top sheet of wrap. Carefully spread jelly over cream cheese. Sprinkle with figs and apricots to within ½ inch of edges. Sprinkle with cheese.

2. Using bottom sheet of wrap to help lift and, starting at a long side, carefully roll up cheese mixture into a log. Carefully press walnuts into outside of log, rolling slightly to cover all sides. Wrap tightly in plastic wrap. Refrigerate at least 2 hours to set.

3. To serve, place roulade on serving plate. Sprinkle with chives. Serve with crackers.

10 servings (4 crackers and 2 tablespoons spread each).
1 Serving: Calories 170 (Calories from Fat 100); Fat 1g (Saturated 5g); Cholesterol 20mg; Sodium 160mg; Carbohydrate 14g (Dietary Fiber 1g); Protein 4g
% Daily Value: Vitamin A 10%; Vitamin C 0%; Calcium 6%; Iron 4%
Exchanges: 1 Starch, 2 Fat
Carbohydrate Choices: 1

Roll cream cheese (between 2 sheets of plastic wrap) into 9 × 6-inch rectangle with rolling pin.

Using bottom sheet of wrap to help lift, carefully roll up cheese mixture into a log.

Dried Fruit and Cream Cheese Roulade

Ham and Swiss Appetizer Cheesecake

Prep: 30 min Bake: 55 min Cool: 1 hr Refrigerate: 2 hr
(Photo on page 23)

1 cup crushed round wheat crackers (about 28 crackers)

3 tablespoons butter or margarine, melted

2 packages (8 ounces each) cream cheese, softened

1/4 cup whipping (heavy) cream

2 eggs

2 cups finely shredded Swiss cheese (8 ounces)

1 cup chopped fully cooked ham

1/2 cup chopped drained roasted red bell peppers (from 7.25-ounce jar)

4 medium green onions, sliced (1/4 cup)

2 tablespoons chopped fresh or 1/2 teaspoon dried thyme leaves

1 package (13 ounces) assorted crackers

1. Heat oven to 350°. Mix crushed crackers and butter until well blended. Press evenly in bottom of springform pan, 9 × 3 inches. Bake 8 to 10 minutes or until golden brown.

2. Meanwhile, beat cream cheese in large bowl with electric mixer on medium speed until smooth. Add whipping cream and eggs; beat until smooth. Stir in cheese, ham, bell peppers, onions and thyme. Spoon evenly over crust in pan.

3. Bake 45 to 55 minutes or until center is set. Run knife around edge of cheesecake to loosen. Cool completely, about 1 hour. Cover and refrigerate at least 2 hours but no longer than 48 hours.

4. Remove side of pan. Place cheesecake on serving platter. Cut into wedges. Serve with crackers.

24 servings.
1 Serving: Calories 230 (Calories from Fat 155); Fat 17g (Saturated 9g); Cholesterol 55mg; Sodium 30mg; Carbohydrate 12g (Dietary Fiber 1g); Protein 7g
% Daily Value: Vitamin A 14%; Vitamin C 6%; Calcium 10%; Iron 6%
Exchanges: 1 Starch, 1/2 High-Fat Meat, 2 Fat
Carbohydrate Choices: 1

BETTY'S TIPS

⊛ **Substitution**
You can use fresh marjoram instead of the thyme if you like.

⊛ **Success Hint**
This cheesecake is perfect to tote to a gathering. Just leave it in the springform pan until you're ready to serve. Pack your garnishes separately, and decorate at the party.

⊛ **Special Touch**
Arrange the cheesecake on a pretty platter. Top with roasted red pepper cutouts of poinsettia leaves and the thyme sprigs.

Cheesy Onion and Tomato Puffs

Prep: 15 min Cook: 20 min

1 sheet frozen puff pastry (from 17.3-ounce package), thawed

2 tablespoons butter or margarine

1 sweet onion, cut lengthwise into quarters and thinly sliced (2$\frac{1}{2}$ cups)

2 teaspoons packed brown sugar

$\frac{1}{4}$ cup sun-dried tomatoes in oil and herbs, drained and finely chopped

1 round (4 ounces) Camembert cheese, cut into $\frac{3}{4} \times \frac{3}{4} \times \frac{1}{4}$-inch pieces

1. Heat oven to 400°. Spray 2 cookie sheets with cooking spray. Unfold pastry on lightly floured surface. Roll into 12-inch square, trimming edges to make even. Cut into 6 rows by 6 rows to make 36 (2-inch) squares. Place on cookie sheets. Bake 12 to 15 minutes, rearranging cookie sheets after 6 minutes, until puffed and golden brown. Remove from cookie sheets to wire rack. Cool until slightly warm.

2. Meanwhile, melt butter in 8-inch skillet over medium heat. Cook onion in butter 15 to 20 minutes, stirring occasionally, until tender. Stir in brown sugar. Cook and stir until onions are coated. Stir in tomatoes. Remove from heat; keep warm.

3. Place cooled pastry squares on same cookie sheets. Press cheese piece into center of each pastry square. Fill with about 1 teaspoon onion mixture. Bake about 1 minute or until cheese is melted.

36 appetizers.
1 Appetizer: Calories 50 (Calories from Fat 35); Fat 4g (Saturated 2g); Cholesterol 10mg; Sodium 45mg; Carbohydrate 3g (Dietary Fiber 0g); Protein 1g
% Daily Value: Vitamin A 0%; Vitamin C 0%; Calcium 0%; Iron 2%
Exchanges: 1 Fat
Carbohydrate Choices: 0

BETTY'S TIPS

❂ **Substitution**
A regular yellow onion can be substituted for the sweet onion.

❂ **Do-Ahead**
The onion filling can be cooked, covered and refrigerated up to 24 hours ahead. Just before serving, assemble appetizers and bake as directed.

❂ **Special Touch**
Sprinkle some chopped fresh parsley on top of these puffed bites. Add a few sprigs of fresh marjoram and sliced grape tomatoes to the serving platter for an instant touch of holiday.

Cheesy Onion and Tomato Puffs

Cranberry-Chicken Salad Puffs

Prep: 25 min Bake: 20 min

$^1/_2$ cup water

$^1/_4$ cup butter or margarine

$^1/_2$ cup Gold Medal all-purpose flour

2 eggs

Cranberry-Chicken Salad Filling (below)

1. Heat oven to 400°. Grease cookie sheet with shortening or spray with cooking spray. Heat water and butter to rolling boil in 2$^1/_2$-quart saucepan. Stir in flour; reduce heat to low. Stir vigorously over low heat about 1 minute or until mixture forms a ball; remove from heat.

2. Beat in eggs all at once with spoon; continue beating until smooth. Drop dough by heaping teaspoonfuls about 2 inches apart onto cookie sheet.

3. Bake about 18 minutes or until puffed and golden brown. Remove from oven; cut small slit with knife in side of each puff to allow steam to escape. Return to oven; bake 2 minutes longer. Cool away from draft about 10 minutes.

4. While puffs are baking, make Cranberry-Chicken Salad Filling.

5. Cut off top third of each puff; pull out any strands of dough. Spoon heaping teaspoonful of chicken salad into each puff.

20 puffs.

Cranberry-Chicken Salad Filling

1 cup deli chicken salad spread

$^1/_4$ cup dried cranberries

$^1/_4$ cup chopped pistachio nuts

1 teaspoon chopped fresh or $^1/_4$ teaspoon dried marjoram leaves

Mix all ingredients.

1 Puff: Calories 75 (Calories from Fat 45); Fat 5g (Saturated 2g); Cholesterol 30mg; Sodium 50mg; Carbohydrate 5g (Dietary Fiber 0g); Protein 3g
% Daily Value: Vitamin A 2%; Vitamin C 2%; Calcium 0%; Iron 2%
Exchanges: $^1/_2$ Medium-Fat Meat, 1 Fat
Carbohydrate Choices: 0

BETTY'S TIPS

⊙ **Substitution**
To save time, this flavorful chicken spread can be served on crackers or used to stuff Belgian endive leaves.

⊙ **Do-Ahead**
You can assemble these appetizers and refrigerate up to 2 hours before serving. Relax and enjoy the party!

Cranberry-Chicken Salad Puffs

Gorgonzola- and Hazelnut-Stuffed Mushrooms

Prep: 30 min Bake: 20 min

1 pound fresh whole mushrooms

$^{1}/_{3}$ cup crumbled Gorgonzola cheese

$^{1}/_{4}$ cup Progresso® Italian-style bread crumbs

$^{1}/_{4}$ cup chopped hazelnuts (filberts)

$^{1}/_{4}$ cup finely chopped red bell pepper

4 medium green onions, chopped ($^{1}/_{4}$ cup)

$^{1}/_{2}$ teaspoon salt

1. Heat oven to 350°. Remove stems from mushroom caps; reserve caps. Finely chop enough stems to measure about $^{1}/_{2}$ cup. Discard remaining stems.

2. Mix chopped mushroom stems and remaining ingredients in small bowl until well blended. Spoon into mushroom caps, mounding slightly. Place in ungreased jelly roll pan, 15$^{1}/_{2}$ × 10$^{1}/_{2}$ × 1 inch.

3. Bake 15 to 20 minutes or until thoroughly heated. Serve warm.

About 35 mushrooms.
1 Mushroom: Calories 20 (Calories from Fat 10); Fat 1g (Saturated 0g); Cholesterol 0mg; Sodium 60mg; Carbohydrate 1g (Dietary Fiber 0g); Protein 1g
% Daily Value: Vitamin A 0%; Vitamin C 0%; Calcium 0%; Iron 0%
Exchanges: Free Food
Carbohydrate Choices: 0

BETTY'S TIPS

⊛ **Substitution**
Walnuts or pistachios can be used instead of the hazelnuts if you like.

⊛ **Special Touch**
Arrange the warm mushrooms on a serving platter, and add whole hazelnuts and oregano sprigs for a festive flair.

⊛ **Did You Know?**
Italian Gorgonzola is rich and creamy with a mild, yet slightly pungent flavor and aroma. If you can't find Gorgonzola, use blue cheese instead.

Gorgonzola- and Hazlenut-Stuffed Mushrooms

Basil- and Crabmeat-Topped Cucumbers

Prep: 40 min

1 medium English cucumber
1 package (3 ounces) cream cheese, softened
2 tablespoons mayonnaise or salad dressing
1/4 cup chopped fresh basil leaves
2 tablespoons finely chopped red onion
2 teaspoons grated lemon peel
1 cup frozen cooked crabmeat, thawed and flaked
2 tablespoons capers, if desired
Small basil leaves or chopped fresh basil, if desired

1. Score cucumber lengthwise with tines of fork if desired. Cut into thirty-six 1/4-inch slices.

2. Beat cream cheese in small bowl with electric mixer on low speed until creamy. Mix in mayonnaise until well blended. Stir in chopped basil, onion, lemon peel and crabmeat.

3. Spread or pipe about 1 teaspoon crabmeat mixture on each cucumber slice. Sprinkle with capers. Garnish with basil leaves.

36 appetizers.
1 Appetizer: Calories 20 (Calories from Fat 20); Fat 2g (Saturated 1g); Cholesterol 5mg; Sodium 3_ ˥; Carbohydrate 0g (Dietary Fiber 0g); Protein 1g
% Daily Value: Vitamin A 2%; Vi in C 0%; Calcium 0%; Iron 0%
Exchanges: 1/2 Fat
Carbohydrate Choices: 0

BETTY'S TIPS

⊚ **Substitution**
You can use a 6-ounce can of crabmeat, drained ad of the frozen crabmeat. Or try using imitation crab chunks (also called surimi) instead.

⊚ **Special Touch**
Arrange the topped cucumbers on your platter, and add basil sprigs and long strips of fresh lemon peel as a colorful garnish.

⊚ **Did You Know?**
English, or hothouse, cucumbers have a mild flavor, very few seeds and are long and thin. Because they are usually not waxed, you don't need to peel them before using. They're perfect for this refreshing appetizer.

Basil- and Crabmeat-Topped Cucumbers

Quick

Hot Crab Crostini

Prep: 20 min Bake: 10 min

1/2 French baguette, cut into 1/4-inch slices (24 slices)

1 tablespoon olive or vegetable oil

1 can (6 ounces) crabmeat, well drained and flaked

1 jar (2 ounces) diced pimientos, well drained

2 ounces shredded Swiss cheese (1/2 cup)

1/2 cup grated Parmesan cheese

1/4 cup chive and onion cream cheese spread (from 8-ounce container)

1/4 teaspoon red pepper sauce

1 tablespoon chopped fresh chives

1. Heat oven to 400°. Place bread slices on large un-greased cookie sheet. Brush tops lightly with oil. Bake 3 to 5 minutes or until crisp and very light brown.

2. Meanwhile, mix remaining ingredients except chives in medium bowl. Spread 1 rounded tablespoonful crabmeat mixture on each bread slice.

3. Bake about 5 minutes or until filling is hot and cheese is melted. Sprinkle with chives.

24 appetizers.
1 Appetizer: Calories 125 (Calories from Fat 35); Fat 4g (Saturated 2g); Cholesterol 10mg; Sodium 260mg; Carbohydrate 16g (Dietary Fiber 1g); Protein 6g
% Daily Value: Vitamin A 2%; Vitamin C 2%; Calcium 8%; Iron 6%
Exchanges: 1 Starch, 1/2 High-Fat Meat
Carbohydrate Choices: 1

Hot Crab Crostini

BETTY'S TIPS

⊗ **Substitution**
If an imported cheese shop is available to you, try a different firm and flavorful cheese such as manchego or Asiago in place of the Swiss cheese.

⊗ **Success Hint**
Baguettes vary in width. If your baguette is very narrow, you may need 30 slices to hold all of the filling.

⊗ **Do-Ahead**
The bread can be baked ahead, covered and stored at room temperature. Prepare the crab mixture the day before; cover and refrigerate. Assemble the appetizers just before baking them.

Chipotle Chicken Drummettes

Prep: 15 min Marinate: 30 min Bake: 35 min

1/4 cup chili sauce

2 tablespoons soy sauce

2 chipotle chiles in adobo sauce (from 7-ounce can), chopped

2 teaspoons adobo sauce from can

1/4 teaspoon garlic powder

1/8 teaspoon coarsely ground pepper

2 pounds chicken drummettes (20 to 24)

Avocado Mayonnaise (right)

1. Mix all ingredients except drummettes and Avocado Mayonnaise in shallow dish. Add drummettes; turn to coat. Cover and refrigerate 30 minutes to marinate.

2. Heat oven to 375°. Line jelly roll pan, 15 1/2 × 10 1/2 × 1 inch, with aluminum foil. Spray foil with cooking spray. Remove drummettes from marinade; place in pan. Brush with remaining marinade. Bake 30 to 35 minutes or until chicken is no longer pink when centers of thickest pieces are cut.

3. Meanwhile, make Avocado Mayonnaise. Serve with warm drummettes.

20 to 24 appetizers.

Avocado Mayonnaise

1 medium ripe avocado, peeled and pitted

2 tablespoons mayonnaise or salad dressing

1/4 cup chopped fresh cilantro

1 teaspoon lime juice

Dash of salt

Mash avocado in small bowl. Stir in remaining ingredients until well blended. Refrigerate until serving.

1 Appetizer: Calories 85 (Calories from Fat 45); Fat 5g (Saturated 1g); Cholesterol 20mg; Sodium 135mg; Carbohydrate 4g (Dietary Fiber 1g); Protein 6g
% Daily Value: Vitamin A 2%; Vitamin C 2%; Calcium 0%; Iron 4%
Exchanges: 1 Medium-Fat Meat
Carbohydrate Choices: 0

BETTY'S TIPS

⚙ **Do-Ahead**
You can prepare and bake these yummy drummettes up to 24 hours ahead; cover with foil and refrigerate. Reheat in a covered pan at 350° for 20 to 25 minutes.

⚙ **Special Touch**
Place the Avocado Mayonnaise in a small serving bowl in the center of the platter with the warm drummettes. Garnish with shredded lime peel and cilantro.

⚙ **Did You Know?**
Chipotle chiles are smoked jalapeño chiles. They are available dried or canned in a spicy adobo sauce that we've used for this recipe.

Chipotle Chicken Drummettes

Low Fat

Spiced Pork Tenderloin Crostini

Prep: 30 min Bake: 45 min

$1/2$ teaspoon seasoned salt

$1/2$ teaspoon garlic pepper

$1/2$ teaspoon dried marjoram leaves

$1/4$ teaspoon ground sage

1 pound pork tenderloin

36 slices ($1/4$- to $1/2$-inch thick) baguette-style French bread (from 10-ounce loaf)

$1/4$ cup Dijon mustard

$3/4$ cup apple-cranberry chutney (from 8.5-ounce jar)

$1/3$ cup crumbled blue cheese

Fresh marjoram leaves

1. Heat oven to 425°. Mix seasoned salt, garlic pepper, marjoram and sage. Rub mixture over pork. Place pork in shallow roasting pan. Insert meat thermometer so tip is in thickest part of pork. Bake uncovered 20 to 25 minutes or until thermometer reads 155°. Cover pork with aluminum foil and let stand 10 to 15 minutes until thermometer reads 160°.

2. Meanwhile, reduce oven temperature to 375°. Place bread slices in ungreased jelly roll pan, $15^1/2 \times 10^1/2 \times 1$ inch. Bake about 5 minutes or until crisp; cool.

3. Cut pork into very thin slices. Spread each bread slice with about $1/4$ teaspoon mustard. Top each with a thin slice of pork, 1 teaspoon chutney, about $1/2$ teaspoon cheese and marjoram leaves.

36 crostini.
1 Crostini: Calories 55 (Calories from Fat 10); Fat 1g (Saturated 0g); Cholesterol 10mg; Sodium 140mg; Carbohydrate 7g (Dietary Fiber 0g); Protein 4g
% Daily Value: Vitamin A 0%; Vitamin C 0%; Calcium 2%; Iron 2%
Exchanges: $1/2$ Starch, $1/2$ Very Lean Meat
Carbohydrate Choices: $1/2$

BETTY'S TIPS

✿ **Substitution**
If you like, go ahead and use crumbled goat cheese instead of the blue cheese.

✿ **Do-Ahead**
All the components of this recipe can be prepared ahead of time. The pork can be cooked and in the refrigerator up to 24 hours in advance. The crostini slices can be baked up to 2 hours in advance. However, it's best to assemble the appetizers close to serving time.

✿ **Special Touch**
Use your prettiest platter for these elegant appetizers! Arrange the topped crostini, then garnish with sprigs of fresh marjoram and fresh currants or cranberries.

Spiced Pork Tenderloin Crostini

Caramelized-Onion Bruschetta

Prep: 15 min Cook: 16 min Cool: 10 min Broil: 4 min

½ cup butter or margarine

3 large red onions, cut in half and thinly sliced

¼ cup sugar

3 tablespoons raspberry or balsamic vinegar

1 loaf (1 pound) baguette bread, cut into ½-inch slices

1 tub (8 ounces) soft cream cheese with herbs or vegetables

2 tablespoons chopped fresh parsley

1. Melt butter in 12-inch heavy skillet over medium-high heat until sizzling. Cook onions in butter 5 to 6 minutes, stirring frequently, until onions are softened. Stir in sugar and vinegar. Cook 9 to 10 minutes, stirring frequently, until onions are very soft and light golden brown. Cool onion mixture slightly, about 10 minutes.

2. Set oven control to broil. Place bread slices on cookie sheet. Broil with tops 4 inches from heat 1 to 2 minutes or until lightly browned. Turn bread; broil 1 to 2 minutes longer or until lightly browned.

3. Spread about 2 teaspoons cream cheese on each bread slice. Top each with 1 tablespoon onion mixture; sprinkle with small amount of parsley.

12 servings (2 slices each).
1 Serving: Calories 270 (Calories from Fat 145); Fat 16g (Saturated 9g); Cholesterol 40mg; Sodium 330mg; Carbohydrate 27g (Dietary Fiber 2g); Protein 5g
% Daily Value: Vitamin A 12%; Vitamin C 4%; Calcium 6%; Iron 8%
Exchanges: 2 Starch, 2½ Fat
Carbohydrate Choices: 2

BETTY'S TIPS

⊗ **Variation**
The caramelized onion mixture is also great on sandwiches and grilled meat.

⊗ **Do-Ahead**
The onion mixture can be made two or three days ahead and kept refrigerated. Then just toast the bread, assemble and serve.

Caramelized-Onion Bruschetta

Low Fat

Nacho Cheese Pinwheels

Prep: 25 min Refrigerate: 1 hr

- 4 spinach-flavor, tomato-flavor or plain flour tortillas (8 to 10 inches in diameter)
- 1/2 cup bean dip
- 1/2 cup nacho cheese dip
- 3 to 4 tablespoons chopped green onions or chopped fresh cilantro

1. Spread each tortilla with about 2 tablespoons bean dip and 2 tablespoons cheese dip. Sprinkle each with onions.

2. Tightly roll up tortillas; wrap individually in plastic wrap. Refrigerate at least 1 hour but no longer than 24 hours. To serve, cut off ends from each roll and discard. Cut rolls into 1/2- to 3/4-inch slices. Secure with toothpicks if desired.

36 appetizers.
1 Appetizer: Calories 25 (Calories from Fat 10); Fat 1g (Saturated 1g); Cholesterol 0mg; Sodium 65mg; Carbohydrate 3g (Dietary Fiber 0g); Protein 1g
% Daily Value: Vitamin A 0%; Vitamin C 0%; Calcium 0%; Iron 0%
Exchanges: 1 Free Food
Carbohydrate Choices: 0

BETTY'S TIPS

⚙ **Substitution**
You could use jalapeño-flavored process cheese sauce instead of the nacho cheese dip.

⚙ **Success Hint**
These tasty morsels are easy to tote. You can take them to your destination before cutting, or go ahead and cut them and arrange on a platter. Cover tightly with plastic wrap. Garnish just before serving.

⚙ **Special Touch**
Use two colors of tortillas to make the pinwheels, then arrange them on a holiday platter. Pierce each pinwheel with a frilly toothpick, and add some fresh cilantro sprigs to the arrangement. A few pickled chile peppers would add to the festive look.

Brie and Cherry Pastry Cups

Prep: 30 min Bake: 23 min

- 1 sheet frozen puff pastry (from 17.3-ounce package), thawed
- 1/3 to 1/2 cup red cherry preserves
- 4 ounces Brie cheese, cut into 1/2 × 1/2-inch pieces (36 pieces)
- 1/4 cup chopped pecans
- 2 tablespoons chopped fresh chives

1. Heat oven to 375°. Spray 36 miniature muffin cups, 1 3/4 × 1 inch, with cooking spray. Cut pastry into 36 (1 1/2-inch) squares. Lightly press each square into muffin cup; press center with finger.

2. Bake 10 minutes. Press center with handle of wooden spoon. Bake 6 to 8 minutes longer or until golden brown. Immediately press again in center. Fill each with about 1/2 teaspoon preserves. Top with cheese piece, pecans and chives.

3. Bake 3 to 5 minutes or until cheese is melted. Serve warm.

36 appetizers.
1 Appetizer: Calories 60 (Calories from Fat 35); Fat 4g (Saturated 1g); Cholesterol 10mg; Sodium 35mg; Carbohydrate 5g (Dietary Fiber 0g); Protein 1g
% Daily Value: Vitamin A 0%; Vitamin C 0%; Calcium 0%; Iron 2%
Exchanges: 1/2 Other Carbohydrate, 1/2 Fat
Carbohydrate Choices: 0

BETTY'S TIPS

⚙ **Substitution**
If you like spicy foods, try substituting red or green jalapeño jelly for the cherry preserves. It's a delicious touch of sweet and spice!

⚙ **Do-Ahead**
Go ahead and assemble the cups and bake up to 4 hours in advance, omitting the final bake time for melting the cheese. Cover with plastic wrap and refrigerate until ready to bake. Right before serving, heat at 375° just until warm and cheese is melted.

⚙ **Special Touch**
Arrange these pretty appetizer cups on tiered serving plates with fresh rosemary and cherries.

Brie and Cherry Pastry Cups

Nacho Cheese Pinwheels

Citrus-Marinated Olives with Roasted Peppers

Prep: 15 min Marinate: 1 hr

¼ cup olive or vegetable oil

¼ cup balsamic vinegar

1 teaspoon grated orange peel

1 teaspoon grated lemon peel

1 tablespoon chopped fresh rosemary leaves

1 teaspoon fennel seed, crushed

1 cup drained pitted Kalamata olives

1 cup drained pitted Spanish olives

¼ cup sliced roasted yellow bell peppers (from 12-ounce jar)

Fresh rosemary sprigs, if desired

Orange and/or lemon peel spirals or wedges, if desired

1. Mix oil, vinegar, orange peel, lemon peel, rosemary and fennel seed in medium bowl until blended. Stir in olives. Cover and refrigerate at least 1 hour to marinate.

2. Just before serving, stir in bell peppers. Garnish with rosemary sprigs and orange spirals.

16 servings.
1 Serving: Calories 40 (Calories from Fat 35); Fat 4g (Saturated 1g); Cholesterol 0mg; Sodium 300mg; Carbohydrate 1g (Dietary Fiber 0g); Protein 0g
% Daily Value: Vitamin A 8%; Vitamin C 16%; Calcium 0%; Iron 2%
Exchanges: 1 Fat
Carbohydrate Choices: 0

BETTY'S TIPS

✪ **Substitution**
Go ahead and use other olives if you like. You can also use olives with pits instead of the pitted variety.

✪ **Success Hint**
If you want to tote this appetizer to a get-together, package the olives separately from the roasted peppers. When you arrive at your destination, combine them in your serving bowl and garnish with the rosemary and orange spirals.

✪ **Did You Know?**
Greek Kalamata olives are large, rich and fruity and are a dark eggplant color. The flavors in this recipe are a perfect match for them.

Citrus-Marinated Olives with Roasted Peppers

Olive and Herb Deviled Eggs

Prep: 1 hr

8 hard-cooked eggs

1/3 cup mayonnaise or salad dressing

2 tablespoons finely chopped parsley

2 tablespoons finely chopped fresh marjoram leaves

2 tablespoons finely chopped fresh chives

1/2 teaspoon garlic pepper

1/2 cup chopped ripe olives

8 pitted ripe olives, sliced

Fresh parsley or marjoram sprigs or leaves, if desired

1. Cut peeled egg lengthwise in half with rippled vegetable cutter or sharp knife. Carefully remove yolks and place in small bowl; mash with fork. Reserve egg white halves.

2. Mix mashed yolks, mayonnaise, chopped herbs, garlic pepper and chopped olives. Carefully spoon mixture into egg white halves, mounding lightly. Top each egg half with olive slices. Garnish with small herb sprig or leaves.

16 appetizers.
1 Appetizer: Calories 80 (Calories from Fat 65); Fat 7g (Saturated 1g); Cholesterol 110mg; Sodium 110mg; Carbohydrate 1g (Dietary Fiber 0g); Protein 3g
% Daily Value: Vitamin A 4%; Vitamin C 0%; Calcium 2%; Iron 2%
Exchanges: 1/2 Medium-Fat Meat, 1 Fat
Carbohydrate Choices: 0

Olive and Herb Deviled Eggs

BETTY'S TIPS

✿ **Substitution**
Go ahead and substitute basil for the parsley or marjoram if you like.

✿ **Success Hint**
Don't be tempted to use Kalamata or other specialty olives in this recipe because the flavor would be too strong. The ripe olives are mild enough to add just a pleasant olive flavor without overpowering the egg flavor.

✿ **Do-Ahead**
Prepare the stuffed eggs up to 24 hours in advance. Refrigerate in a tightly covered container until serving time.

✿ **Special Touch**
Instead of an olive slice, top each egg half with a cherry tomato wedge.

Honey-Cardamom Mixed Nuts

Honey-Cardamom Mixed Nuts

Prep: 10 min Bake: 45 min

$^1/_4$ cup honey

2 tablespoons butter or margarine, melted

$^3/_4$ teaspoon ground cardamom

$^1/_2$ teaspoon salt

$^1/_2$ teaspoon ground cinnamon

$^1/_4$ teaspoon ground cloves

$^1/_4$ teaspoon ground ginger

2 containers (10 ounces each) deluxe salted mixed nuts without peanuts

1. Heat oven to 275°. Spray jelly roll pan, $15^1/_2 \times 10^1/_2 \times 1$ inch, with cooking spray. Mix all ingredients except nuts in large bowl. Add nuts; stir to coat.

2. Spread nuts in pan. Bake 45 minutes, stirring every 15 minutes. Cool in pan, stirring occasionally.

24 servings (2 tablespoons each).
1 Serving: Calories 175 (Calories from Fat 125); Fat 14g (Saturated 3g); Cholesterol 5mg; Sodium 220mg; Carbohydrate 8g (Dietary Fiber 1g); Protein 4g
% Daily Value: Vitamin A 0%; Vitamin C 0%; Calcium 2%; Iron 4%
Exchanges: $^1/_2$ Other Carbohydrate, $^1/_2$ High-Fat Meat, 2 Fat
Carbohydrate Choices: $^1/_2$

BETTY'S TIPS

◉ **Substitution**
You can use a combination of whatever salted nuts you have. Almonds and cashews are especially elegant and are very nice together.

◉ **Special Touch**
These spiced nuts are great to serve at a party at home or away, or to give as a special gift. Package them in a pretty jar or in their own serving dish, then add a bow and a copy of the recipe to present to the recipient.

◉ **Did You Know?**
Cardamom is known for its spicy sweet flavor and pungent aroma. It's used extensively in Scandinavian and East Indian cooking.

Quick

Gingerbread Popcorn Snack

Prep: 10 min Bake: 10 min Cool: 10 min
(Photo on page xii)

12 cups lightly salted popped popcorn

$^1/_2$ cup butter or margarine

2 tablespoons molasses

2 teaspoons ground ginger

1 teaspoon ground cinnamon

$^1/_4$ teaspoon salt

1. Heat oven to 350°. Divide popcorn between 2 ungreased rectangular pans, $13 \times 9 \times 2$ inches each.

2. Heat remaining ingredients in 1-quart saucepan over medium heat, stirring occasionally, until butter is melted. Pour over popcorn, tossing until completely coated.

3. Bake uncovered 10 minutes, stirring after 5 minutes. Cool 10 minutes.

10 cups.
$^1/_2$ Cup: Calories 80 (Calories from Fat 55); Fat 6g (Saturated 3g); Cholesterol 10mg; Sodium 120mg; Carbohydrate 5g (Dietary Fiber 1g); Protein 1g
% Daily Value: Vitamin A 4%; Vitamin C 0%; Calcium 0%; Iron 0%
Exchanges: $^1/_2$ Starch, 1 Fat
Carbohydrate Choices: 0

BETTY'S TIPS

◉ **Do-Ahead**
You can make the popcorn up to 48 hours in advance. Just remember to cool completely, then store tightly covered.

◉ **Special Touch**
For added festive flavor, add 1 to 2 cups of pecans or almonds to the popcorn before baking. This popcorn, with or without the nuts, makes a nice gift. Wrap in a pretty tin and tie with a bow to present to a special friend or relative.

Betty Crocker
ON WHAT'S NEW

The Cheese Plate

Holiday appetizer fare doesn't have to be involved and complicated. Instead, it can be simple and unadorned—and delicious! Creating a cheese plate or cheese display will simplify your holiday meal planning—with mouthwatering results.

Cheese ABC's

Specialty shops and farmers' markets, in addition to your local supermarket, are invaluable resources when shopping for cheese. Stores that offer the largest variety, such as wine shops, gourmet food stores and food co-ops, may also offer you samples to taste. This is a great way to explore cheeses you aren't familiar with and taste the differences among cheeses you like. Sample sharp Cheddar and mild Cheddar, and note the differences. Be sure to ask lots of questions. Cheese experts will be able to answer questions and suggest the right cheeses for your entertaining plans.

A If you will be serving cheese as an appetizer, choose three to five cheeses and plan on 1 to 2 ounces of each cheese per person.

B Remove cheese from the refrigerator no more than 2 hours before guests arrive, so the cheese can warm to room temperature, the optimal serving temperature.

C Arrange the cheeses however you like, perhaps according to size, color, shape or flavor. As a general rule, first sample milder, younger cheeses with less complexity, such as Havarti, and work your way up to more mature, bolder, heavier cheeses, such as Asiago or Limburger. Or if you prefer, serve a "flight," samples of cheeses with something in common, such as texture or cheeses from the same family, perhaps Cheddar. A flight of soft or semisoft cheeses might include Fontina, Camembert, Havarti and Brie.

D Display cheeses in large wedges, or whole for softer cheeses such as Brie. Let guests serve themselves, using an assortment of sharp knives, cheese spreaders and cheese slicers.

E Label cheeses for your guests. Be creative by using toothpicks with flags, individual place cards, ceramic markers or any other type of marker. Knowing which cheeses guests enjoyed most will be helpful for future entertaining.

Great Go-Togethers

▶ **Cheese** is wonderful by itself, but it's even better when accompanied by foods that cleanse the palate, add texture and taste, and complement the cheese. Serve your cheese with

▶ **Assorted bread cubes** or slices (dark breads, nut breads) or assorted crackers

▶ **Fresh or dried fruits** (apples, apricots, cherries, dates, figs, grapes, melon, pears)

▶ **Vegetables** (roasted red bell peppers or raw bell pepper strips, raw carrots, cooked green beans, olives, marinated vegetable salad)

▶ **Nuts** (roasted or smoked whole almonds, cashews, hazelnuts, pecans)

▶ **Meats** (capicola, chorizo, ham, prosciutto, salami, almost any cured meat)

Betty Crocker
MAKES IT EASY

Cheese Primer

Cheese is most commonly made from cow, sheep or goat milk, but it can also be made from yak, buffalo and camel milk! Even when stored at optimal conditions, all cheeses continue to ripen. Younger, fresher cheeses will have a short life (less than a week) than harder, aged cheeses, which may keep up to 2 months. Cheese can be classified in a variety of ways, but it is loosely grouped into the six main categories below.

Fresh or soft ripened cheeses are either not aged at all or are aged for a very short time. Those that are aged may have edible rinds. These cheeses develop more intense flavors as they continue to age. Fresh cheeses include cream cheese, crème fraîche, mascarpone and fresh mozzarella. Soft ripened cheeses include Boursin, Brie, feta, **Camembert** (pictured), and queso blanco.

Semihard cheeses are firm in texture but are not crumbly. They have more moisture than hard cheeses. They are good sliced and can be grated as well. Semihard cheeses include brick, **Cheddar** (pictured), Emmental, kasseri, Monterey Jack and provolone.

Hard cheeses are very firm and crumbly in texture with more intense flavors. Often eaten out of hand, many are also shredded and used in recipes. Hard cheeses include Myzithra, **Parmigiano-Reggiano** (pictured), Romano and Swiss, as well as aged Gouda and aged dry Monterey Jack.

Washed rind cheeses are typically soft cheeses that are aged for a short time. During the ripening process, the cheese is washed weekly with a liquid such as brine, wine or beer. This washing produces a rusty orange rind (that is not eaten) with a pungent, strong aroma. Although the rind is robust, the cheese inside is usually creamy and mild. Washed rind cheeses include Limburger, **Muenster** (pictured), and Taleggio.

Semisoft cheeses are firm enough to slice but are still soft and creamy. These cheeses include Edam, **Fontina** (pictured bottom), baby Gouda, Havarti, **Port-Salut** (pictured top) and baby Swiss.

Blue cheeses have had mold introduced to them during process and as a result have blue-green veins that run throughout the cheese. Depending on the aging conditions, blue cheeses can vary from creamy to firm and from very mild to robust and strong. Common blues include Danish blue, **Gorgonzola** (pictured), Maytag blue, Roquefort and Stilton.

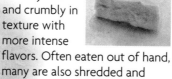

Sandwiches and Pizza

Midday Meals that Shine

Chicken Pizza Mexicana (page 75)

Open-Face Turkey Diner Sandwiches (page 75)

Tex-Mex Veggie Hoagies

Prep: 20 min

6 hoagie buns, split

6 slices (³/₄ ounce each) Monterey jack cheese, cut diagonally in half

¹/₂ cup finely chopped cucumber

¹/₄ cup mayonnaise or salad dressing

¹/₄ cup Old El Paso Thick 'n Chunky salsa

1 teaspoon finely chopped seeded jalapeño chile pepper

¹/₂ teaspoon ground cumin

¹/₄ teaspoon salt

2 medium tomatoes, seeded and finely chopped (1¹/₂ cups)

1 medium green bell pepper, finely chopped (1 cup)

2 medium green onions, thinly sliced (2 tablespoons)

1. Scoop out bread from bottoms of buns; reserve for another use. Line bottom of each bun with 2 triangles of cheese.

2. Mix remaining ingredients. Divide evenly among buns. Serve immediately.

6 sandwiches.
1 Sandwich: Calories 425 (Calories from Fat 155); Fat 17g (Saturated 6g); Cholesterol 26mg; Sodium 910mg; Carbohydrate 54g (Dietary Fiber 4g); Protein 14g
% Daily Value: Vitamin A 14%; Vitamin C 48%; Calcium 24%; Iron 16%
Exchanges: 3 Starch, 2 Vegetable, 3 Fat
Carbohydrate Choices: 3¹/₂

BETTY'S TIPS

☺ **Success Hint**
We suggest using hoagie buns or other buns with a firm, crusty outside. This filling is moist, so soft breads, such as hot dog buns, aren't the best choice.

☺ **Health Twist**
These sandwiches are packed with veggies, which makes them high in fiber and vitamin C. Use reduced-fat mayonnaise and reduced-fat cheese to trim the fat to 10 grams and the calories to 370 per serving.

☺ **Did You Know?**
Savor the heat of Southwest cooking. Use a little more jalapeño chile pepper, and add a hot shot by using medium or hot salsa.

Tex-Mex Veggie Hoagies

Quick

Dilled Shrimp and Egg Salad Wraps

Prep: 10 min

4 hard-cooked eggs, chopped
1 cup chopped cooked shrimp
1 tablespoon chopped fresh dill weed
2 tablespoons finely chopped red onion
3 tablespoons creamy mustard-mayonnaise
   sauce
1/4 teaspoon salt
4 flour tortillas (8 inches in diameter)
2 cups shredded lettuce

1. Mix all ingredients except tortillas and lettuce in medium bowl.

2. Spread mixture evenly on each tortilla; top with lettuce. Fold in sides of each wrap; roll up. Cut each in half.

3. Serve immediately or wrap each sandwich in plastic wrap. Refrigerate until serving time or up to 24 hours.

4 wraps.
1 Wrap: Calories 310 (Calories from Fat 110); Fat 12g (Saturated 3g); Cholesterol 335mg; Sodium 630mg; Carbohydrate 28g (Dietary Fiber 2g); Protein 23g
% Daily Value: Vitamin A 10%; Vitamin C 4%; Calcium 10%; Iron 22%
Exchanges: 2 Starch, 2 1/2 Lean Meat
Carbohydrate Choices: 2

BETTY'S TIPS

⊛ **Success Hint**
Shredding the lettuce makes rolling the wraps easier. To shred the lettuce, cut the leaves into thin strips with a sharp knife.

⊛ **Time-Saver**
Pressed for time? Look for hard-cooked eggs in the deli or dairy area of the grocery store.

Dilled Shrimp and Egg Salad Wraps

Peppercorn Beef Pitas

Prep: 15 min

- 4 cups romaine and leaf lettuce mix (from 10-ounce bag)
- $1/2$ pound cubed cooked roast beef ($1^1/_3$ cups)
- 4 roma (plum) tomatoes, cut lengthwise in half, then sliced
- $1/2$ cup peppercorn ranch dressing
- 2 pita breads (8 inches in diameter), cut in half to form pockets
- $1/4$ cup sliced red onion, if desired

1. Toss lettuce, beef, tomatoes and dressing.

2. Spoon mixture evenly into pita bread halves. Top with onion. Serve immediately or wrap each sandwich in plastic wrap. Refrigerate until serving or up to 1 hour.

4 pita pockets.
1 Pocket: Calories 415 (Calories from Fat 205); Fat 23g (Saturated 5g); Cholesterol 55mg; Sodium 580mg; Carbohydrate 31g (Dietary Fiber 3g); Protein 22g
% Daily Value: Vitamin A 32%; Vitamin C 38%; Calcium 10%; Iron 20%
 Exchanges: 2 Starch, 2 Medium-Fat Meat, 2 Fat
Carbohydrate Choices: 2

BETTY'S TIPS

⚙ **Substitution**
  Cubed cooked turkey or smoked turkey from the deli can be used instead of the beef. Halved cherry tomatoes can be used instead of the roma variety.

⚙ **Variation**
  For a terrific salad, omit the pita breads and toss the remaining ingredients together. You can also spoon the mixture onto flour tortillas and roll up.

Turkey Cucumber Dill Sandwiches

Prep: 15 min

- $1/4$ cup mayonnaise or salad dressing
- 1 tablespoon dried dill weed
- 8 slices multigrain bread
- $1/2$ pound sliced cooked deli turkey
- 4 slices (1 ounce each) dill Havarti or Muenster cheese
- 16 thin slices cucumber
- 4 lettuce leaves

1. Mix mayonnaise and dill weed. Spread on one side of each bread slice.

2. Top 4 slices with turkey, cheese, cucumber and lettuce. Top with remaining bread.

4 sandwiches.
1 Sandwich: Calories 420 (Calories from Fat 215); Fat 24g (Saturated 9g); Cholesterol 65mg; Sodium 1,200mg; Carbohydrate 28g (Dietary Fiber 4g); Protein 23g
% Daily Value: Vitamin A 14%; Vitamin C 8%; Calcium 22%; Iron 16%
Exchanges: 2 Starch, $2^1/_2$ High-Fat Meat
Carbohydrate Choices: 2

BETTY'S TIPS

⚙ **Substitution**
  If you have fresh dill growing in the garden, use 2 teaspoons chopped fresh dill weed in place of the dried dill weed.

⚙ **Serve-With**
  Add carrot and celery sticks with your favorite dip for an easy summer meal. Serve ice cream and fresh berries for dessert.

Peppercorn Beef Pitas

Turkey Cucumber Dill Sandwiches

Betty Crocker
ON BASICS

Quick
Basil Chicken Salad

Prep: 10 min

2 cups chopped cooked chicken
1/4 cup finely chopped celery
1/4 cup finely chopped red bell pepper
2 tablespoons chopped fresh basil leaves
3 tablespoons mayonnaise or salad dressing
1/4 teaspoon onion powder
1/8 teaspoon salt
   Dash of pepper

1. Mix all ingredients in small bowl.

2. Cover and refrigerate until ready to serve.

4 servings.
1 Serving: Calories 200 (Calories from Fat 115); Fat 13g (Saturated 3g); Cholesterol 65mg; Sodium 200mg; Carbohydrate 1g (Dietary Fiber 0g); Protein 20g
% Daily Value: Vitamin A 14%; Vitamin C 30%; Calcium 2%; Iron 4%
Exchanges: 3 Lean Meat, 1 Fat
Carbohydrate Choices: 0

Use kitchen scissors to cut basil into very small pieces.

Basil Chicken Salad

Basil Chicken Salad Sandwiches

Prep: 10 min

1 cup shredded lettuce

4 pita breads (6 inches in diameter), cut in half to form pockets

2 cups Basil Chicken Salad (opposite page) or deli chicken salad spread

16 thin cucumber slices

¼ cup cashew halves

1. Place about 2 tablespoons lettuce in each pita bread half; top each with ¼ cup Basil Chicken Salad.

2. Place cucumber slices in pitas. Top salad with cashews. Serve immediately, or wrap each sandwich in plastic wrap and refrigerate until serving.

8 sandwiches.
1 Sandwich: Calories 40 (Calories from Fat 160); Fat 18g (Saturated 3g); Cholesterol 65mg; Sodium 450mg; Carbohydrate 33g (Dietary Fiber 2g); Protein 26g
% Daily Value: Vitamin A 16%; Vitamin C 34%; Calcium 6%; Iron 16%
Exchanges: 2 Starch, 3 Medium-Fat Meat
Carbohydrate Choices: 2

BETTY'S TIPS

⊘ **Substitution**
Slivered almonds or chopped peanuts would also be a good topper for the sandwiches.

⊘ **Variation**
The Basil Chicken Salad is also delicious in other bread choices. Or try a scoop on a bed of shredded lettuce.

Basil Chicken Salad Sandwiches

Turkey, Bacon and Guacamole Wraps

Prep: 15 min

1 ripe avocado, pitted, peeled and mashed

1 tablespoon Old El Paso taco sauce

1/4 teaspoon garlic salt

4 flour tortillas (8 to 10 inches in diameter)

8 ounces thinly sliced cooked turkey

8 slices precooked bacon

4 romaine lettuce leaves

1/4 cup drained roasted red bell peppers (from 7-ounce jar), large pieces cut up

1. Mix avocado, taco sauce and garlic salt in small bowl. Spread about 1 tablespoon on each tortilla.

2. Top tortillas with turkey; spread with any remaining avocado mixture. Top with bacon, romaine and bell peppers. Fold in sides of each wrap; roll up. Cut each in half. Serve immediately or wrap each sandwich in plastic wrap. Refrigerate until serving or up to 24 hours.

8 wraps.
1 Wrap: Calories 385 (Calories from Fat 160); Fat 18g (Saturated 5g); Cholesterol 40mg; Sodium 1,210mg; Carbohydrate 36g (Dietary Fiber 4g); Protein 20g
% Daily Value: Vitamin A 16%; Vitamin C 36%; Calcium 8%; Iron 16%
Exchanges: 2 Starch, 2 Medium-Fat Meat, 1 Vegetable, 1 1/2 Fat
Carbohydrate Choices: 2 1/2

BETTY'S TIPS

✿ **Success Hint**
For the best results and flavor, purchase avocados that are slightly soft to the touch. If they are still firm, let stand at room temperature for a couple of days.

✿ **Time-Saver**
To save prep time, use refrigerated guacamole instead of the avocado.

✿ **Serve-With**
Plan to have small bags of tortilla or corn chips ready to send off with these sandwiches.

Turkey, Bacon and Guacamole Wraps

Quick

Ham and Cheese Tortilla Roll-Ups

Prep: 10 min

1¹/₂ cups shredded Cheddar cheese (6 ounces)

¹/₄ cup mayonnaise or salad dressing

¹/₄ cup sour cream

1 can (11 ounces) Green Giant Mexicorn whole kernel corn, red and green peppers, drained

10 flour tortillas (6 to 8 inches in diameter)

10 slices (1 ounce each) fully cooked deli ham
Cilantro sprigs, if desired

1. Mix cheese, mayonnaise, sour cream and corn in medium bowl.

2. Top each tortilla with 1 slice ham. Spread 2 rounded tablespoonfuls corn mixture over ham. Top with cilantro. Roll up tortillas.

10 roll-ups.

1 Roll-Up: Calories 335 (Calories from Fat 155); Fat 17g (Saturated 7g); Cholesterol 40mg; Sodium 840mg; Carbohydrate 30g (Dietary Fiber 2g); Protein 15g
% Daily Value: Vitamin A 6%; Vitamin C 2%; Calcium 14%; Iron 10%
Exchanges: 2 Starch, 1 Medium-Fat Meat, 2 Fat
Carbohydrate Choices: 3

BETTY'S TIPS

⚙ **Substitution**
Smoked deli turkey can be used instead of the ham.

⚙ **Success Hint**
Make sure the corn is thoroughly drained. After pouring liquid from the can, drain the corn on a paper towel to help absorb the juices.

Ham and Cheese Tortilla Roll-Ups

Cheese and Veggie Sandwiches

Prep: 15 min

4	hoagie buns
1/2	cup hummus (from 7-ounce container)
4	slices (1 ounce each) Cheddar cheese
4	slices (1 ounce each) Swiss cheese
1	medium cucumber, cut into 16 slices
1	medium tomato, cut into 4 slices
4	thin slices red onion, if desired

1. Cut buns horizontally in half. Spread hummus over bottom of each bun.

2. Fill buns with cheeses, cucumber, tomato and onion.

4 sandwiches.
1 Sandwich: Calories 530 (Calories from Fat 205); Fat 23g (Saturated 12g); Cholesterol 55mg; Sodium 940mg; Carbohydrate 60g (Dietary Fiber 6g); Protein 27g
% Daily Value: Vitamin A 18%; Vitamin C 16%; Calcium 54%; Iron 22%
 Exchanges: 4 Starch, 2 High-Fat Meat, 1/2 Fat
Carbohydrate Choices: 4

BETTY'S TIPS

⊕ **Serve-With**
These robust vegetable sandwiches go well with watermelon wedges and lemonade.

⊕ **Variation**
Use your favorite cheese—provolone, Muenster, Monterey Jack or Monterey Jack with jalapeño peppers—or a slice of each.

Cheese and Veggie Sandwiches

Quick

Beef and Provolone Focaccia Sandwiches

Prep: 10 min

1 round loaf (12 ounces) focaccia bread
  (9 inches in diameter)
1/4 cup refrigerated basil pesto
8 ounces thinly sliced cooked deli roast beef
1 medium tomato, thinly sliced
8 slices (3/4 ounce each) provolone cheese
2 or 3 romaine lettuce leaves

1. Cut focaccia horizontally in half to make 2 layers. Spread pesto over cut sides.

2. Layer beef, tomato, cheese and romaine between layers. Cut filled focaccia into 6 wedges. Serve immediately or wrap each wedge in plastic wrap. Refrigerate until serving or up to 24 hours.

Beef and Provolone Focaccia Sandwiches

6 sandwiches.
1 Sandwich: Calories 400 (Calories from Fat 190); Fat 21g (Saturated 7g); Cholesterol 60mg; Sodium 870mg; Carbohydrate 29g (Dietary Fiber 2g); Protein 24g
% Daily Value: Vitamin A 12%; Vitamin C 8%; Calcium 26%; Iron 18%
Exchanges: 2 Starch, 2 1/2 Medium-Fat Meat, 1 Fat
Carbohydrate Choices: 2

BETTY'S TIPS

⚙ **Substitution**
You can use another green instead of the romaine. Arugula would be delicious, or try leaf or Bibb lettuce for a flavor change.

⚙ **Did You Know?**
If you've never had focaccia, you're in for a treat. It's a wonderful round loaf of Italian bread that has been seasoned with olive oil, salt and sometimes spices. It's available fresh at many bakeries and often can be found packaged in the deli or bakery area of large grocery stores.

Betty Crocker

MAKES IT EASY

Corn-Stuffed Turkey Burgers

Prep: 15 min Grill: 15 min

1¼ pounds ground turkey

½ cup Progresso plain bread crumbs

1 tablespoon chopped chipotle chiles in adobo sauce (from 7-ounce can)

½ cup fresh corn kernels or Green Giant Niblets frozen corn

2 tablespoons Old El Paso Thick 'n Chunky salsa

1 tablespoon chopped fresh cilantro

½ teaspoon salt

4 slices (¾ ounce each) Cheddar cheese

4 hamburger buns, split

Shape turkey mixture into ¼-inch-thick patties. Spoon 2 tablespoons corn mixture onto center of 4 patties.

1. Heat coals or gas grill for direct heat. Mix turkey, bread crumbs and chiles. Shape mixture into 8 patties, about ¼ inch thick.

2. Mix corn, salsa, cilantro and salt in small bowl. Spoon about 2 tablespoons corn mixture onto center of 4 patties. Top with remaining patties; press edges to seal.

3. Grill patties uncovered 4 to 6 inches from medium heat 12 to 14 minutes, turning once, until no longer pink in center. Top patties with cheese. Cover and grill about 1 minute or until cheese is melted. Serve burgers on buns. Serve with additional salsa and chopped cilantro if desired.

Top with remaining patties; press edges to seal.

4 sandwiches.
1 Sandwich: Calories 535 (Calories from Fat 225); Fat 25g (Saturated 9g); Cholesterol 115mg; Sodium 960mg; Carbohydrate 37g (Dietary Fiber 2g); Protein 40g
% Daily Value: Vitamin A 8%; Vitamin C 2%; Calcium 22%; Iron 20%
Exchanges: 2½ Starch, 4½ Medium-Fat Meat
Carbohydrate Choices: 2½

Corn-Stuffed Turkey Burgers

Baked Turkey, Cheddar and Bacon Sandwich

Baked Turkey, Cheddar and Bacon Sandwich

Prep: 10 min Bake: 32 min Stand: 5 min

2	cups Original Bisquick mix
1	cup milk
1	egg
4	ounces thinly sliced deli turkey breast
1½	cups shredded Cheddar cheese (6 ounces)
5	slices precooked bacon

1. Heat oven to 400°. Spray square baking dish, 8 × 8 × 2 inches, with cooking spray.

2. Stir Bisquick mix, milk and egg until blended. Spread half of the batter into baking dish. Top with turkey and 1 cup cheese. Top with bacon. Spread remaining batter over bacon.

3. Bake uncovered about 29 minutes or until golden brown and center is set. Sprinkle with remaining ½ cup cheese. Bake about 3 minutes until cheese is melted. Let stand 5 minutes before cutting.

6 servings.
1 Serving: Calories 355 (Calories from Fat 180); Fat 20g (Saturated 9g); Cholesterol 80mg; Sodium 1,080mg; Carbohydrate 27g (Dietary Fiber 0g); Protein 17g
% Daily Value: Vitamin A 8%; Vitamin C 0%; Calcium 26%; Iron 10%
Exchanges: 2 Starch, 1½ Medium-Fat Meat, 2 Fat
Carbohydrate Choices: 2

BETTY'S TIPS

✪ **Substitution**
You can purchase turkey from the deli or use packaged sliced turkey breast found with the luncheon meats.

✪ **Did You Know?**
This hot sandwich, reminiscent of a club sandwich, makes an awesome casual meal. Wrap each serving in a sheet of aluminum foil, and then tote with fresh fruit and cookies for a hot portable meal.

Betty Crocker
ON BASICS

Low Fat

Summer Refrigerator Relish

Prep: 20 min Chill: 24 hr

6 cups finely chopped cabbage
1 cup sugar
½ cup white or cider vinegar
1½ teaspoons salt
1 teaspoon mustard seed
½ teaspoon celery seed
2 medium cucumbers, shredded (3 cups)
1 medium red bell pepper, chopped (1 cup)

1. Mix all ingredients in large bowl. Spoon into 1-quart jar and 1-pint jar.

2. Cover and refrigerate at least 24 hours but no longer than 2 weeks.

6 cups relish.
¼ Cup: Calories 40 (Calories from Fat 0); Fat 0g (Saturated 0g); Cholesterol 0mg; Sodium 150mg; Carbohydrate 10g (Dietary Fiber 1g); Protein 0g
% Daily Value: Vitamin A 6%; Vitamin C 26%; Calcium 0%; Iron 0%
Exchanges: 2 Vegetable
Carbohydrate Choices: ½

To chop cabbage, place flat side of ¼ head of cabbage on cutting board. Cut into thin slices with large sharp knife. Cut slices several times to make smaller pieces.

Summer Refrigerator Relish

Country Brats

Prep: 5 min Cook: 15 min

6 fully cooked bratwurst

1 can or bottle (12 ounces) beer

3 tablespoons spicy brown or Dijon mustard

6 bratwurst buns, split

³/₄ cup Summer Refrigerator Relish (opposite page) or sweet pickle relish

6 sandwiches.
1 Sandwich: Calories 485 (Calories from Fat 245); Fat 27g (Saturated 9g); Cholesterol 50mg; Sodium 1,620mg; Carbohydrate 44g (Dietary Fiber 2g); Protein 16g
% Daily Value: Vitamin A 2%; Vitamin C 0%; Calcium 10%; Iron 16%
Exchanges: 3 Starch, 1 Medium-Fat Meat, 3 Fat
Carbohydrate Choices: 3

1. Pierce each bratwurst with fork 3 or 4 times. Heat beer and bratwurst to boiling in 2-quart saucepan; reduce heat. Cover and simmer about 10 minutes or until heated through; drain.

2. Spread mustard on buns. Place bratwursts in buns. Spoon 2 tablespoons relish over top of each bratwurst.

BETTY'S TIPS

✪ **Success Hint**

Don't let a rainy day dampen the look of the brats. To give them a browned, grilled look, drain the beer and heat the cooked bratwursts in the bottom of the saucepan over medium heat until browned.

Country Brats

London Broil Sandwiches with Lemon Mayonnaise

Prep: 15 min Grill: 9 min

Lemon Mayonnaise (below)
1 loaf (1 pound) rustic baguette bread
2 tablespoons olive or vegetable oil
1 tablespoon grated lemon peel
1 tablespoon soy sauce
1/2 teaspoon lemon pepper seasoning salt
1 pound beef boneless sirloin steak, 1 inch thick
1 1/2 cups shredded romaine lettuce

1. Heat coals or gas grill for direct heat. Make Lemon Mayonnaise.

2. Cut bread horizontally in half. Drizzle 1 tablespoon oil over cut sides of bread. Mix remaining 1 tablespoon oil, lemon peel, soy sauce and lemon pepper seasoning salt. Rub both sides of beef with oil mixture.

3. Cover and grill beef 4 to 6 inches from medium heat 8 to 9 minutes, turning once or twice, until desired doneness. Add bread, cut sides down, for last 2 minutes of grilling or until toasted.

4. Spread Lemon Mayonnaise on bottom half of bread. Cut beef crosswise into thin slices. Layer romaine and beef on bottom half of bread. Add top half of bread; cut crosswise into 4 sandwiches.

4 sandwiches.

Lemon Mayonnaise
1/4 cup mayonnaise or salad dressing
1 teaspoon grated lemon peel
1/4 teaspoon lemon pepper seasoning salt

Mix all ingredients.

1 Sandwich: Calories 590 (Calories from Fat 225); Fat 25g (Saturated 5g); Cholesterol 70mg; Sodium 1,270mg; Carbohydrate 58g (Dietary Fiber 3g); Protein 33g
% Daily Value: Vitamin A 10%; Vitamin C 10%; Calcium 10%; Iron 32%
Exchanges: 4 Starch, 3 Medium-Fat Meat, 1 Fat
Carbohydrate Choices: 4

BETTY'S TIPS

⌖ **Success Hint**
One medium lemon will yield 1 to 2 tablespoons of peel. Grate the lemon peel carefully so that you use only the yellow part of the skin and not the bitter white pith that is underneath.

⌖ **Serve-With**
Serve these hearty sandwiches with deli potato salad and fresh tomato slices. Top off the meal with fresh strawberries and whipped cream.

London Broil Sandwiches with Lemon Mayonnaise

Reuben Sandwiches

Prep: 15 min Cook: 11 hr

1 package (2 pounds) refrigerated sauerkraut
1 package (2 to 3 pounds) corned beef brisket
1 cup Thousand Island dressing
16 slices pumpernickel rye bread, toasted
8 slices (1 ounce each) Swiss cheese

1. Place sauerkraut in 3- to 4-quart slow cooker. Place beef brisket on sauerkraut. (If brisket includes packet of spices, sprinkle spices over brisket.)

2. Cover and cook on Low heat setting 9 to 11 hours.

3. Remove beef from cooker; place on cutting board. Cut beef into slices. To serve, spread 1 tablespoon dressing on each toast slice. Using slotted spoon to remove sauerkraut from cooker, top 8 slices toast with ½ cup sauerkraut each. Top sauerkraut with beef slices and cheese slice. Top with remaining toast.

8 sandwiches.
1 Sandwich: Calories 540 (Calories from Fat 315); Fat 35g (Saturated 12g); Cholesterol 110mg; Sodium 2,390mg; Carbohydrate 33g (Dietary Fiber 6g); Protein 29g
% Daily Value: Vitamin A 6%; Vitamin C 14%; Calcium 36%; Iron 26%
Exchanges: 2 Starch, 1 Vegetable, 3 High-Fat Meat, 1 Fat
Carbohydrate Choices: 2

BETTY'S TIPS

⚙ **Serve-With**
This cries out for a good garlic dill pickle, some crunchy potato chips and a side of deli slaw.

⚙ **Variation**
To make this a portable potluck sandwich, stir the sliced beef into the sauerkraut. Place the dressing in a squeeze bottle (like for ketchup), and set out a basket of rye buns and smaller slices of Swiss cheese to make it easy for guests to make their own sandwiches.

⚙ **Special Touch**
Need a hearty party snack? Build the sandwiches on slices of party rye for a three-bite treat.

Reuben Sandwiches

Big and Spicy Chicken Hoagies

Prep: 15 min Cook: 8 hr

3 tablespoons Caribbean jerk seasoning

3 pounds boneless skinless chicken thighs

1 large red or green bell pepper, chopped (1½ cups)

1 large onion, chopped (1 cup)

½ cup chicken broth

¼ cup ketchup

8 hoagie buns (7 to 8 inches), split

1. Rub jerk seasoning generously over chicken. Place bell pepper and onion in bottom of 3½- to 4-quart slow cooker. Place chicken over vegetables. Mix broth and ketchup in small bowl; pour over chicken.

2. Cover and cook on Low heat setting 6 to 8 hours.

3. Remove chicken from cooker; place on cutting board. Shred chicken, using 2 forks. Return chicken to cooker and mix well. Using slotted spoon to remove chicken mixture from cooker, fill buns with chicken mixture.

8 sandwiches.
1 Sandwich: Calories 560 (Calories from Fat 155); Fat 17g (Saturated 5g); Cholesterol 105mg; Sodium 990mg; Carbohydrate 57g (Dietary Fiber 4g); Protein 45g
% Daily Value: Vitamin A 12%; Vitamin C 18%; Calcium 12%; Iron 32%
Exchanges: 4 Starch, 4½ Lean Meat
Carbohydrate Choices: 4

BETTY'S TIPS

⚙ **Serve-With**
Serve this party-friendly sandwich with coleslaw and sliced fresh fruit for a complete meal.

⚙ **Variation**
If you like, reheat leftovers and serve in flour tortillas.

Big and Spicy Chicken Hoagies

Open-Face Turkey Diner Sandwiches

Prep: 15 min Cook: 10 hr
(Photo on page 53)

1 package (2 pounds) turkey breast tenderloins
$^1/_2$ teaspoon rubbed sage
2 jars (12 ounces each) roasted turkey gravy
1 package (28 ounces) frozen home-style mashed potatoes
$^1/_2$ teaspoon poultry seasoning
1 teaspoon Worcestershire sauce
6 slices white bread, toasted
Paprika

1. Place turkey in 3- to 4-quart slow cooker. Sprinkle with sage. Top with gravy.

2. Cover and cook on Low heat setting 8 to 10 hours.

3. About 10 minutes before serving, cook mashed potatoes as directed on package for 3 servings.

4. Remove turkey from cooker; place on cutting board. Cut turkey into $^1/_4$-inch slices. Stir poultry seasoning and Worcestershire sauce into gravy in cooker.

5. Place 2 pieces turkey on each toast slice. Top with $^1/_4$ cup mashed potatoes. Spoon gravy over potatoes. Sprinkle with paprika.

6 sandwiches.
1 Sandwich: Calories 475 (Calories from Fat 145); Fat 16g (Saturated 4g); Cholesterol 105mg; Sodium 1,160mg; Carbohydrate 41g (Dietary Fiber 3g); Protein 42g
% Daily Value: Vitamin A 24%; Vitamin C 6%; Calcium 10%; Iron 20%
Exchanges: 3 Starch, $4^1/_2$ Lean Meat
Carbohydrate Choices: 3

BETTY'S TIPS

✪ **Substitution**
Use leftover mashed potatoes or Potato Buds instant mashed potatoes in place of the frozen potatoes.

✪ **Serve-With**
Serve with a side of cranberry sauce.

✪ **Variation**
In place of potatoes, use stuffing.

Quick
Chicken Pizza Mexicana

Prep: 10 min Grill: 10 min
(Photo on page 53)

2 cups shredded taco-seasoned cheese (8 ounces)
1 package (16 ounces) ready-to-serve original Italian pizza crust (12 inches in diameter)
$1^1/_2$ cups chopped cooked chicken
2 roma (plum) tomatoes, thinly sliced
1 small jalapeño chile pepper, seeded and finely chopped

1. Heat coals or gas grill for direct heat. Sprinkle cheese evenly over pizza crust. Top with remaining ingredients.

2. Cover and grill pizza 4 to 6 inches from medium heat 8 to 10 minutes or until crust is crisp and cheese is melted. (If crust browns too quickly, place a piece of aluminum foil between crust and grill.)

4 servings.
1 Serving: Calories 640 (Calories from Fat 245); Fat 27g (Saturated 14g); Cholesterol 105mg; Sodium 1,060mg; Carbohydrate 59g (Dietary Fiber 3g); Protein 39g
% Daily Value: Vitamin A 16%; Vitamin C 10%; Calcium 38%; Iron 24%
Exchanges: 4 Starch, 4 Lean Meat, 2 Fat
Carbohydrate Choices: 4

BETTY'S TIPS

✪ **Success Hint**
Keep a spray bottle filled with water near the grill. Use it to douse any flare-ups that might occur.

✪ **Variation**
For individual pizzas, use two 6-inch Italian pizza crusts and simply divide ingredients equally between the two crusts. Grilling time should be about the same.

Quick

Bell Pepper and Cheese Pizza

Prep: 10 min Grill: 10 min

$^3/_4$ cup pizza sauce

1 package (16 ounces) ready-to-serve original Italian pizza crust (12 inches in diameter)

1 cup shredded mozzarella cheese (4 ounces)

1 large bell pepper (any color), thinly sliced and cut into bite-size pieces (1 cup)

1 small sweet onion (Bermuda, Maui, Spanish, Walla Walla), thinly sliced ($^1/_2$ cup)

1 tablespoon chopped fresh or 1$^1/_2$ teaspoons dried basil leaves

$^1/_4$ cup grated Parmesan cheese

1. Heat coals or gas grill for direct heat. Spread pizza sauce on pizza crust. Sprinkle with mozzarella cheese. Arrange bell pepper, onion and basil on top. Sprinkle with Parmesan cheese.

2. Place pizza on sheet of heavy-duty aluminum foil or pizza pan. Cover and grill 4 to 6 inches from medium-low heat 8 to 10 minutes or until cheese is melted and pizza is thoroughly heated.

4 servings.
1 Serving: Calories 465 (Calories from Fat 135); Fat 15g (Saturated 8g); Cholesterol 35mg; Sodium 1,050mg; Carbohydrate 58g (Dietary Fiber 4g); Protein 24g
% Daily Value: Vitamin A 16%; Vitamin C 40%; Calcium 32%; Iron 22%
Exchanges: 3$^1/_2$ Starch, 1 Vegetable, 2 Medium-Fat Meat
Carbohydrate Choices: 4

BETTY'S TIPS

⚙ **Time-Saver**
When minutes count, use 2 cups of frozen bell pepper and onion stir-fry, thawed, in place of the fresh bell pepper and onion.

⚙ **Serve-With**
It's hard to resist fresh-baked pizza! Add a tossed salad with Italian dressing and an assortment of crisp relishes.

⚙ **Variation**
Grilling is a great way to make this pizza, but you can bake it, too. Bake in a 450° oven for 8 to 10 minutes or until cheese is melted.

Bell Pepper and Cheese Pizza

Quick

Family-Favorite Cheese Pizza

Prep: 10 min Bake: 12 min Stand: 2 min

1¹/₂ cups Original or Reduced Fat Bisquick mix

¹/₃ cup very hot water

¹/₂ cup pizza sauce

¹/₂ teaspoon Italian seasoning

2 cups shredded mozzarella cheese (8 ounces)

5 slices (³/₄ ounce each) reduced-fat processed American cheese

1. Move oven rack to lowest position. Heat oven to 450°. Grease 12-inch pizza pan with shortening.

2. Mix Bisquick mix and very hot water until soft dough forms; beat vigorously 20 strokes. Press dough in pizza pan, using fingers dipped in Bisquick mix; pinch edge to form ¹/₂-inch rim. Spread pizza sauce over dough. Sprinkle with Italian seasoning and mozzarella cheese.

3. Bake 10 to 12 minutes or until crust is golden and cheese is bubbly.

4. Cut American cheese slices into any shape you like with 2-inch cookie cutters. Arrange shapes on pizza. Let stand 1 to 2 minutes or until American cheese is melted.

8 servings.
1 Serving: Calories 210 (Calories from Fat 90); Fat 10g (Saturated 5g); Cholesterol 20mg; Sodium 740mg; Carbohydrate 18g (Dietary Fiber 1g); Protein 12g
% Daily Value: Vitamin A 8%; Vitamin C 2%; Calcium 30%; Iron 4%
Exchanges: 1 Starch, 1¹/₂ Medium-Fat Meat
Carbohydrate Choices: 1

Family-Favorite Cheese Pizza

BETTY'S TIPS

⊕ **Time-Saver**
In a hurry? Use shredded cheese available in the dairy section of the supermarket.

⊕ **Health Twist**
For a saving of 2 grams of fat and 70 calories per serving, use Reduced Fat Bisquick mix.

Betty Crocker
MAKES IT EASY

Pizza Dough

Prep: 20 min Rise: 45 min

2³/₄ to 3¹/₄ cups Gold Medal all-purpose flour
   2 packages active dry yeast
   2 tablespoons chopped fresh or
     ¹/₄ teaspoon dried basil leaves
 ¹/₂ teaspoon salt
   1 cup warm water (105° to 115°)
   2 tablespoons olive or vegetable oil

1. Place 2³/₄ cups flour, the yeast, basil and salt in food processor. Cover and process 10 seconds. Add water and oil. Cover and process 30 to 45 seconds or until dough pulls away from side of bowl. If dough is sticky, add flour, ¹/₄ cup at a time, until dough is no longer sticky.

2. Lightly oil medium bowl. Place dough in bowl, turning to coat. Cover with plastic wrap and place in warm place about 45 minutes or until doubled in size.

3. Use as directed for Fresh Tomato Pizza on the Grill (opposite page).

4 servings.
1 Serving: Calories 380 (Calories from Fat 70); Fat 8g (Saturated 1g); Cholesterol 0mg; Sodium 300mg; Carbohydrate 67g (Dietary Fiber 3g); Protein 10g
% Daily Value: Vitamin A 0%; Vitamin C 0%; Calcium 2%; Iron 26%
Exchanges: 4 Starch, 1¹/₂ Fat
Carbohydrate Choices: 4¹/₂

Press dough into 6-inch round on heavy-duty foil

BETTY'S TIPS

⊕ **Success Hint**
   To test that the dough has risen sufficiently, push two fingers into it; the depression should remain.
   This pizza dough can be prepared, divided into pieces and frozen. Just thaw and grill.

⊕ **Special Touch**
   For a fun do-it-yourself party, set out a variety of topping ingredients for your guests. Give them each a piece of dough, and let them make their own pizzas.

Fresh Tomato Pizza on the Grill

Prep: 20 min Grill: 10 min

Pizza Dough (opposite page)
Cornmeal
8   teaspoons olive or vegetable oil
2   medium tomatoes, thinly sliced
1/4 cup chopped fresh or 2 teaspoons dried basil leaves
1   cup shredded mozzarella cheese (4 ounces)

1. Make Pizza Dough. While dough is rising, heat coals or gas grill for direct heat. Place pizza stone on grill if using.

2. Divide dough into 4 parts. Place each part on piece of heavy-duty aluminum foil lightly sprinkled with cornmeal. Press each part into 6-inch round. Brush with oil. Place foil directly on grill rack.

3. Cover and grill pizza dough 4 to 6 inches from medium heat 3 to 4 minutes or until no longer doughy. Remove from grill. Top with tomatoes, basil and cheese. Cover and grill 5 to 6 minutes longer or until cheese is melted and crust is lightly browned.

4 pizzas.
1 Pizza: Calories 560 (Calories from Fat 200); Fat 22g (Saturated 5g); Cholesterol 15mg; Sodium 450mg; Carbohydrate 71g (Dietary Fiber 4g); Protein 19g
% Daily Value: Vitamin A 20%; Vitamin C 10%; Calcium 22%; Iron 28%
 Exchanges: 4 1/2 Starch, 1/2 High-Fat Meat, 1 Vegetable, 3 Fat
Carbohydrate Choices: 5

Fresh Tomato Pizza on the Grill

Betty Crocker
ON WHAT'S NEW

Speedy Sandwiches

The Earl of Sandwich, from whom the sandwich gets its name, would be awestruck if he could see his namesake now! Pick and choose from these lists to make your favorite.

THE SPREADS
What sandwich would be complete without a spread?

- ▶ hummus (plain, garlic, sun-dried tomato)

- ▶ tahini

- ▶ pesto

- ▶ mustard (honey, sweet onion, horseradish, dill, jalapeño)

- ▶ flavored mayonnaise (lemon, salsa, herb-garlic)

- ▶ barbecue sauce (mesquite, zesty, hot and spicy)

THE BREADS
Start with one of these.

- ▶ focaccia bread

- ▶ pita bread or pita wrap

- ▶ bagel

- ▶ sweet Hawaiian bread

- ▶ crustless bread (a children's favorite)

- ▶ frozen pretzels, heated

- ▶ Italian bread

- ▶ buttermilk bread

- ▶ potato buns

THE ESSENTIALS
It's what goes between the bread.

- ▶ assorted cracker-size luncheon meats and cheeses (layer in sandwiches)

- ▶ deli-style sliced cheeses (provolone, Cheddar, mozzarella)

- ▶ refrigerated cooked shredded barbecue pork, beef or chicken

- ▶ Old El Paso refried beans (fat-free, vegetarian)

- ▶ precooked bacon strips

- ▶ frozen cooked meatballs (Italian, plain)

- ▶ refrigerated roasted chicken breasts

- ▶ canned chicken breast meat

- ▶ vacuum-packed tuna (no draining)

- ▶ sliced fresh mozzarella cheese

THE FIXIN'S
Extras give a sandwich a taste all its own.

- ▶ roasted vegetables (from deli)

- ▶ baby greens

- ▶ tabbouleh (from deli)

- ▶ roasted red bell peppers

- ▶ spicy olives

- ▶ pickled vegetables

Chill-Chasing Soups, Stews and Chilis

Dishes to Warm the Heart

Fish and Tomato Soup (page 88)

Corn and Shrimp Chowder (page 94)

Minestrone with Italian Sausage

Prep: 25 min Cook: 21 min

1 tablespoon olive or vegetable oil

1 pound bulk sweet Italian sausage

1 medium onion, chopped (1/2 cup)

2 medium carrots, coarsely chopped (1 cup)

2 teaspoons dried basil leaves

2 teaspoons finely chopped garlic

3 cans (14 ounces each) beef broth

1 can (14.5 ounces) diced tomatoes, undrained

1 can (15 to 16 ounces) great northern beans, rinsed and drained

1 cup uncooked small elbow macaroni (3 1/2 ounces)

1 medium zucchini, cut lengthwise in half, then cut into 1/4-inch slices (1 cup)

1 cup Green Giant frozen cut green beans

1. Heat oil in 5-quart Dutch oven over medium-high heat. Cook sausage, onion, carrots, basil and garlic in oil 5 to 7 minutes, stirring frequently, until sausage is no longer pink; drain.

2. Stir broth, tomatoes and great northern beans into sausage mixture. Heat to boiling; reduce heat to medium-low. Cover and cook 7 to 8 minutes, stirring occasionally.

3. Stir in macaroni, zucchini and frozen green beans; heat to boiling. Cook over medium-high heat 5 to 6 minutes, stirring occasionally, until vegetables are hot and macaroni is tender.

7 servings (1 1/2 cups each).
1 Serving: Calories 345 (Calories from Fat 135); Fat 15g (Saturated 5g); Cholesterol 35mg; Sodium 1,060mg; Carbohydrate 37g (Dietary Fiber 6g); Protein 21g
% Daily Value: Vitamin A 20%; Vitamin C 12%; Calcium 12%; Iron 26%
Exchanges: 2 Starch, 1 Vegetable, 2 Medium-Fat Meat
Carbohydrate Choices: 2 1/2

Minestrone with Italian Sausage

BETTY'S TIPS

❂ **Serve-With**
Serve this robust soup bubbling hot with savory Herb Focaccia (page 16). Sliced pears drizzled with warm maple syrup and topped with whipped cream or ice cream make a quick-to-eat after-dinner treat.

❂ **Variation**
It's easy to make this soup meatless. Simply substitute an additional can of great northern beans or your favorite canned beans for the sausage and use vegetable broth instead of beef broth.

❂ **Special Touch**
Try topping each serving with a little chopped fresh basil or a fresh basil sprig for an extra burst of color and flavor.

Creamy Beef, Mushroom and Noodle Soup

Prep: 20 min Cook: 34 min

2	tablespoons butter or margarine
1	medium onion, coarsely chopped ($^1/_2$ cup)
2	teaspoons finely chopped garlic
1	package (8 ounces) sliced fresh mushrooms
$1^1/_2$	pounds beef boneless top sirloin steak, cut into 2 × $^3/_4$ × $^1/_4$-inch pieces
6	cups beef broth
$^1/_2$	cup dry sherry or beef broth
$^1/_4$	cup ketchup
$^3/_4$	teaspoon salt
$^1/_8$	teaspoon pepper
2	cups uncooked medium egg noodles
1	container (8 ounces) sour cream

1. Melt butter in 5- to 6-quart Dutch oven over medium-high heat. Cook onion, garlic and mushrooms in butter 5 to 6 minutes, stirring frequently, until mushrooms are softened.

2. Stir in beef. Cook 5 to 6 minutes, stirring frequently, until beef is no longer pink. Stir in remaining ingredients except noodles and sour cream. Heat to boiling; reduce heat to medium-low. Cover and cook 10 minutes, stirring occasionally. Stir in noodles. Cover and cook 5 to 7 minutes, stirring occasionally, until noodles are tender.

3. Stir in sour cream. Cook 3 to 5 minutes, stirring frequently, until well blended.

7 servings ($1^1/_2$ cups each).
1 Serving: Calories 290 (Calories from Fat 125); Fat 14g (Saturated 7g); Cholesterol 90mg; Sodium 1,100mg; Carbohydrate 15g (Dietary Fiber 1g); Protein 26g
% Daily Value: Vitamin A 10%; Vitamin C 2%; Calcium 6%; Iron 16%
Exchanges: 1 Starch, $3^1/_2$ Lean Meat, $^1/_2$ Fat
Carbohydrate Choices: 1

BETTY'S TIPS

⊙ **Success Hint**
A slick way to slice beef is to place the beef in the freezer for about 30 minutes or until very firm. Using a sharp knife makes it easier to thinly slice the beef.

⊙ **Serve-With**
More than a soup, this hearty meal-in-a-bowl goes well with Parmesan–Black Pepper Breadsticks (page 18) and a side of steamed broccoli.

⊙ **Special Touch**
Just before serving this creamy soup, stir in a little chopped fresh parsley.

Creamy Beef, Mushroom and Noodle Soup

Wild Rice Soup

Prep: 20 min Cook: 20 min

2	tablespoons butter or margarine
2	medium stalks celery, sliced (1 cup)
1	medium carrot, coarsely shredded (1 cup)
1	medium onion, chopped ($^1/_2$ cup)
1	small green bell pepper, chopped ($^1/_2$ cup)
3	tablespoons Gold Medal all-purpose flour
$^1/_4$	teaspoon pepper
1	pouch (from 10-ounce package) frozen cooked wild rice ($1^1/_4$ cups)
1	cup water
1	can ($10^1/_2$ ounces) condensed chicken broth
1	cup half-and-half
$^1/_3$	cup slivered almonds, toasted, if desired
$^1/_4$	cup chopped fresh parsley

1. Melt butter in 3-quart saucepan over medium-high heat. Cook celery, carrot, onion and bell pepper in butter about 4 minutes, stirring occasionally, until tender.

2. Stir in flour and pepper. Stir in wild rice, water and broth. Heat to boiling; reduce heat to low. Cover and simmer 15 minutes, stirring occasionally.

3. Stir in half-and-half, almonds and parsley. Heat just until hot (do not boil or soup may curdle).

3 servings ($1^1/_2$ cups each).
1 Serving: Calories 365 (Calories from Fat 170); Fat 19g (Saturated 11g); Cholesterol 50mg; Sodium 740mg; Carbohydrate 36g (Dietary Fiber 4g); Protein 12g
% Daily Value: Vitamin A 100%; Vitamin C 28%; Calcium 12%; Iron 10%
Exchanges: 2 Starch, 1 Vegetable, 1 Medium-Fat Meat, $2^1/_2$ Fat
Carbohydrate Choices: $2^1/_2$

BETTY'S TIPS

⊛ **Substitution**
If you can't find the frozen cooked wild rice, use $1^1/_4$ cups from a 15-ounce can of cooked wild rice. Want to cook the wild rice yourself? Heat $^1/_2$ cup uncooked wild rice and $1^1/_4$ cups water to boiling in 2-quart saucepan; reduce heat to low. Cover and simmer 40 to 50 minutes until wild rice is tender.

⊛ **Health Twist**
For 2 grams of fat and 245 calories per serving, omit the butter and spray the saucepan with cooking spray before heating. Substitute 1 cup evaporated fat-free milk for the half-and-half.

⊛ **Special Touch**
Top servings of this hearty soup with Toasted Cheese Slices (page 96).

Wild Rice Soup

Beefy French Onion Soup

Prep: 15 min Cook: 10 hr + 10 min

- 7 small onions, cut in half and thinly sliced (about 7 cups)
- 1 tablespoon butter or margarine, melted
- 2 tablespoons sugar
- 2 dried bay leaves
- 1½ pounds beef stew meat
- 3 cans (10½ ounces each) condensed beef consommé
- ¼ cup dry sherry or apple juice
- 1 cup apple juice
- ¼ teaspoon dried thyme leaves
- 8 slices (½ inch thick) French bread, toasted
- 2 cups shredded Swiss cheese (8 ounces)

1. Toss onions, butter and sugar in 5- to 6-quart slow cooker. Top with bay leaves and beef.

2. Cover and cook on low heat setting 9 to 10 hours or until onions are deep brown.

3. Stir in beef consommé, sherry, apple juice and thyme. Increase heat setting to high. Cover and cook 10 minutes or until hot. Remove bay leaves.

4. To serve, spoon into overproof soup bowls and top each serving with slice of toast and ¼ cup cheese. If desired, broil with tops 6 inches from heat 3 to 5 minutes or until cheese is bubbly and begins to brown.

8 servings (1 cup each).
1 Serving: Calories 440 (Calories from Fat 180); Fat 20g (Saturated 10g); Cholesterol 80 mg; Sodium 910 mg; Carbohydrate 31g (Dietary Fiber 2g); Protein 34g
% Daily Value: Vitamin A 10%; Vitamin C 6%; Calcium 32%; Iron 20%
Exchanges: 1½ Starch, 2 Vegetable, 4 Lean Meat, 1 Fat
Carbohydrate Choices: 2

Beefy French Onion Soup

BETTY'S TIPS

☺ **Success Hint**
For best results, don't double this recipe. If the onions are packed too deeply in the slow cooker, they steam and stay pale and boiled tasting instead of caramelizing. They would eventually caramelize, but not before the beef would become dried out and overcooked.

☺ **Serve-With**
A fresh tossed salad with a vinaigrette would taste great with this rich soup. Spoil your family with a small fancy French pastry from the bakery for dessert.

☺ **Special Touch**
If you broil the soup with cheese on top, place the soup bowls on pretty plates to protect fingers and your table from the hot bowls.

Betty Crocker ON BASICS

Low Fat

Slow Cooker Chicken Broth

Prep: 10 min Cook: 8 hr

3- to 3¹/₂-pound cut-up broiler-fryer chicken
10 cups water
2 medium ribs celery, coarsely chopped (1 cup)
2 medium carrots, coarsely chopped (1 cup)
2 medium onions, coarsely chopped (1 cup)
2 teaspoons chopped fresh thyme leaves
2 teaspoons salt
¹/₄ teaspoon pepper

1. Combine all ingredients in 6-quart slow cooker.

2. Cover and cook on Low heat setting 6 to 8 hours.

3. Remove chicken and vegetables from broth; cool. To make broth clear, strain through a cheesecloth-lined colander. Remove skin and bones from chicken. Discard skin, bones and vegetables. Refrigerate broth and chicken separately to use in recipes.

Coarsely chop celery, carrots and onions into similar size pieces.

10 cups broth; about 4 cups chicken.
1 Cup Broth: Calories 10 (Calories from Fat 0); Fat 0g (Saturated 0g); Cholesterol 5mg; Sodium 340mg; Carbohydrate 0g (Dietary Fiber 0g); Protein 1g
% Daily Value: Vitamin A 0%; Vitamin C 0%; Calcium 0%; Iron 0%
Exchanges: 1 Serving Free
Carbohydrate Choices: 0

Chicken and Spinach Tortellini Soup

Prep: 20 min Cook: 12 min

1 tablespoon olive or vegetable oil

$1/3$ cup chopped green onions (about 5 medium)

$1/3$ cup julienne strips (matchstick-size) carrots

1 teaspoon finely chopped garlic

6 cups Slow Cooker Chicken Broth (opposite page) or canned chicken broth

2 cups shredded cooked chicken

1 cup small frozen cheese-filled tortellini

$1/4$ teaspoon ground nutmeg, if desired

$1/8$ teaspoon pepper

3 cups chopped fresh spinach

1. Heat oil in 4$1/2$- to 5-quart Dutch oven over medium-high heat. Cook onions, carrots and garlic in oil 3 to 4 minutes, stirring frequently, until onions are softened.

2. Stir in broth and chicken. Heat to boiling. Stir in tortellini; reduce heat to medium. Cover and cook 3 to 5 minutes or until tortellini are tender.

3. Stir in nutmeg, pepper and spinach. Cover and cook 2 to 3 minutes or until spinach is hot.

5 servings (1$1/2$ cups each).
1 Serving: Calories 240 (Calories from Fat 100); Fat 11g (Saturated 3g); Cholesterol 80mg; Sodium 1,320mg; Carbohydrate 10g (Dietary Fiber 1g); Protein 25g
% Daily Value: Vitamin A 70%; Vitamin C 6%; Calcium 8%; Iron 14%
Exchanges: $1/2$ Starch, 3$1/2$ Lean Meat
Carbohydrate Choices: $1/2$

BETTY'S TIPS

✿ **Time-Saver**
Simplify your life! Instead of chopping the carrots yourself, look for packaged julienne-cut carrots in the produce section of the supermarket.

✿ **Serve-With**
Large cracker sheets and a crunchy, munchy vegetable tray of carrots, celery and cucumbers round out this easy-to-make soup.

Chicken and Spinach Tortellini Soup

Low Fat

Fish and Tomato Soup

Prep: 15 min Total: 50 min
(Photo on page 81)

1	tablespoon olive or vegetable oil
1	teaspoon finely chopped garlic
2	medium stalks celery, coarsely chopped (1 cup)
1	medium onion, coarsely chopped ($^1/_2$ cup)
1	tablespoon chopped fresh parsley
1	dried bay leaf
2	cans (28 ounces each) Italian-style plum tomatoes, undrained
2	cans (14 ounces each) vegetable or chicken broth
1	cup dry white wine or vegetable broth
1$^1/_2$	pounds assorted fish fillets (such as bass, cod, haddock, ocean perch or red snapper), cut into 2-inch pieces
1$^1/_2$	teaspoons salt
$^1/_2$	teaspoon pepper
	Grated lemon peel, if desired

1. Heat oil in 5- to 6-quart Dutch oven over medium heat. Cook garlic, celery, onion, parsley and bay leaf in oil 5 to 6 minutes, stirring frequently, until celery is crisp-tender.

2. Stir in tomatoes, broth and wine. Heat to boiling over high heat; reduce heat to medium-low. Cover and simmer 20 minutes, stirring occasionally.

3. Stir in fish, salt and pepper. Cover and simmer 8 to 10 minutes or until fish flakes easily with a fork. Remove bay leaf. Top soup with lemon peel.

8 servings (1$^1/_2$ cups each).
1 Serving: Calories 165 (Calories from Fat 45); Fat 5g (Saturated 1g); Cholesterol 45mg; Sodium 1300mg; Carbohydrate 12g (Dietary Fiber 3g); Protein 18g
% Daily Value: Vitamin A 22%; Vitamin C 26%; Calcium 8%; Iron 8%
Exchanges: 2 Vegetable, 2 Very Lean Meat, 1 Fat
Carbohydrate Choices: 1

BETTY'S TIPS

⊛ **Serve-With**
Serve this easy "catch" with a mixed-greens salad drizzled with an herb vinaigrette and a loaf of crusty bread.

⊛ **Variation**
For shellfish lovers, try shrimp, clams or mussels as part of the fish in this recipe. Cook 8 to 10 minutes until shrimp are pink and firm or until clams and mussels open.

⊛ **Special Touch**
Toasted bread slices brushed with a little olive oil and sprinkled with shredded Parmesan cheese and chopped fresh parsley make a crunchy and tasty soup topper.

Slow Cooker Mediterranean Chicken Stew

Prep: 10 min Cook: 6 hr

- 2 teaspoons olive or vegetable oil
- 2 pounds boneless, skinless chicken thighs
- 1 teaspoon garlic salt
- 1/4 teaspoon pepper
- 2 teaspoons dried oregano leaves
- 2 cans (14.5 ounces each) diced tomatoes with garlic and onion, undrained
- 1 can (14 ounces) quartered artichoke hearts, drained
- 1 package (10 ounces) couscous (1 1/2 cups)
- 1 can (6 ounces) pitted medium ripe olives, drained

1. Heat oil in 12-inch skillet over medium-high heat. Sprinkle chicken with garlic salt, pepper and oregano. Cook chicken in oil 8 minutes, turning once, until brown on both sides; drain. Place chicken, tomatoes and artichokes in 4- to 4 1/2-quart slow cooker.

2. Cover and cook on Low heat setting 5 to 6 hours.

3. Cook couscous as directed on package. Stir olives into stew. To serve, spoon stew over couscous.

5 servings (1 1/2 cups each).
1 Serving: Calories 605 (Calories from Fat 190); Fat 21g (Saturated 5g); Cholesterol 115mg; Sodium 1,040mg; Carbohydrate 64g (Dietary Fiber 10g); Protein 50g
% Daily Value: Vitamin A 14%; Vitamin C 24%; Calcium 16%; Iron 38%
Exchanges: 4 Starch, 1 Vegetable, 5 Lean Meat
Carbohydrate Choices: 4

BETTY'S TIPS

✪ Substitution
Not an onion lover? Diced tomatoes with roasted garlic can be substituted for the diced tomatoes with garlic and onion.

✪ Serve-With
For a medley of Mediterranean flavors, serve this stew with a fresh spinach salad topped with crumbled feta cheese and sliced fresh figs. Sesame or poppy seed-topped bread makes a great accompaniment.

✪ Variation
Take a tour through the grocery store, and you're sure to find quite an assortment of olives. Take your pick—any of the pitted varieties will work well in this recipe.

Slow Cooker Mediterranean Chicken Stew

Continental Pork Stew

Prep: 15 min Cook: 49 min

1	tablespoon olive or vegetable oil
1	tablespoon butter or margarine
2	teaspoons finely chopped garlic
1	package (8 ounces) sliced fresh mushrooms
1½	pounds pork boneless loin roast, cut into 1-inch pieces
2½	cups chicken broth
1	cup white wine or chicken broth
1½	cups frozen pearl onions
3	medium carrots, cut lengthwise in half, then cut into ¼-inch slices
1	small onion studded with 4 whole cloves
1	teaspoon salt
⅛	teaspoon pepper
1	cup whipping (heavy) cream
⅓	cup Gold Medal Wondra® quick-mixing flour
	Chopped parsley, if desired

BETTY'S TIPS

⚙ **Substitution**
If your family likes the flavor of veal, you can substitute 1½ pounds of veal boneless loin roast for the pork.

⚙ **Success Hint**
To make the studded onion for the stew, peel the onion, then gently push 4 whole cloves into it.

⚙ **Serve-With**
You'll want to have plenty of crusty rolls or thick slices of bread to soak up all of the flavorful juices in this savory stew.

1. Heat oil and butter in 4½- to 5-quart Dutch oven over medium-high heat. Cook garlic and mushrooms in oil mixture 5 to 6 minutes, stirring frequently, until mushrooms are softened.

2. Stir in pork. Cook 6 to 7 minutes, stirring frequently, until pork is lightly browned.

3. Stir in broth, wine, pearl onions, carrots, onion with cloves, salt and pepper. Heat to boiling; reduce heat to medium-low. Cover and cook 25 to 30 minutes, stirring occasionally, until pork is tender and no longer pink in center.

4. Remove onion with cloves; discard. Beat in whipping cream and flour with wire whisk. Cook 5 to 6 minutes, stirring constantly, until hot and slightly thickened. Sprinkle with parsley.

6 servings (1⅓ cups each).
1 Serving: Calories 450 (Calories from Fat 270); Fat 30g (Saturated 13g); Cholesterol 120mg; Sodium 910mg; Carbohydrate 15g (Dietary Fiber 2g); Protein 31g
% Daily Value: Vitamin A 100%; Vitamin C 4%; Calcium 6%; Iron 12%
Exchanges: 1 Starch, 4 Lean Meat, 3½ Fat
Carbohydrate Choices: 1

Continental Pork Stew

Low Fat

Caribbean Turkey Stew

Prep: 20 min Cook: 36 min

1	tablespoon olive or vegetable oil
1	medium onion, coarsely chopped ($^1\!/_2$ cup)
2	teaspoons finely chopped garlic
$1^1\!/_2$	pounds turkey breast tenderloins, cut into 1-inch pieces
$^1\!/_2$	teaspoon salt
$^1\!/_2$	teaspoon ground nutmeg
$^1\!/_4$	teaspoon pepper
1	dark-orange sweet potato, peeled and cut into 1-inch pieces ($1^1\!/_2$ cups)
2	dried bay leaves
4	small red potatoes, cut into eighths ($1^1\!/_2$ cups)
2	cups chicken broth
2	cups Green Giant frozen sweet peas

Caribbean Turkey Stew

1. Heat oil in $4^1\!/_2$-quart Dutch oven over medium-high heat. Cook onion and garlic in oil 4 to 5 minutes, stirring frequently, until onion is softened.

2. Sprinkle turkey pieces with salt, nutmeg and pepper. Stir into onion mixture. Cook 5 to 6 minutes, stirring occasionally, until turkey is no longer pink.

3. Stir in remaining ingredients except peas. Heat to boiling; reduce heat to medium-low. Cover and cook 18 to 20 minutes or until potatoes are tender.

4. Stir in frozen peas. Cover and cook 4 to 5 minutes, stirring occasionally, until peas are hot. Remove bay leaves.

5 servings ($1^1\!/_2$ cups each).
1 Serving: Calories 320 (Calories from Fat 45); Fat 5g (Saturated 1g); Cholesterol 90mg; Sodium 760mg; Carbohydrate 34g (Dietary Fiber 6g); Protein 39g
% Daily Value: Vitamin A 96%; Vitamin C 18%; Calcium 4%; Iron 21%
Exchanges: 2 Starch, $4^1\!/_2$ Lean Meat
Carbohydrate Choices: 2

BETTY'S TIPS

☺ **Serve-With**
A tropical salad of mango, papaya and bananas drizzled with fresh lime juice adds to the Caribbean flavor of this sweet and spicy stew.

☺ **Special Touch**
For an extra taste treat, add a lime wedge and chopped parsley or a sprinkle of coconut just before serving.

☺ **Did You Know?**
The sweetest sweet potatoes have a dark-orange, thick outer skin and a bright orange, sweet flesh inside. When cooked, their texture is very moist and tender.

Tomato-Vegetable Stew with Cheddar Cheese Dumplings

Prep: 20 min Cook: 45 min

2 tablespoons vegetable oil

2 large onions, coarsely chopped (3$^1/_2$ cups)

2 medium ribs celery, coarsely chopped ($^3/_4$ cup)

2 cups frozen Italian green beans

1 can (28 ounces) diced tomatoes, undrained

1 can (14 ounces) chicken broth

1 teaspoon dried basil leaves

$^1/_4$ teaspoon pepper

Cheddar Cheese Dumplings (right)

1. Heat oil in 4$^1/_2$- to 5-quart Dutch oven over medium-high heat. Cook onions and celery in oil, stirring frequently, until tender.

2. Stir in remaining ingredients except Cheddar Cheese Dumplings. Heat to boiling; reduce heat to low. Simmer uncovered 15 to 20 minutes or until beans are tender.

3. Meanwhile, make Cheddar Cheese Dumplings. Drop dough by rounded tablespoonfuls onto simmering stew. Cover and cook over medium-low heat 20 to 25 minutes or until dumplings are firm when pressed.

6 servings (1 cup each).

Cheddar Cheese Dumplings

1$^1/_2$ cups Gold Medal self-rising flour

$^1/_2$ teaspoon ground mustard

$^1/_4$ cup shortening

$^1/_2$ cup shredded sharp Cheddar cheese (2 ounces)

$^2/_3$ cup milk

Stir together flour and mustard in medium bowl. Cut in shortening, using pastry blender or fork, until mixture looks like coarse crumbs. Stir in cheese. Add milk; stir just until dry ingredients are moistened.

1 Serving: Calories 360 (Calories from Fat 160); Fat 18g (Saturated 5g); Cholesterol 10mg; Sodium 580mg; Carbohydrate 39g (Dietary Fiber 4g); Protein 10g
% Daily Value: Vitamin A 18%; Vitamin C 20%; Calcium 16%; Iron 16%
Exchanges: 2 Starch, 2 Vegetable, 3 Fat
Carbohydrate Choices: 2$^1/_2$

BETTY'S TIPS

✪ **Success Hint**
Resist the urge to stir too much! Dumplings require very little mixing when the milk is added to the dry ingredients. If the dough is overmixed, the dumplings can become heavy and tough, so mix just until the dry ingredients are moistened.

✪ **Serve-With**
For a great go-along with this meatless meal, add sunflower nuts and matchstick-cut carrots to your favorite salad greens and toss with ranch dressing.

✪ **Special Touch**
For the final touch, pass around bowls of extra shredded Cheddar cheese to serve with this yummy stew.

Tomato-Vegetable Stew with Cheddar Cheese Dumplings

Corn and Shrimp Chowder

Prep: 15 min Cook: 33 min

 4 slices bacon, cut into $1/2$-inch pieces

 1 medium onion, coarsely chopped ($1/2$ cup)

 1 medium rib celery, coarsely chopped ($1/2$ cup)

 6 small red potatoes, cut into $1/2$-inch pieces

 2 cups Green Giant Niblets frozen corn

$1/4$ teaspoon dried thyme leaves

 4 cups chicken broth

$1/4$ cup Gold Medal Wondra quick-mixing flour

 2 cups half-and-half

 1 package (12 ounces) frozen uncooked medium shrimp, peeled, deveined and tails removed (do not thaw)

$1/2$ teaspoon salt

$1/8$ teaspoon pepper

1. Cook bacon in 5- to 6-quart Dutch oven over medium-high heat 5 to 6 minutes, stirring frequently, until crisp. Stir in onion, celery, potatoes, frozen corn and thyme. Cook 5 to 6 minutes, stirring frequently, until onion and celery are softened.

2. Beat in broth and flour with wire whisk. Heat to boiling; reduce heat to medium. Cover and boil about 15 minutes, stirring occasionally, until potatoes are tender and soup is slightly thickened.

3. Stir in half-and-half, shrimp, salt and pepper. Cover and cook 5 to 6 minutes, stirring occasionally, until shrimp are pink and firm.

7 servings ($1^{1}/_{3}$ cups each).
1 Serving: Calories 280 (Calories from Fat 100); Fat 11g (Saturated 6g); Cholesterol 100mg; Sodium 930mg; Carbohydrate 31g (Dietary Fiber 3g); Protein 16g
% Daily Value: Vitamin A 10%; Vitamin C 8%; Calcium 10%; Iron 14%
Exchanges: 2 Starch, $1^{1}/_{2}$ Very Lean Meat, $1^{1}/_{2}$ Fat
Carbohydrate Choices: 2

BETTY'S TIPS

❂ **Serve-With**
Make this cozy soup the star of a simple meal. A basket of hearty whole-grain or sourdough rolls or breadsticks is the only accompaniment needed.

❂ **Special Touch**
Perk up the presentation of this chunky chowder by sprinkling each serving with chopped fresh thyme or parsley.

❂ **Did You Know?**
The term chowder is used to describe a thick, rich soup that contains chunks of food. The name comes from the French Chaudière, or "cauldron."

Corn and Shrimp Chowder

Skillet Nacho Chili

Prep: 30 min

1 pound lean ground beef

1 medium onion, chopped ($^1/_2$ cup)

1 can (19 ounces) Progresso hearty tomato soup

1 can (15 ounces) spicy chili beans in sauce, undrained

1 can (4.5 ounces) Old El Paso chopped green chiles, undrained

1 cup Green Giant Niblets frozen corn (from 1-pound bag)

1 cup shredded Cheddar cheese (4 ounces)

2 cups corn chips

1. Spray 12-inch nonstick skillet with cooking spray; heat over medium-high heat. Cook beef and onion in skillet 10 to 12 minutes, stirring frequently, until beef is brown and onion is tender; drain.

2. Stir soup, chili beans, green chiles and corn into beef mixture. Heat to boiling; reduce heat to medium. Cook 8 to 10 minutes, stirring occasionally, until sauce is slightly thickened and corn is cooked.

3. Sprinkle each serving with cheese. Serve with corn chips.

4 servings.
1 Serving: Calories 585 (Calories from Fat 260); Fat 29g (Saturated 11g); Cholesterol 95mg; Sodium 1,790mg; Carbohydrate 45g (Dietary Fiber 8g); Protein 37g
% Daily Value: Vitamin A 26%; Vitamin C 28%; Calcium 20%; Iron 30%
Exchanges: 3 Starch, 4 Medium-Fat Meat, 1 Fat
Carbohydrate Choices: 3

BETTY'S TIPS

⊕ **Substitution**
Ground turkey can be used in place of the ground beef in this recipe.

⊕ **Success Hint**
Garnish this dinnertime treat with chopped fresh cilantro for an extra south-of-the-border taste.

⊕ **Serve-With**
Warm corn bread, butter and honey are great accompaniments to this stick-to-your-ribs meal.

Skillet Nacho Chili

Betty Crocker
ON WHAT'S NEW

"Souper" Soup Toppers

Chase the chill out of winter by adding a terrific topper to a bowl of steaming soup, stew or chili. Check out these easy ideas.

CROSTINI

Heat oven to 375°. Place 12 slices Italian bread, $1/2$-inch thick, on ungreased cookie sheet. Drizzle 1 teaspoon olive oil over each slice of bread. Mix $1/2$ cup chopped tomato, 1 tablespoon chopped fresh basil leaves, $1/4$ teaspoon salt and $1/4$ teaspoon pepper. Spread over bread slices. Sprinkle 1 tablespoon shredded Parmesan cheese over each slice. Bake about 8 minutes or until bread is hot.

EASY CHEESE BISCUITS

Heat oven to 450°. Mix 1 cup Original Bisquick mix, $1/2$ cup milk and $1/4$ cup shredded Cheddar cheese until soft dough forms; beat vigorously 30 seconds. Drop dough (6 to 8 spoonfuls) about 2 inches apart onto ungreased cookie sheet. Bake 6 to 8 minutes or until golden brown.

SEASONED CROUTONS

Cut dry (not hard) bread into $1/2$-inch cubes, and toss with olive oil to lightly coat (or spread one side of dry bread with softened butter or margarine, and cut into $1/2$-inch cubes). Sprinkle with grated Parmesan cheese and Italian seasoning or your favorite herbs or seasoning. Cook in ungreased skillet over medium heat 4 to 7 minutes, stirring frequently, until golden brown.

TORTILLA STRIPS

Heat oven to 375°. Brush 4 small corn or flour tortillas with melted butter or margarine. Sprinkle with chili powder, if desired. Cut each tortilla into $2 \times 1/2$-inch strips or 12 wedges, or cut into shapes with cookie cutters. Place in single layer on 2 ungreased cookie sheets. Bake 6 to 8 minutes or until light brown and crisp. Cool slightly.

TOASTED CHEESE SLICES

Set oven control to broil. Place 8 slices French bread, $3/4$- to 1-inch thick, on ungreased cookie sheet. Broil with tops about 5 inches from heat 1 to 2 minutes or until golden brown. Turn bread slices over; top each slice with 2 tablespoons shredded cheese or 1 slice of cheese. Broil 1 to 2 minutes longer or until cheese is melted and golden brown.

Get Garnished

Garnishes are a simple way to add color, texture, flavor and, of course, eye appeal to soups and stews. As a rule, the stronger or more varied the flavors or textures in a soup or stew, the simpler the garnish should be so it won't compete with the soup. If you don't know where to start, consider using an ingredient in the soup, stew or chili such as an herb or vegetable.

Top with . . .

VEGGIES

▶ chopped avocado

▶ chopped bell pepper

▶ chopped broccoli

▶ chopped tomato

▶ sliced cucumber

▶ sliced green onion

▶ sliced mushrooms

---

*How to make bell pepper cutouts
Cut bell pepper into quarters, and remove seeds. Using a small sharp knife or small canapé cutter, cut desired shapes from pepper.

**How to pipe mashed potatoes
Place mashed potatoes in decorating bag with large star tip. Gently squeeze to form rosettes or to pipe a border around the edge of a soup or stew.

NUTS OR SEEDS

▶ cashews

▶ pine nuts

▶ popcorn

▶ sliced or slivered almonds

▶ sunflower nuts

▶ toasted sesame seed

FRUIT

▶ sliced apple

▶ sliced mango

▶ sliced pear

SOMETHING SALTY

▶ crumbled cooked bacon

▶ crumbled feta or blue cheese

▶ crushed corn or tortilla chips

▶ pretzels

▶ shredded cheese

Swirl in or dollop with . . .

▶ guacamole

▶ pesto

▶ salsa

▶ sour cream or yogurt

Arrange on top . . .

▶ bagel chips

▶ bell pepper cutouts*

▶ chopped crystallized ginger

▶ edible flowers (pansies, nasturtiums, citrus blossoms, marigolds, petunias)

▶ fresh herbs (parsley, dill weed, fennel, cilantro, rosemary)

▶ lemon or lime peel strips

▶ lime wedges or slices

▶ piped mashed potatoes**

▶ tiny or small whole shrimp, cooked

Chipotle Pork Chili

Prep: 20 min Cook: 53 min

1 tablespoon olive or vegetable oil

2 medium onions, cut in half, then cut into
$^1/_4$-inch slices and slices separated

2 teaspoons finely chopped garlic

1 teaspoon salt

1 tablespoon ground cumin

$^1/_8$ teaspoon pepper

2 pounds pork boneless loin roast, cut into
1-inch pieces

1 chipotle chili in adobo sauce, finely
chopped, plus 1 teaspoon adobo sauce
(from 7- to 11-ounce can)

3 cans (14.5 ounces each) diced tomatoes with
geen chiles, undrained

1. Heat oil in 4$^1/_2$- to 5-quart Dutch oven over medium-high heat. Cook onions and garlic in oil 4 to 5 minutes, stirring occasionally, until onions are softened.

2. Stir in salt, cumin, pepper and pork. Cook 6 to 8 minutes, stirring frequently, until pork is lightly browned.

3. Stir in chipotle chili, adobo sauce and tomatoes. Heat to boiling; reduce heat to medium-low. Cover and cook 35 to 40 minutes, stirring occasionally, until pork is no longer pink in center.

5 servings (1$^1/_2$ cups each).
1 Serving: Calories 400 (Calories from Fat 160); Fat 18g (Saturated 5g); Cholesterol 115mg; Sodium 1,300mg; Carbohydrate 16g (Dietary Fiber 4g); Protein 43g
% Daily Value: Vitamin A 20%; Vitamin C 32%; Calcium 10%; Iron 22%
Exchanges: 1 Starch, 6 Lean Meat
Carbohydrate Choices: 1

Chipotle Pork Chili

BETTY'S TIPS

⊛ **Serve-With**
Warm flour tortillas make great dippers for this rich, smoky chili. A fresh vegetable plate of carrot, jicama and cucumber sticks and a creamy dip make a cooling side dish.

⊛ **Special Touch**
Laced with chipotle chiles for smoky kicks, this chili begs for a topper of sour cream and a few slices of fresh avocado.

⊛ **Did You Know?**
Chipotle chiles are dried smoked jalapeño chiles. They can be purchased dried, pickled or in adobo sauce.

Chili with Corn Dumplings

Prep: 25 min Cook: 45 min
(Photo on page iv)

1½ pounds ground beef

¾ cup chopped onion

1 can (15.25 ounces) Green Giant Niblets whole kernel sweet corn, undrained

1 can (14.5 ounces) stewed tomatoes, undrained

1 can (15 ounces) tomato sauce

2 tablespoons chili powder

1 teaspoon red pepper sauce

Corn Dumplings (right)

1. Cook beef and onion in 4½- to 5-quart Dutch oven over medium-high heat, stirring frequently, until beef is brown; drain.

2. Reserve ½ cup corn for dumplings. Stir remaining corn with liquid, tomatoes, tomato sauce, chili powder and pepper sauce into beef mixture. Heat to boiling; reduce heat to low. Cover and simmer 15 minutes.

3. Meanwhile, make Corn Dumplings. Drop dough by rounded tablespoonfuls onto simmering chili. Cover and cook 25 to 30 minutes or until dumplings are firm when pressed.

6 servings (about 1 cup each).

Corn Dumplings

1⅓ cups Original Bisquick mix

⅔ cup cornmeal

⅔ cup milk

3 tablespoons chopped fresh cilantro

Reserved ½ cup whole kernel corn

Stir together Bisquick mix and cornmeal in medium bowl. Stir in milk, cilantro and corn just until dry ingredients are moistened.

1 Serving: Calories 515 (Calories from Fat 200); Fat 22g (Saturated 8g); Cholesterol 65mg; Sodium 1,300mg; Carbohydrate 56g (Dietary Fiber 6g); Protein 20g
% Daily Value: Vitamin A 36%; Vitamin C 22%; Calcium 12%; Iron 28%
Exchanges: 3 Starch, 2 Vegetable, 2½ High-Fat Meat, 1 Fat
Carbohydrate Choices: 4

BETTY'S TIPS

☺ **Substitution**
You can use either white or yellow cornmeal to make the dumplings for this mildly spicy meal-in-a-bowl.

☺ **Serve-With**
Bubbling away under pillows of tender dumplings, this saucy chili is a great finish to a long day. Pair with a salad of mixed greens, grapes and toasted walnuts, and dinner is served.

☺ **Special Touch**
Dress up this great chili with sprigs of fresh cilantro and a sprinkle of your favorite shredded cheese.

Low Fat

Vegetable and Bean Chili

Prep: 20 min Cook: 25 min

1 tablespoon olive or vegetable oil

2 medium onions, coarsely chopped (1 cup)

2 teaspoons finely chopped garlic

1 bag (1 pound) Green Giant Select® frozen broccoli, carrots and cauliflower

1 can (15 to 16 ounces) red beans, rinsed and drained

1 can (15 to 16 ounces) garbanzo beans, rinsed and drained

2 cans (14.5 ounces each) diced tomatoes with green chiles, undrained

1 can (8 ounces) tomato sauce

2 cups Green Giant Niblets frozen whole kernel sweet corn (from 1-pound bag)

2 tablespoons chili powder

1 tablespoon ground cumin

³/₄ teaspoon salt

¹/₈ teaspoon ground red pepper (cayenne)

1. Heat oil in 4¹/₂- to 5-quart Dutch oven over medium-high heat. Cook onions and garlic in oil 4 to 5 minutes, stirring frequently, until onions are softened.

2. Stir in remaining ingredients. Heat to boiling; reduce heat to medium-low. Cover and cook 15 to 20 minutes, stirring occasionally, until chili is hot and vegetables are crisp-tender.

6 servings (1¹/₂ cups each).
1 Serving: Calories 315 (Calories from Fat 55); Fat 6g (Saturated 1g); Cholesterol 0mg; Sodium 1,210mg; Carbohydrate 64g (Dietary Fiber 17g); Protein 18g
% Daily Value: Vitamin A 76%; Vitamin C 46%; Calcium 14%; Iron 38%
Exchanges: 3¹/₂ Starch, 2 Vegetable
Carbohydrate Choices: 4

BETTY'S TIPS

⚙ Time-Saver
Keep a variety of canned beans on your kitchen shelf and a mix of frozen vegetables in the freezer. Then when the question, "What's for dinner?" is asked, this hearty chili is the less-than-an-hour-away answer.

⚙ Serve-With
For a chill-chasing meal, serve this zesty chili with Pepper Jack Cheese Quick Bread (page 12) and a crisp green salad topped with sliced tomatoes and red onions.

Variation
Any combination of your favorite vegetables or canned beans will work well in this recipe. Try canned black beans, black-eyed peas or butter beans.

Vegetable and Bean Chili

Sensational Salads

Fresh Selections for Every Meal

Gyro Salad (page 122)

Cashew Curry Shrimp Salad (page 105)

Raspberry-Poppy Seed Salad

Apple-Pear Salad

Quick
Raspberry-Poppy Seed Salad

Prep: 15 min

Poppy Seed Dressing (below)
1 bag (10 ounces) heart of romaine salad mix (about 10 cups)
2 cups fresh raspberries
2 kiwifruit, peeled, sliced and cut in half
1/2 red onion, thinly sliced

1. Make Poppy Seed Dressing.

2. Toss remaining ingredients in large bowl. Pour dressing over salad; toss. Serve immediately.

6 servings.

Poppy Seed Dressing
1/2 cup mayonnaise or salad dressing
1/3 cup sugar
1/4 cup milk
1 tablespoon poppy seed
2 tablespoons white vinegar

Beat all ingredients in small bowl with wire whisk.

1 Serving: Calories 245 (Calories from Fat 145); Fat 6g (Saturated 2g); Cholesterol 10mg; Sodium 125mg; Carbohydrate 23g (Dietary Fiber 5g); Protein 2g
% Daily Value: Vitamin A 30%; Vitamin C 72%; Calcium 8%; Iron 6%
Exchanges: 1/2 Fruit, 1 Vegetable, 1/2 Other Carbohydrate, 3 Fat
Carbohydrate Choices: 1 1/2

BETTY'S TIPS

✿ **Time-Saver**
Pressed for time? Skip the scratch dressing, and toss the salad with your favorite bottled poppy seed dressing.

✿ **Health Twist**
Reduce the fat and calories in this salad by using reduced-fat mayonnaise.

✿ **Do-Ahead**
Cut up the kiwifruit and onion ahead, package separately and refrigerate until serving time. Prepare the dressing, cover and refrigerate. Whisk before tossing

Quick
Apple-Pear Salad

Prep: 25 min

1 large red apple, cut into quarters, then cut crosswise into thin slices
1 large pear, cut into quarters, then cut crosswise into thin slices
1 medium rib celery, cut diagonally into thin slices (1/2 cup)
4 ounces Havarti cheese, cut into matchstick-size strips
3 tablespoons olive or vegetable oil
2 tablespoons frozen (thawed) apple juice concentrate
1 tablespoon chopped fresh chives
3 tablespoons chopped cashews, if desired

1. Mix apple, pear, celery and cheese in medium salad bowl.

2. Thoroughly mix oil, juice concentrate and chives in small bowl. Pour over apple mixture; toss to coat. Sprinkle with cashews.

8 servings.
1 Serving: Calories 150 (Calories from Fat 100); Fat 11g (Saturated 4g); Cholesterol 15mg; Sodium 110mg; Carbohydrate 10g (Dietary Fiber 1g); Protein 3g
% Daily Value: Vitamin A 4%; Vitamin C 4%; Calcium 8%; Iron 0%
Exchanges: 1/2 Fruit, 1/2 High-Fat Meat, 1 1/2 Fat
Carbohydrate Choices: 1/2

BETTY'S TIPS

✿ **Substitution**
Instead of Havarti, try Swiss or Muenster cheese for a change of pace.

✿ **Do-Ahead**
The celery and cheese can be cut ahead of time, and the dressing can be made in advance. Be sure to cut the apple and pear at the last minute to avoid darkening.

✿ **Special Touch**
Serve this salad in a pretty bowl lined with leaf lettuce.

Chicken Pasta Salad with Roasted Red Pepper Dressing

Prep: 20 min Cook: 22 min

3 cups uncooked farfalle (bow-tie) pasta (8 ounces)

1 bag (14 ounces) Green Giant Select frozen broccoli florets

²/₃ cup refrigerated Alfredo sauce (from 10-ounce container)

1 jar (7 ounces) roasted red bell peppers, drained and finely chopped

¹/₄ teaspoon salt

1 package (6 ounces) refrigerated diced cooked chicken breast

1 can (11 ounces) Green Giant Mexicorn whole kernel corn, red and green peppers, drained

1. Cook and drain pasta as directed on package, adding broccoli for last 3 minutes of cooking. Rinse with cold water; drain.

2. Mix Alfredo sauce, bell peppers and salt in small bowl. Mix pasta, broccoli, chicken and corn in large bowl. Add pepper mixture to pasta mixture; toss until coated. Serve immediately, or refrigerate until serving.

6 servings.
1 Serving: Calories 375 (Calories from Fat 100); Fat 11g (Saturated 6g); Cholesterol 60mg; Sodium 380mg; Carbohydrate 45g (Dietary Fiber 5g); Protein 24g
% Daily Value: Vitamin A 52%; Vitamin C 54%; Calcium 12%; Iron 14%
Exchanges: 3 Starch, 2 Lean Meat, ¹/₂ Fat
Carbohydrate Choices: 3

BETTY'S TIPS

⚙ **Substitution**
If you like, you can use frozen diced cooked chicken breast. Be sure to thaw before using. Or if you have left-over cooked chicken or turkey in the refrigerator, measure about 1¹/₄ cups for this recipe.

⚙ **Time-Saver**
If you like, don't chop the roasted red bell peppers. Instead, process the dressing mixture in a small food processor until well mixed.

⚙ **Serve-With**
Sliced fresh tomatoes are a tasty, easy addition to this salad supper.

Chicken Pasta Salad with Roasted Red Pepper Dressing

Cashew Curry Shrimp Salad

Prep: 15 min Chill: 2 hr
(Photo on page 101)

Curry Dressing (right)

1 cup Green Giant frozen sweet peas
(from 1-pound bag)

1 package (12 ounces) frozen cooked, peeled
and deveined shrimp, thawed, drained and
tails removed

2 medium ribs celery, thinly sliced (³⁄₄ cup)

1 can (1³⁄₄ ounces) shoestring potatoes
(1¹⁄₄ cups)

¹⁄₂ cup cashew halves

1 head Belgian endive

1. Make Curry Dressing. Cook and drain peas as
directed on bag. Rinse with cold water; drain.

2. Place shrimp, celery and peas in medium bowl. Add
dressing; toss to coat. Cover and refrigerate at least
2 hours to blend flavors.

3. Just before serving, gently stir shoestring potatoes
and cashews into shrimp mixture. Arrange endive
leaves, pointed ends out, around edge of medium
serving platter or 4 plates. Spoon shrimp mixture
into center of platter or divide among 4 plates.
Sprinkle with additional cashews and shoestring
potatoes if desired.

4 servings (1¹⁄₄ cups each).

Curry Dressing

¹⁄₂ cup reduced-fat mayonnaise
or salad dressing

2 tablespoons lemon juice

1 tablespoon milk

1 teaspoon curry powder

¹⁄₈ teaspoon pepper

Mix all ingredients in small bowl.

1 Serving: Calories 390 (Calories from Fat 215); Fat 24g (Saturated 5g);
Cholesterol 175mg; Sodium 570mg; Carbohydrate 25g (Dietary Fiber
6g); Protein 25g
% Daily Value: Vitamin A 42%; Vitamin C 34%; Calcium 12%; Iron 28%
Exchanges: 1 Starch, 2 Vegetable, 3 Lean Meat, 2 Fat
Carbohydrate Choices: 1¹⁄₂

BETTY'S TIPS

❂ **Substitution**
Chow mein noodles can be used instead of shoestring
potatoes.

❂ **Do-Ahead**
The shrimp mixture can be made up to 24 hours ahead
of time; add cashews and potatoes just before serving.
Also, the endive leaves can be separated, washed,
wrapped in a damp paper towel and stored in a plastic
bag up to 24 hours before serving.

❂ **Did You Know?**
You may find several types of curry powder in your
grocery store, but the most common blends are labeled
either curry powder (mild) or Madras curry powder
(a bit hotter).

Lemon Pepper Tuna with Orzo

Prep: 25 min Chill: 1 hr

1½   cups uncooked orzo or rosamarina pasta (10 ounces)

2   pouches (5 ounces each) zesty lemon pepper-flavored marinated chunk light tuna

1   medium green bell pepper, chopped (1 cup)

1   cup diced dilled Havarti cheese (4 ounces)

1   cup reduced-fat mayonnaise or salad dressing

1   tablespoon grated lemon peel

1   tablespoon lemon juice

½   teaspoon salt

    Lemon slices, if desired

    Dill weed sprigs, if desired

1. Cook and drain pasta as directed on package. Rinse with cold water; drain.

2. Mix pasta and remaining ingredients except lemon slices and dill weed in large bowl. Cover and refrigerate at least 1 hour to blend flavors. Garnish with lemon slices and dill weed.

5 servings (1⅓ cups each).
1 Serving: Calories 550 (Calories from Fat 225); Fat 25g (Saturated 7g); Cholesterol 55mg; Sodium 700mg; Carbohydrate 53g (Dietary Fiber 3g); Protein 28g
% Daily Value: Vitamin A 8%; Vitamin C 38%; Calcium 14%; Iron 18%
Exchanges: 3 Starch, 1 Vegetable, 2½ Lean Meat, 3 Fat
Carbohydrate Choices: 3½

Lemon Pepper Tuna with Orzo

BETTY'S TIPS

⚙ **Substitution**
Elbow macaroni, small macaroni rings or small shell pasta can be substituted for the orzo. If you can't find the lemon pepper-flavored tuna, use regular tuna and add 1 teaspoon lemon pepper seasoning or your favorite seasoning blend. Regular Havarti or any cheese can be used in place of the dilled Havarti cheese.

⚙ **Did You Know?**
Tuna is now packaged in tightly sealed, vacuum-packed pouches. The flavored or plain tuna is ready to serve with no draining. These flat pouches store easily and can go anywhere.

Southwest Potato Salad

Prep: 20 min Cook: 40 min Cool: 15 min Chill: 2 hr

4 unpeeled medium round red or white potatoes (1$^1/_2$ pounds)

4 unpeeled small sweet potatoes (1$^1/_2$ pounds)

1$^1/_4$ cups reduced-fat mayonnaise or salad dressing

2 tablespoons milk

1 teaspoon cumin seed

$^1/_2$ teaspoon salt

1 or 2 chipotle chiles in adobo sauce, finely chopped

1 large red bell pepper, chopped (1 cup)

8 medium green onions, sliced ($^1/_2$ cup)

1. Place red or white potatoes and sweet potatoes in 4-quart Dutch oven; add enough water just to cover potatoes. Cover and heat to boiling; reduce heat to low. Cook covered 20 to 25 minutes or until sweet potatoes are tender; remove sweet potatoes from Dutch oven. Cook red or white potatoes 10 to 15 minutes longer, if necessary, until tender. Drain potatoes. Let stand about 15 minutes or until cool enough to handle. Peel potatoes; cut into cubes.

2. Mix mayonnaise, milk, cumin seed, salt and chiles in large glass or plastic bowl. Add potatoes, bell pepper and onions; stir gently to coat. Cover and refrigerate at least 2 hours to blend flavors.

12 servings ($^3/_4$ cup each).
1 Serving: Calories 200 (Calories from Fat 80); Fat 9g (Saturated 1g); Cholesterol 10mg; Sodium 290mg; Carbohydrate 28g (Dietary Fiber 3g); Protein 2g
% Daily Value: Vitamin A 100%; Vitamin C 38%; Calcium 2%; Iron 6%
Exchanges: 1$^1/_2$ Starch, 1 Vegetable, 1$^1/_2$ Fat
Carbohydrate Choices: 2

BETTY'S TIPS

⊕ **Substitution**
There is no substitute for the flavor of chipotles, so leave them out if you can't find them. You can, though, duplicate their hot kick by adding $^1/_4$ teaspoon ground red pepper (cayenne) to the mayonnaise mixture.

⊕ **Success Hint**
Round red or round white potatoes usually take longer to cook than sweet potatoes, so note in our directions that you may have to cook those a little longer.

⊕ **Did You Know?**
Chipotles are smoked, dried jalapeños with a wonderful rich, smoky flavor. They are sold dried whole, ground and in cans with spicy adobo sauce.

Southwest Potato Salad

Betty Crocker
ON WHAT'S NEW

Leaves of Green

Look beyond iceberg lettuce and you will find an increasing variety of greens. These leaves of green offer a range of textures and flavors, from mild and subdued to bold and distinctive. Blend these unique greens with traditional salad greens to create one-of-a-kind salads.

GATHERING GREENS

▶ Be sure to thoroughly wash greens to remove all dirt and grit. Fill the sink with water and gently rinse the greens, or use a sprayer. Repeat until all the dirt is removed.

▶ Remove roots and stems, if necessary, and any brown or wilted spots.

▶ Pat dry with paper towels, or spin in a salad spinner to remove excess water.

▶ Store in damp paper towels in either a salad spinner or plastic bag with holes, and refrigerate up to a week. To help prevent browning and keep greens at their freshest, the refrigerator should be between 34° and 36°.

MILD GREENS	APPEARANCE	FLAVOR
Boston Lettuce (butterhead)	Small, soft, buttery leaves	Mild, delicate flavor
Chinese Cabbage (napa)	Thin, crinkly, cream-colored leaves with light green tips	Delicate, mild cabbage flavor
Mâche (corn salad)	Spoon-shaped medium to dark green leaves with velvety texture	Mild, subtly sweet and nutty

Chinese cabbage

Mâche

Boston lettuce

Mustard greens

Arugula

Chard

Watercress

BOLD GREENS	APPEARANCE	FLAVOR
Arugula (rocket)	Medium green, spike-shaped leaves	Peppery, slightly bitter, pungent
Red/Green Chard	Large, thick green leaves or red-tinted leaves with bright red stalks	Strong, bitter
Mustard Greens	Dark green or maroon-hued leaves	Assertive, spicy, mustard flavor
Watercress	Small, dark green heart-shaped leaves	Peppery, spicy

IN THE MIX

▶ Mix mild-flavored greens with more assertive ones. Try tossing Boston or butterhead with mâche and arugula. Or mix a bit of pretty red chard with a bowl of romaine and iceberg lettuces. A salad of spicy, pungent greens alone may be too much, but combining them with mild greens creates an unforgettable salad.

▶ When dressing greens, or tossing with a dressing, start with a small amount of dressing and add more if needed. Toss just before serving so greens won't become wilted and limp.

▶ As a rule, stronger, more assertive greens will need a bit more dressing than mild, delicate greens. Stronger greens will work better with stronger-flavored dressings. Mild greens will pair well with lighter dressings, such as vinaigrettes. A tangy balsamic vinaigrette or fruit vinaigrette will complement a salad of romaine, iceberg and Chinese cabbage. For a combination of spinach and watercress, consider a more robust Russian dressing.

Grilled Salmon and Asparagus Salad (page 119)

Texas Coleslaw

Prep: 15 min Chill: 1 hr

    1   bag (16 ounces) coleslaw mix
$^1/_2$ cup chopped fresh cilantro
    2   cans (11 ounces each) Green Giant Mexicorn
        whole kernel corn, red and green peppers,
        drained
$^1/_4$ cup vegetable oil
    3   tablespoons lime or lemon juice
$^3/_4$ teaspoon ground cumin
$^1/_2$ teaspoon salt

1. Toss coleslaw mix, cilantro and corn in very large
   (4-quart) bowl. Place oil, lime juice, cumin and salt
   in tightly covered container; shake well. Pour over
   coleslaw mixture; toss.

2. Cover and refrigerate 1 to 2 hours to blend flavors.

16 servings ($^1/_2$ cup each).
1 Serving: Calories 75 (Calories from Fat 35); Fat 4g (Saturated 10g);
Cholesterol 0mg; Sodium 170mg; Carbohydrate 9g (Dietary Fiber 2g);
Protein 1g
% Daily Value: Vitamin A 2%; Vitamin C 24%; Calcium 2%; Iron 2%
Exchanges: $^1/_2$ Starch, 1 Fat
Carbohydrate Choices: $^1/_2$

BETTY'S TIPS

⚙ **Substitution**
Two cups Green Giant Niblets frozen corn, cooked as
directed on the package and rinsed with cold water, can
be used instead of the canned corn.

⚙ **Variation**
If your family likes things hot and spicy, add 1 jalapeño
chile pepper, seeded and finely chopped, to the
coleslaw mixture.

⚙ **Did You Know?**
Mysteriously, coleslaw always seems to shrink in the
refrigerator! This version also shrinks a bit in the fridge,
and as is typical with vinaigrette-based slaws, some of
the cabbage pieces become translucent during storage.

Quick

Smoked Turkey Jarlsberg Salad Supreme

Prep: 20 min

$1^1/_2$ pounds smoked turkey breast cut into
         $1 \times ^1/_4$-inch strips (5 cups)
     8   ounces Jarlsberg or Swiss cheese, cut into
         $1 \times ^1/_4$-inch strips (2 cups)
     2   cups seedless red grapes, whole or cut in
         half
$1^1/_2$ cups slivered almonds, toasted
$^2/_3$ cup mayonnaise or salad dressing
$^2/_3$ cup sour cream
2 to 4   tablespoons milk
         Salt and pepper to taste, if desired
         Lettuce, if desired

1. Mix turkey, cheese, grapes and almonds in very large
   (4-quart) bowl.

2. Mix remaining ingredients except lettuce in medium
   bowl. Pour over turkey mixture; mix gently. Cover
   and refrigerate until serving. Serve on lettuce.

8 servings (1 cup each).
1 Serving: Calories 575 (Calories from Fat 360); Fat 40g (Saturated 11g);
Cholesterol 120mg; Sodium 240mg; Carbohydrate 14g (Dietary Fiber
3g); Protein 40g
% Daily Value: Vitamin A 8%; Vitamin C 8%; Calcium 38%; Iron 14%
Exchanges: 1 Fruit, 6 Medium-Fat Meat, $1^1/_2$ Fat
Carbohydrate Choices: 1

BETTY'S TIPS

⚙ **Substitution**
You can substitute 1 cup dried cherries or cranberries
for the grapes. Because the dried fruit is smaller and will
distribute nicely throughout the salad, just 1 cup is
enough to substitute for the 2 cups of grapes.

⚙ **Success Hint**
To toast nuts, spread them in an ungreased shallow pan
and bake at 350° for 6 to 10 minutes, stirring frequently,
until light brown. Or sprinkle in an ungreased heavy
skillet and cook over medium heat 5 to 7 minutes,
stirring frequently until nuts begin to brown, then
stirring constantly until nuts are light brown.

Smoked Turkey Jarlsberg Salad Supreme

Texas Coleslaw

Vegetable Parmesan Toss

Prep: 30 min Chill: 2 hr

4   cups broccoli florets

4   cups cauliflowerets

1   large sweet onion (Bermuda, Maui, Spanish, Walla Walla), thinly sliced and separated into rings

2   cups mayonnaise or salad dressing

$^1/_3$ cup grated Parmesan cheese

$^1/_4$ cup sugar

$^1/_2$ teaspoon salt

$^1/_2$ teaspoon dried basil leaves

1   pound bacon, crisply cooked and crumbled

1   large head lettuce, torn into bite-size pieces (12 cups)

2   cups onion-and-garlic-flavored croutons

1   can (8 ounces) sliced water chestnuts, drained

1. Mix broccoli, cauliflower and onion in very large (4-quart) bowl.

2. Mix mayonnaise, cheese, sugar, salt and basil in small bowl. Add mayonnaise mixture to vegetables; toss gently to coat. Cover and refrigerate at least 2 hours or overnight.

3. Just before serving, add bacon, lettuce, croutons and water chestnuts; toss lightly. Store leftovers covered in refrigerator.

20 servings (1 cup each).
1 Serving: Calories 260 (Calories from Fat 200); Fat 22g (Saturated 4g); Cholesterol 20mg; Sodium 380mg; Carbohydrate 11g (Dietary Fiber 2g); Protein 5g
% Daily Value: Vitamin A 8%; Vitamin C 46%; Calcium 6%; Iron 4%
Exchanges: 2 Vegetable, 4$^1/_2$ Fat
Carbohydrate Choices: 1

BETTY'S TIPS

✪ Substitution
Red onion can be substituted for the sweet onion.

✪ Health Twist
To reduce the fat in this recipe, crisply cook only 4 to 6 strips of bacon instead of using 1 pound. Just before serving, sprinkle the crumbled bacon on top of the salad instead of tossing it in. Also, select reduced-fat mayonnaise, reduced-fat grated Parmesan cheese, and look for reduced-fat croutons.

✪ Did You Know?
The type of sweet onions available in the supermarket will vary depending on where you live and the time of year. Maui and Walla Walla are two of the most common varieties.

Vegetable Parmesan Toss

Quick

Tropical Fruit and Spinach Salad

Prep: 20 min

Candied Macadamia Nuts (below)

4 cups bite-size pieces baby spinach leaves

1 cup sliced strawberries

12 slices mango (from 24-ounce jar), drained

2 kiwifruit, peeled and sliced

$^1/_2$ cup raspberry vinaigrette

1. Make Candied Macadamia Nuts.

2. Divide spinach among 4 plates. Arrange strawberries, mango and kiwifruit on spinach. Sprinkle with nuts. Drizzle with vinaigrette.

4 servings.

Candied Macadamia Nuts

$^1/_4$ cup macadamia nuts, coarsely chopped

1 tablespoon plus 1 teaspoon sugar

Cook nuts and sugar in 1-quart saucepan over low heat, stirring frequently, until sugar is melted and nuts are coated (some sugar may clump and not dissolve). Cool and break apart.

1 Serving: Calories 155 (Calories from Fat 55); Fat 6g (Saturated 1g); Cholesterol 0mg; Sodium 400mg; Carbohydrate 23g (Dietary Fiber 4g); Protein 2g
% Daily Value: Vitamin A 64%; Vitamin C 100%; Calcium 4%; Iron 6%
Exchanges: 1 Fruit, 2 Vegetable, 1 Fat
Carbohydrate Choices: $1^1/_2$

BETTY'S TIPS

⊛ **Substitution**

Slivered almonds may be substituted for the macadamia nuts. One large ripe mango, peeled and sliced, may be substituted for the jarred mango slices.

⊛ **Variation**

Try the creamy Poppy Seed Dressing on page 103 instead of the raspberry vinaigrette for a change of flavor in this vibrantly colored salad.

⊛ **Did You Know?**

Bags of triple-washed regular and baby spinach leaves are now available in the produce section of most large supermarkets.

Tropical Fruit and Spinach Salad

Betty Crocker
ON WHAT'S NEW

Speedy Salads

Although you can create a salad with just iceberg lettuce, why not be creative and let some of these products star as the "supporting cast" of your salad?

THE GREENS

Prepackaged salad mixes are the quickest way to start your salad.

▶ hearts of romaine

▶ baby spring mix greens

▶ herb salad mix

▶ three-color deli coleslaw

▶ veggie blend salad mix

▶ baby spinach leaves

VERY VEGGIE

These foods add zing and zest to salads with no effort.

- ▶ roasted red bell peppers

- ▶ shredded red cabbage

- ▶ spicy olives (jalapeño and garlic, habanero)

- ▶ pickled vegetables (mushrooms, asparagus, green beans)

- ▶ hot pickled chiles

MEATS & CHEESES

Check out the meat and freezer cases as well as canned meats for these items.

- ▶ assorted cracker-size luncheon meats and cheeses (the perfect size for salads)

- ▶ cooked marinated tuna (herb-garlic, lemon-pepper, hickory-smoked)

- ▶ refrigerated cooked taco-seasoned shredded chicken or beef

- ▶ refrigerated cooked shredded barbecue pork, beef or chicken

- ▶ frozen cooked chicken breast strips or diced chicken

- ▶ frozen cooked seasoned beef strips or south-western-style chicken breast strips

- ▶ precooked bacon strips, broken into pieces, or real bacon bits (in jars)

FRUIT BASKET

If you're craving a fruit salad, use some of these ideas.

- ▶ canned tropical fruit salad shapes

- ▶ fresh pineapple

- ▶ dried figs

- ▶ flavored dried cranberries (orange, cherry)

- ▶ cinnamon-covered raisins

JUST FOR FUN

Extra ingredients give any salad a special twist.

- ▶ cheese cubes

- ▶ flavored almonds (roasted-garlic, honey-roasted, ranch, Italian Parmesan, bacon-Cheddar, oven-roasted)

- ▶ flavored croutons (garlic, ranch, cheese, Caesar, herb)

- ▶ refrigerated cooked stir-fry noodles

Italian Chopped Salad

Prep: 25 min

1/4 pound prosciutto (8 to 10 slices), cut into 1/8-inch strips

4 cups bite-size pieces mixed salad greens

1 cup bite-size pieces arugula

1 small head radicchio, cut into thin strips (1 cup)

1/3 cup red wine vinaigrette

1/2 cup crumbled Gorgonzola cheese

6 pepperoncini peppers (bottled Italian peppers), drained, if desired

1. Cook prosciutto in 10-inch nonstick skillet over medium-high heat 5 minutes, stirring occasionally. Reduce heat to medium. Cook 5 to 10 minutes longer, stirring frequently, until prosciutto becomes mostly crisp. Drain on paper towel.

2. Place remaining ingredients except cheese and pepperoncini peppers in large bowl; toss to coat. Sprinkle with prosciutto and cheese. Garnish with pepperoncini peppers.

6 servings.
1 Serving: Calories 130 (Calories from Fat 90); Fat 10g (Saturated 3g); Cholesterol 20mg; Sodium 530mg; Carbohydrate 3g (Dietary Fiber 1g); Protein 7g
% Daily Value: Vitamin A 28%; Vitamin C 12%; Calcium 10%; Iron 4%
Exchanges: 1/2 Vegetable, 1 High-Fat Meat, 1/2 Fat
Carbohydrate Choices: 0

BETTY'S TIPS

⊗ **Substitution**
If prosciutto isn't available in your area, very thinly sliced deli ham can be substituted. Make sure to pat the ham dry with paper towels before cooking it. The ham may not become as crisp and chewy and may remain in larger pieces. Another substitution is 6 slices of crisply cooked bacon, crumbled.

⊗ **Serve-With**
This robust, full-flavored salad would be delicious alongside grilled steak or lamb chops.

⊗ **Did You Know?**
Prosciutto is a dry-cured Italian ham that is usually sliced paper thin. It can be found in the deli area of most large supermarkets, at meat markets and at Italian markets.

Italian Chopped Salad

Quick

California BLT Salad

Prep: 15 min

Lemon Ranch Dressing (below)
1   bag (10 ounces) ready-to-eat American blend salad greens (iceberg lettuce, romaine, red cabbage, carrots and radishes)
12 slices ready-to-eat cooked bacon, cut into pieces
1   large tomato, cut into wedges
1   avocado, pitted, peeled and cut into wedges

1. Make Lemon Ranch Dressing.

2. Toss salad greens and bacon with dressing until coated. Garnish with tomato and avocado.

4 servings.

Lemon Ranch Dressing
$1/3$ cup ranch dressing
$1/2$ teaspoon grated lemon peel

Beat ingredients with wire whisk until smooth.

1 Serving: Calories 295 (Calories from Fat 225); Fat 25g (Saturated 5g); Cholesterol 25mg; Sodium 510mg; Carbohydrate 9g (Dietary Fiber 4g); Protein 9g
% Daily Value: Vitamin A 18%; Vitamin C 50%; Calcium 6%; Iron 8%
Exchanges: $1/2$ High-Fat Meat, 2 Vegetable, $4^1/_2$ Fat
Carbohydrate Choices: $1/2$

BETTY'S TIPS

⊛ **Success Hint**
Look for already-cooked bacon in the supermarket with the regular bacon. Just reheat it in the microwave.

⊛ **Serve-With**
Toast your favorite bread and add some watermelon wedges, and you'll have a cool summer meal. Try root beer floats for desserts.

California BLT Salad

Layered Seafood Chef Salads

Prep: 15 min

6 cups romaine and iceberg lettuce mix (from 10-ounce bag)

4 cups broccoli slaw mix (from 8-ounce bag)

1 cup sliced drained roasted red bell peppers (from 12-ounce jar)

1 package (8 ounces) refrigerated imitation crabmeat chunks, large pieces cut up

4 hard-cooked eggs, sliced

1 cup 1 × ¼-inch strips Cheddar cheese

1 cup 1 × ¼-inch strips cucumber

1 cup Thousand Island dressing

2 tablespoons chopped fresh chives

1. For each salad, use a 4- to 5-cup container. In each container, layer ingredients in this order: 1½ cups lettuce, 1 cup broccoli slaw, ¼ cup bell peppers, ¼ cup crabmeat, 1 egg, ¼ cup cheese strips and ¼ cup cucumber strips. Drizzle ¼ cup dressing over each salad. Sprinkle with chives. Serve immediately or cover and refrigerate up to 24 hours.

2. To serve, toss salads.

4 salads.
1 Salad: Calories 510 (Calories from Fat 340); Fat 38g (Saturated 12g); Cholesterol 275mg; Sodium 1,410mg; Carbohydrate 19g (Dietary Fiber 5g); Protein 29g
% Daily Value: Vitamin A 96%; Vitamin C 100%; Calcium 30%; Iron 14%
Exchanges: 3 Lean Meat, 4 Vegetable, 5 Fat
Carbohydrate Choices: 1

BETTY'S TIPS

⚙ **Substitution**

Shredded cheese can be used instead of the strips. Go ahead and vary the cheese flavor if you like, too; suggestions include mozzarella, Monterey Jack and Colby.

⚙ **Success Hint**

When you prepare a layered salad to be tossed at a later time, place the dressing on top to help keep the lettuce and other ingredients firm and crisp until you are ready to eat.

Layered Seafood Chef Salads

Quick

Grilled Salmon and Asparagus Salad

Prep: 15 min Grill: 15 min
(Photo on page 109)

Maple Dijon Dressing (right)
1 pound salmon fillet, $1/2$-inch thick
1 pound asparagus spears
4 cups fresh baby salad greens
1 cup shredded carrots
2 hard-cooked eggs, cut into 8 wedges
Freshly ground black pepper, if desired

1. Heat coals or gas grill for direct heat. Make Maple Dijon Dressing.

2. Cut salmon crosswise into 4 pieces. Brush with 1 tablespoon of the dressing. Toss asparagus and 1 tablespoon of the dressing. Place asparagus in grill basket or vegetable tray.

3. Place salmon, skin side down, on grill. Cover and grill salmon and vegetables 4 to 6 inches from medium heat, cooking asparagus 7 to 10 minutes and salmon 10 to 15 minutes, shaking grill basket or turning asparagus occasionally, until salmon flakes easily with fork and asparagus is crisp-tender.

4. Slide pancake turner between salmon and skin to remove each piece from skin. Divide salad greens, carrots and eggs among 4 plates. Top each with salmon and asparagus. Sprinkle with pepper. Serve with remaining dressing.

4 servings.

Maple Dijon Dressing

$1/3$ cup maple-flavored syrup
2 tablespoons Dijon mustard
2 tablespoons olive or vegetable oil

Mix all ingredients in small bowl with wire whisk.

1 Serving: Calories 385 (Calories from Fat 155); Fat 17g (Saturated 4g); Cholesterol 180mg; Sodium 340mg; Carbohydrate 28g (Dietary Fiber 3g); Protein 30g
% Daily Value: Vitamin A 100%; Vitamin C 46%; Calcium 8%; Iron 12%
Exchanges: 1 Starch, 3 Vegetable, 3 Lean Meat, 1 Fat
Carbohydrate Choices: 2

BETTY'S TIPS

⊕ **Success Hint**
No more greenish-gray ring around the yolk! Place eggs in a saucepan, add enough cold water just to cover eggs and heat to boiling. Remove from heat; cover and let stand 18 minutes. Immediately drain, rinse with cold water and peel.

⊕ **Serve-With**
Crusty hard rolls or chewy rustic artisan bread would be a delicious partner for this salad.

⊕ **Do-Ahead**
This salad can be served cold. Grill the salmon and asparagus, cook the eggs and make the dressing up to one day ahead of time. Cover and refrigerate until serving.

Easy Chicken Tostada Salads

Prep: 20 min

8   tostadas (from 4.8-ounce package)

4   cups shredded lettuce

1   can (15 ounces) black beans, rinsed and drained

2   boneless, skinless chicken breast halves (about $^1/_2$ pound), cooked and cut into $^1/_2$-inch slices

1   cup Old El Paso Thick 'n Chunky salsa

$^1/_4$ cup sliced ripe olives

$^1/_2$ cup shredded taco-seasoned cheese (2 ounces)

$^1/_4$ cup sour cream

$^1/_4$ cup chopped fresh cilantro

1. Place 2 tostadas, slightly overlapping, on each of 4 plates.

2. Top tostadas with remaining ingredients. Serve with additional salsa if desired.

4 servings.
1 Serving: Calories 465 (Calories from Fat 170); Fat 19g (Saturated 7g); Cholesterol 85mg, Sodium 1,000mg; Carbohydrate 48g (Dietary Fiber 11g); Protein 36g
% Daily Value: Vitamin A 20%; Vitamin C 20%; Calcium 24%; Iron 28%
Exchanges: 3 Starch, 1 Vegetable, $3^1/_2$ Lean Meat
Carbohydrate Choices: 3

BETTY'S TIPS

⊛ **Substitution**
Kidney beans or pinto beans can be substituted for the black beans.

⊛ **Time-Saver**
Look for preshredded lettuce in the produce department of your grocery store.

⊛ **Variation**
Use refrigerated grilled beef strips, cut into pieces, instead of the chicken. Add a little heat kick by using Monterey Jack cheese with jalapeño peppers instead of the taco-seasoned cheese.

Easy Chicken Tostada Salads

Tossed Steak Salad

Prep: 20 min Grill: 20 min

Spicy Garlic Dressing (below)

2 medium green onions, thinly sliced
  (2 tablespoons)

2 large roma (plum) tomatoes, chopped

1 pound beef boneless top sirloin steak
  (1 to 1¹/₂ inches thick)

1 large red or yellow bell pepper

¹/₄ teaspoon salt

¹/₈ teaspoon pepper

6 cups bite-size pieces salad greens

1 cup sliced mushrooms (3 ounces)

1. Heat coals or gas grill for direct heat. Make Spicy Garlic Dressing; reserve ¹/₄ cup dressing. Stir onions and tomatoes into remaining dressing; set aside.

2. Cover and grill beef steak and bell pepper 4 to 5 inches from medium heat 15 to 20 minutes, turning beef once and bell pepper frequently, until beef is desired doneness. Sprinkle beef with salt and pepper. Cut beef into ¹/₄-inch slices. Toss beef and reserved dressing. Cut bell pepper into strips.

3. Place salad greens, bell pepper, mushrooms and beef in large bowl. Add tomato mixture; toss.

6 servings.

Spicy Garlic Dressing

¹/₄ cup olive or vegetable oil

2 tablespoons chopped parsley

3 tablespoons red wine vinegar

1 tablespoon lemon juice

1 teaspoon chopped fresh or ¹/₂ teaspoon dried oregano leaves

¹/₂ teaspoon crushed red pepper flakes

2 cloves garlic, finely chopped

Shake all ingredients in tightly covered container.

1 Serving: Calories 200 (Calories from Fat 110); Fat 12g (Saturated 2g); Cholesterol 40mg; Sodium 150mg; Carbohydrate 6g (Dietary Fiber 2g); Protein 17g
% Daily Value: Vitamin A 72%; Vitamin C 100%; Calcium 4%; Iron 14%
Exchanges: 1 Vegetable, 2 Lean Meat, 1¹/₂ Fat
Carbohydrate Choices: ¹/₂

BETTY'S TIPS

❂ **Substitution**
Cider vinegar can be substituted for the red wine vinegar in the dressing.

❂ **Serve-With**
Enjoy this sizzling summer salad with a crusty French baguette and a tall glass of iced tea.

❂ **Did You Know?**
Our Spicy Garlic Dressing is a version of Argentina's classic chimichurri sauce, which will give you a zesty, bold and spicy taste sensation. It is fondly referred to as Argentina's version of Italian pesto.

Tossed Steak Salad

Gyro Salad

Prep: 20 min Cook: 5 min
(Photo on page 101)

Yogurt Dressing (right)

- 1 pound beef boneless sirloin steak, 1 to 1$1/2$ inches thick
- 1 tablespoon olive or vegetable oil
- 1$1/4$ teaspoons Greek seasoning
- 8 cups bite-size pieces mixed salad greens
- 1 medium cucumber, thinly sliced
- 1 small red onion, thinly sliced and separated into rings
- 1 large tomato, chopped (1 cup)

1. Make Yogurt Dressing.

2. Cut beef steak into 4 × $1/4$-inch strips. Heat oil in 12-inch nonstick skillet over medium-high heat. Add beef to skillet; sprinkle with Greek seasoning. Cook, stirring frequently, until beef is brown. Drain if necessary.

3. Divide salad greens among 6 plates. Top each with cucumber, onion, tomato and beef. Serve with dressing.

6 servings.

Yogurt Dressing

- $1/2$ cup plain yogurt
- $1/2$ cup reduced-fat sour cream
- $1/4$ cup milk
- 1 teaspoon Greek seasoning

Mix all ingredients in small bowl with wire whisk until creamy.

1 Serving: Calories 185 (Calories from Fat 65); Fat 7g (Saturated 2g); Cholesterol 50mg; Sodium 580mg; Carbohydrate 10g (Dietary Fiber 2g); Protein 20g
% Daily Value: Vitamin A 56%; Vitamin C 36%; Calcium 12%; Iron 14%
Exchanges: 2 Lean Meat, 2 Vegetable, $1/2$ Fat
Carbohydrate Choices: $1/2$

BETTY'S TIPS

✪ **Substitution**
To substitute for the Greek seasoning used to season the beef, use 1$1/4$ teaspoons garlic pepper, $1/4$ teaspoon crumbled dried oregano leaves and $3/4$ teaspoon salt. In the Yogurt Dressing, use $1/2$ teaspoon garlic pepper, $1/8$ teaspoon crumbled dried oregano leaves and $1/2$ teaspoon salt for the Greek seasoning.

✪ **Serve-With**
Warm pita bread, cut into wedges, is the perfect choice to serve with this salad.

Seafood and Vegetable Dishes
Fresh, Light and Delicious

Shrimp Kabobs with Orange Spinach Salad (page 138)

Vegetables in Peanut Sauce with Noodles (page 132)

Quick

Grilled Vegetables and Ravioli

Prep: 10 min Grill: 12 min

1/4 cup olive or vegetable oil

1 teaspoon garlic pepper

1/2 teaspoon salt

2 small zucchini, cut lengthwise in half

2 medium red, yellow or green bell peppers, cut lengthwise in half and seeded

1 small red onion, cut into quarters

1 package (9 ounces) refrigerated cheese-filled ravioli

1 tablespoon chopped fresh or 1 teaspoon dried basil leaves

1 teaspoon chopped fresh or 1/4 teaspoon dried thyme leaves

1/4 cup shredded Parmesan cheese

1. Spray grill rack with cooking spray. Heat coals or gas grill for direct heat. Mix 2 tablespoons oil, garlic pepper and salt. Brush on cut sides of vegetables.

2. Cover and grill zucchini, bell peppers and onion, cut sides down, 10 to 12 minutes, brushing occasionally with oil mixture, until crisp-tender.

3. While vegetables are grilling, cook and drain ravioli as directed on package. Return to saucepan.

4. Cut zucchini crosswise into 1/4-inch slices. Cut bell peppers into slices. Separate onion into pieces. Toss ravioli, vegetables, remaining 2 tablespoons oil, basil and thyme; heat through. Sprinkle with cheese.

4 servings.
1 Serving: Calories 295 (Calories from Fat 180); Fat 20g (Saturated 6g); Cholesterol 70mg; Sodium 940mg; Carbohydrate 18g (Dietary Fiber 3g); Protein 11g
% Daily Value: Vitamin A 84%; Vitamin C 100%; Calcium 22%; Iron 8%
Exchanges: 1 Starch, 1 Medium-Fat Meat, 3 Fat
Carbohydrate Choices: 1

Grilled Vegetables and Ravioli

BETTY'S TIPS

⊕ **Substitution**
You can use a variety of vegetables, depending on your preference. Make sure the total amount of grilled vegetables equals about 4 cups. If you prefer to try a different pasta, go ahead and experiment. We recommend cheese- or meat-filled tortellini or fettuccine.

⊕ **Serve-With**
Fresh doesn't get much better than this! Full of garden goodies, this pasta is perfect served with a light salad, warm breadsticks and an icy sorbet for dessert.

Southwestern Bean Skillet

Prep: 10 min Cook: 16 min

1 cup fresh corn kernels or Green Giant Niblets frozen corn

2 tablespoons chopped fresh cilantro

¹/₂ teaspoon salt

1 small green bell pepper, chopped (¹/₂ cup)

1 small onion, chopped (¹/₄ cup)

1 can (15 ounces) chili beans in sauce, undrained

1 can (15 ounces) black beans, rinsed and drained

1 cup shredded Mexican Cheddar Jack with jalapeño pepper cheese blend (4 ounces)

2 medium tomatoes, chopped (1¹/₂ cups)

1. Mix all ingredients except cheese and tomatoes in 12-inch skillet. Heat to boiling; reduce heat. Cover and simmer 5 minutes.

2. Uncover and simmer 5 to 10 minutes, stirring occasionally, until vegetables are tender. Stir in cheese and tomatoes until cheese is melted.

4 servings.
1 Serving: Calories 425 (Calories from Fat 100); Fat 11g (Saturated 6g); Cholesterol 30mg; Sodium 1,660mg; Carbohydrate 57g (Dietary Fiber 13g); Protein 24g
% Daily Value: Vitamin A 26%; Vitamin C 34%; Calcium 26%; Iron 30%
Exchanges: 3 Starch, 2 Vegetable, 1¹/₂ Lean Meat, 1 Fat
Carbohydrate Choices: 4

BETTY'S TIPS

⊛ **Serve-With**
Keep with the Southwest-flavor theme by serving this meatless skillet meal with warmed tortillas or tortilla chips and sliced avocados and tomatoes.

⊛ **Variation**
For a heartier, meatier meal, you can add cooked ground beef or turkey with the beans.

⊛ **Did You Know?**
Chili beans give a boost of flavor to this recipe, so be sure not to drain. The canned pinto beans are in a sauce of tomato paste, chili powder and other spices.

Southwestern Bean Skillet

Impossibly Easy Quesadilla Pie

Prep: 20 min Bake: 35 min Stand: 10 min

1 tablespoon butter or margarine

1 large onion, chopped (1 cup)

1 large tomato, chopped (1 cup)

1 can (4.5 ounces) Old El Paso chopped green chiles, drained

1 can (4 ounces) sliced ripe olives, drained

2 cups shredded Colby-Monterey Jack cheese (8 ounces)

$1/2$ teaspoon ground cumin

$1/4$ teaspoon salt, if desired

$1/2$ cup Original Bisquick mix

1 cup milk

2 eggs

1. Heat oven to 400°. Spray pie plate, 9 × 1$1/4$ inches, with cooking spray. Melt butter in 10-inch skillet over medium heat. Cook onion in butter, stirring occasionally, until tender; remove from heat. Stir in tomato, chiles, olives, 1 cup cheese, cumin and salt. Spread in pie plate.

2. Stir Bisquick mix, milk and eggs until blended. Pour over vegetable mixture.

3. Bake uncovered 30 minutes. Sprinkle with remaining 1 cup cheese. Bake 3 to 5 minutes or until knife inserted in center comes out clean. Let stand 10 minutes before cutting.

6 servings.
1 Serving: Calories 330 (Calories from Fat 190); Fat 21g (Saturated 11g); Cholesterol 115mg; Sodium 830mg; Carbohydrate 20g (Dietary Fiber 2g); Protein 15g
% Daily Value: Vitamin A 22%; Vitamin C 12%; Calcium 36%; Iron 12%
Exchanges: 1 Starch, 1$1/2$ High-Fat Meat, 1 Vegetable, 2 Fat
Carbohydrate Choices: 1

BETTY'S TIPS

⊛ **Success Hint**
If you'd like an extra kick, use Monterey Jack cheese with jalapeño peppers instead of the Colby-Monterey Jack.

⊛ **Serve-With**
Serve with a mixture of sour cream and salsa or sour cream and Old El Paso taco seasoning mix. Add a relish of jicama sticks, carrots, celery, broccoli and colorful bell pepper strips.

Impossibly Easy Quesadilla Pie

Spanish Rice Bake

Prep: 20 min Bake: 1 hr

 2 tablespoons vegetable oil
 1 cup uncooked regular long-grain rice
 1 medium onion, chopped ($\frac{1}{2}$ cup)
 1 small green bell pepper, chopped ($\frac{1}{2}$ cup)
 1 cup Green Giant Niblets frozen whole kernel corn (from 1-pound bag), thawed
 1 can (10$\frac{3}{4}$ ounces) condensed tomato soup
 2$\frac{1}{2}$ cups boiling water
 1 tablespoon chopped fresh cilantro, if desired
 1 teaspoon chili powder
 $\frac{1}{2}$ teaspoon salt
 2 cups shredded Colby-Monterey Jack cheese (8 ounces)

1. Heat oven to 375°. Spray 2$\frac{1}{2}$-quart casserole with cooking spray.

2. Heat oil in 10-inch skillet over medium heat. Cook rice, onion and bell pepper in oil 6 to 8 minutes, stirring frequently, until rice is light brown and onion is tender. Stir in corn.

3. Mix remaining ingredients except cheese in casserole. Stir in rice mixture and 1 cup cheese.

4. Cover and bake 20 minutes; stir. Cover and bake about 30 minutes longer or until rice is tender; stir. Sprinkle with remaining 1 cup cheese. Bake uncovered 2 to 3 minutes or until cheese is melted.

4 servings (1$\frac{1}{4}$ cups each).
1 Serving: Calories 575 (Calories from Fat 245); Fat 27g (Saturated 13g); Cholesterol 55mg; Sodium 1,080mg; Carbohydrate 63g (Dietary Fiber 3g); Protein 20g
% Daily Value: Vitamin A 24%; Vitamin C 26%; Calcium 44%; Iron 16%
Exchanges: 4 Starch, 1 Medium-Fat Meat, 4 Fat
Carbohydrate Choices: 4

Spanish Rice Bake

BETTY'S TIPS

⚙ **Variation**
Meat lovers can stir in their favorite cooked meat with the rice mixture in step 3. Cooked ground beef, diced pepperoni, crumbled cooked bacon or cooked sausage all work well. Be sure to use a 3-quart casserole, though. This recipe is also perfect served as a side dish with grilled chicken or steak or tacos. It will serve 8 to 10 as a side dish.

⚙ **Special Touch**
Serve this casserole with your favorite fixin's, such as sour cream and chopped avocado or guacamole.

Creamy Tortellini Casserole

Prep: 20 min Bake: 15 min

2 tablespoons butter or margarine

$1/2$ cup shredded carrots

1 medium onion, chopped ($1/2$ cup)

1 package (8 ounces) sliced mushrooms (3 cups)

2 tablespoons Gold Medal all-purpose flour

$1/2$ teaspoon salt

2 cups milk

1 cup shredded Gouda cheese (4 ounces)

$3/4$ cup Green Giant frozen sweet peas (from 1-pound bag), thawed

1 package (9 ounces) refrigerated cheese-filled tortellini

$1/2$ cup finely crushed buttery crackers

1. Heat oven to 350°. Spray 1$1/2$-quart casserole with cooking spray.

2. Melt butter in 3-quart saucepan over medium heat. Cook carrots, onion and mushrooms in butter about 5 minutes, stirring occasionally, until mushrooms are tender.

3. Stir in flour and salt. Gradually add milk, stirring constantly. Cook and stir until mixture is bubbly; remove from heat. Stir in cheese, peas and tortellini. Spoon into casserole. Sprinkle with crackers.

4. Bake uncovered about 15 minutes or until edge begins to bubble.

4 servings (1$1/2$ cups each).
1 Serving: Calories 435 (Calories from Fat 215); Fat 24g (Saturated 13g); Cholesterol 110mg; Sodium 770mg; Carbohydrate 35g (Dietary Fiber 4g); Protein 20g
% Daily Value: Vitamin A 70%; Vitamin C 6%; Calcium 40%; Iron 14%
Exchanges: 2 Starch, 1 Vegetable, 2 Medium-Fat Meat, 2 Fat
Carbohydrate Choices: 2

BETTY'S TIPS

❂ **Substitution**
Quickly dress up this casserole and give it a subtle smoky flavor by using smoked Gouda cheese instead of regular Gouda.

❂ **Serve-With**
This casserole is perfect for those who are looking for a meal without meat. Serve with a crisp Caesar salad and warm breadsticks.

Creamy Tortellini Casserole

Quick & Low-Fat

Minestrone Tortellini

Prep: 10 min Cook: 15 min

1 package (9 ounces) refrigerated cheese-filled tortellini

1 tablespoon olive or vegetable oil

1 medium zucchini, cut lengthwise in half, then cut into $1/4$-inch slices ($1^1/2$ cups)

$1/2$ cup coarsely chopped yellow bell pepper

1 can ($14^1/2$ ounces) diced tomatoes with basil, garlic and oregano, undrained

1 can ($15^1/2$ ounces) Green Giant dark red kidney beans, rinsed and drained

2 tablespoons chili sauce

$1/4$ teaspoon salt

2 tablespoons chopped parsley

1. Cook and drain tortellini as directed on package.

2. While tortellini is cooking, heat oil in 12-inch non-stick skillet over medium-high heat. Cook zucchini and bell pepper in oil 2 to 3 minutes, stirring frequently, until crisp-tender.

3. Stir in tomatoes, beans, chili sauce and salt. Cook 4 to 5 minutes over medium heat, stirring occasionally, until thoroughly heated. Stir in tortellini. Sprinkle with parsley.

4 servings.
1 Serving: Calories 285 (Calories from Fat 80); Fat 9g (Saturated 3g); Cholesterol 55mg; Sodium 710mg; Carbohydrate 46g (Dietary Fiber 9g); Protein 14g
% Daily Value: Vitamin A 24%; Vitamin C 48%; Calcium 12%; Iron 28%
Exchanges: 2 Starch, $1/2$ High-Fat Meat
Carbohydrate Choices: 3

BETTY'S TIPS

⊙ **Substitution**
Any color of bell pepper can be used. Why not try a combination of red, yellow and green? If you have fresh basil in your garden, go ahead and substitute it for the parsley.

⊙ **Special Touch**
Spoon the tortellini mixture into a shallow serving bowl and sprinkle with a little shredded Parmesan cheese before adding the parsley. Then add a couple of fresh parsley sprigs to the side of the dish.

Minestrone Tortellini

Spring Ravioli with Pesto Cream

Prep: 10 min Cook: 8 min

2 teaspoons olive or vegetable oil

8 ounces green beans, cut into 1$\frac{1}{2}$-inch pieces

$\frac{1}{2}$ medium yellow bell pepper, cut into $\frac{1}{2}$-inch pieces ($\frac{1}{2}$ cup)

3 roma (plum) tomatoes, cut into $\frac{1}{2}$-inch pieces (1 cup)

$\frac{1}{2}$ teaspoon salt

16 ounces frozen cheese-filled ravioli (from 24-ounce bag)

$\frac{1}{2}$ cup sour cream

3 tablespoons basil pesto

2 teaspoons grated lemon peel

1. Heat oil in 12-inch nonstick skillet over medium-high heat. Cook green beans and bell pepper in oil about 5 minutes, stirring frequently, until crisp-tender. Stir in tomatoes and salt. Cook 3 minutes.

2. While vegetables are cooking, cook and drain ravioli as directed on package. Mix sour cream, pesto and lemon peel in small bowl.

3. Toss hot cooked ravioli with vegetable mixture and sour cream mixture.

4 servings.
1 Serving: Calories 385 (Calories from Fat 215); Fat 24g (Saturated 9g); Cholesterol 135mg; Sodium 1,350mg; Carbohydrate 26g (Dietary Fiber 3g); Protein 16g
% Daily Value: Vitamin A 24%; Vitamin C 32%; Calcium 32%; Iron 14%
Exchanges: 1$\frac{1}{2}$ Starch, 1$\frac{1}{2}$ High-Fat Meat, 1 Vegetable, 2 Fat
Carbohydrate Choices: 2

BETTY'S TIPS

✪ **Serve-With**
For a lovely early summer supper, serve this meatless dish with wedges of melon, clusters of grapes and garlic breadsticks.

✪ **Variation**
You can use 4 ounces of asparagus, cut into 1-inch pieces, and 4 ounces of snap pea pods instead of the green beans. This dish is delicious just as it is, but if you like, sprinkle the top with shredded Parmesan cheese.

Easy Macaroni and Cheese

Prep: 20 min Total: 20 min

2 packages (7 ounces each) small pasta shells

2 tablespoons butter or margarine

$\frac{1}{4}$ cup Gold Medal all-purpose flour

$\frac{1}{2}$ teaspoon salt

$\frac{1}{2}$ teaspoon ground mustard (dry)

$\frac{1}{4}$ teaspoon pepper

2 cups half-and-half

3 cups shredded Cheddar cheese (12 ounces)

4 medium green onions, sliced ($\frac{1}{4}$ cup)

$\frac{1}{4}$ cup chopped red bell peppers

1. Cook and drain pasta as directed on package.

2. While pasta is cooking, melt butter in 3-quart non-stick saucepan over low heat. Stir in flour, salt, mustard and pepper. Cook over low heat 20 seconds, stirring constantly, until butter is absorbed; remove from heat. Gradually beat in half-and-half with wire whisk. Heat to boiling over medium heat, stirring constantly. Boil and stir 1 minute. Stir in cheese until melted.

3. Stir pasta, onions and bell pepper into sauce. Cook, stirring constantly, until hot.

8 servings.
1 Serving: Calories 465 (Calories from Fat 235); Fat 26g (Saturated 16g); Cholesterol 115mg; Sodium 470mg; Carbohydrate 39g (Dietary Fiber 2g); Protein 19g
% Daily Value: Vitamin A 24%; Vitamin C 8%; Calcium 30%; Iron 14%
Exchanges: 2$\frac{1}{2}$ Starch, 2 High-0Fat Meat, 1$\frac{1}{2}$ Fat
Carbohydrate Choices: 2$\frac{1}{2}$

BETTY'S TIPS

✪ **Substitution**
Use reduced-fat Swiss cheese and a dash of ground nutmeg in place of the Cheddar cheese to bring a whole new flavor to this traditional pasta dish.

✪ **Variation**
Try one of the many new pasta shapes or flavored pasta in this quick recipe.

Spring Ravioli with Pesto Cream

Easy Macaroni and Cheese

Vegetables in Peanut Sauce with Noodles

Prep: 35 min
(Photo on page 123)

1¼ cups water
1 cup creamy peanut butter
¼ cup sugar
½ cup soy sauce
1 tablespoon cornstarch
1 tablespoon grated fresh ginger
8 medium green onions, sliced (½ cup)
2 cups cauliflowerets
2 cups broccoli florets
2 medium carrots, cut into matchstick-size pieces (1 cup)
2 medium ribs celery, sliced (1 cup)
1 bag (8 ounces) fresh bean sprouts
1 can (8 ounces) sliced water chestnuts, drained
5 cups chow mein noodles
Dry-roasted peanuts, if desired

1. Mix water, peanut butter, sugar, soy sauce, cornstarch, ginger and onions in medium bowl; set aside.

2. Spray 4-quart Dutch oven with cooking spray; heat over medium-high heat. Cook cauliflowerets, broccoli, carrots and celery in Dutch oven 5 minutes, stirring frequently. Stir in bean sprouts and water chestnuts. Cook 3 minutes, stirring frequently. Reduce heat to medium; stir in peanut butter mixture. Cover and cook about 5 minutes, stirring occasionally, until sauce is thickened.

3. Serve vegetable mixture over noodles. Sprinkle with peanuts.

6 servings.
1 Serving: Calories 610 (Calories from Fat 325); Fat 36g (Saturated 6g); Cholesterol 0mg; Sodium 1,630mg; Carbohydrate 59g (Dietary Fiber 8g); Protein 22g
% Daily Value: Vitamin A 84%; Vitamin C 42%; Calcium 100%; Iron 26%
Exchanges: 3 Starch, 2 Vegetable, 1 High-Fat Meat, 5 Fat
Carbohydrate Choices: 4

BETTY'S TIPS

❂ **Substitution**
You can use 1 can (14 to 16 ounces) bean sprouts, rinsed and drained, instead of the fresh bean sprouts. Purchase a prepared peanut sauce instead of making your own. Use 2½ cups of peanut sauce for this recipe.

❂ **Did You Know?**
Matchstick-size or julienne carrots can be purchased in the produce section of the supermarket.

Shrimp Pilaf Florentine

Prep: 13 min Cook: 16 min

1   tablespoon olive or vegetable oil

1   small red bell pepper, chopped (¹/₂ cup)

2   medium green onions, sliced (2 tablespoons)

2   cloves garlic, finely chopped

1¹/₂ cups uncooked orzo or rosamarina pasta (8 ounces)

2   teaspoons fresh chopped or ¹/₂ teaspoon dried dill weed

1   teaspoon grated lemon peel

¹/₂ teaspoon salt

1   can (14 ounces) chicken broth

1   cup water

2   cups shredded spinach

1   package (8 ounces) frozen cooked medium shrimp (1¹/₂ cups), thawed and tails removed

¹/₄ cup grated Parmesan cheese

1. Heat oil in 12-inch skillet over medium-high heat. Cook bell pepper, onions and garlic in oil 2 to 3 minutes, stirring frequently, until vegetables are crisp-tender.

2. Stir in pasta, dill weed, lemon peel, salt, broth and water. Heat to boiling; reduce heat. Cover and simmer 8 to 10 minutes or until pasta is tender.

3. Stir in spinach and shrimp. Cook 2 to 3 minutes or until shrimp are tender. Sprinkle with cheese.

4 servings.
1 Serving: Calories 365 (Calories from Fat 70); Fat 8g (Saturated 2g); Cholesterol 115mg; Sodium 1,000mg; Carbohydrate 48g (Dietary Fiber 3g); Protein 25g
% Daily Value: Vitamin A 54%; Vitamin C 34%; Calcium 14%; Iron 26%
Exchanges: 3 Starch, 1 Vegetable, 2 Lean Meat
Carbohydrate Choices: 3

BETTY'S TIPS

⊕ **Substitution**
You can also use fresh shrimp, if you like. You'll need just over half a pound of shrimp in shells. Remove the shells and tails. Cook until shrimp are pink and firm.

⊕ **Serve-With**
Serve with garlic bread and a tossed salad made of your favorite greens. If you like, add a plate of sliced home-grown tomatoes.

⊕ **Did You Know?**
The term Florentine is a reference to the cooking style of Florence, Italy. Typically, dishes with à la Florentine or Florentine in the title are served on a bed of spinach and topped with a rich, cheesy sauce. This skillet meal has the spinach stirred in at the end for an all-in-one meal!

Shrimp Pilaf Florentine

Creamy Salmon with Gemelli and Vegetables

Prep: 5 min Cook: 20 min

1 cup uncooked gemelli (twist) pasta (4 ounces)

1 salmon fillet (1 pound), skin removed and salmon cut into 1-inch pieces

$^1/_4$ teaspoon salt

$1^1/_2$ cups refrigerated new potato wedges (from 1-pound 4-ounce bag)

1 cup fresh whole green beans or Green Giant frozen whole green beans

1 cup Parmesan and mozzarella pasta sauce (from 1-pound jar)

$^1/_4$ teaspoon coarsely ground pepper

2 tablespoons chopped fresh basil leaves

1. Cook and drain pasta as directed on package.

2. While pasta is cooking, spray 12-inch nonstick skillet with cooking spray. Add salmon to skillet; sprinkle with salt. Cook uncovered over medium-high heat 5 to 7 minutes, stirring frequently, until salmon flakes easily with fork. Remove salmon from skillet.

3. Add potatoes, beans, pasta sauce and pepper to same skillet. Heat to boiling; reduce heat. Cover and cook 5 to 7 minutes, stirring occasionally, until vegetables are tender. Stir in pasta, salmon and basil. Cook 2 to 3 minutes, stirring occasionally, just until thoroughly heated.

4 servings.
1 Serving: Calories 495 (Calories from Fat 135); Fat 15g (Saturated 5g); Cholesterol 90mg; Sodium 390mg; Carbohydrate 51g (Dietary Fiber 4g); Protein 39g
% Daily Value: Vitamin A 16%; Vitamin C 8%; Calcium 24%; Iron 18%
Exchanges: 3 Starch, 4 Lean Meat, 1 Vegetable
Carbohydrate Choices: $3^1/_2$

Creamy Salmon with Gemelli and Vegetables

BETTY'S TIPS

⚙ **Substitution**
Salmon steaks will work just as well as the fillet in this recipe.

⚙ **Serve-With**
Warm sliced French bread or Italian rolls would be perfect to serve with this dish. Serve chocolate ice cream sundaes for dessert.

⚙ **Did You Know?**
In Tuscany, combining potatoes and pasta is common. Often this combination is simply seasoned with olive oil, garlic and spices. In this recipe, we've added a cheesy sauce, fresh salmon and basil. The result is delicious!

Quick & Low Fat

Honey Garlic Shrimp and Linguine

Prep: 5 min Cook: 15 min

1 package (9 ounces) refrigerated linguine

1 tablespoon water

1 bag (1 pound) frozen baby peas, carrots, pea pods and corn

1/2 cup coarsely chopped red bell pepper

1 pound uncooked, peeled and deveined medium or large shrimp, thawed if frozen and tails removed

1/2 cup roasted garlic and herb marinade (from 12-ounce bottle)

1 tablespoon honey

1. Cook and drain linguine as directed on package; cover to keep warm.

2. Heat water in 12-inch nonstick skillet over medium-high heat. Add frozen vegetables and bell pepper. Cook 2 to 3 minutes, stirring frequently.

3. Stir in shrimp. Cook, stirring frequently, until vegetables are crisp-tender and shrimp are pink and firm. Stir in marinade and honey. Cook, stirring frequently, until thoroughly heated. Serve over linguine.

4 servings.
1 Serving: Calories 430 (Calories from Fat 20); Fat 2g (Saturated 0g); Cholesterol 160mg; Sodium 1,650mg; Carbohydrate 77g (Dietary Fiber 8g); Protein 33g
% Daily Value: Vitamin A 38%; Vitamin C 38%; Calcium 8%; Iron 40%
Exchanges: 5 Starch, 2 Very Lean Meat
Carbohydrate Choices: 4 1/2

BETTY'S TIPS

✪ **Substitution**
This light shrimp dish is tasty as is, but you can use different frozen vegetables if you like. Why not try Green Giant Select sugar snap peas or broccoli florets? Also, green or yellow bell pepper can be substituted for the red.

✪ **Success Hint**
Uncooked shrimp can usually be purchased at the seafood counter of large grocery stores. Or if you like, purchase frozen shrimp so it's on hand when you need it. Just follow the directions on the package, and thaw before using.

✪ **Serve-With**
To complete the menu, just add whole-grain rolls and sliced watermelon.

Honey Garlic Shrimp and Linguine

Sausage and Shrimp Paella

Prep: 25 min Cook: 35 min

2 cans (14 ounces each) chicken broth

1 teaspoon saffron threads

1 pound cooked smoked chorizo sausage, sliced

1 medium red bell pepper, cut into thin strips

1 medium green bell pepper, cut into thin strips

1 medium onion, chopped ($^1/_2$ cup)

2 cloves garlic, finely chopped

1 can (14$^1/_2$ ounces) herb-flavored diced tomatoes, undrained

2$^1/_4$ cups uncooked Arborio or regular long-grain rice

1 cup dry white wine or nonalcoholic white wine

$^1/_2$ pound cooked, peeled and deveined medium shrimp, thawed if frozen and tails removed

1 cup Green Giant frozen sweet peas

2 tablespoons chopped parsley

1. Heat broth to boiling in 2-quart saucepan; stir in saffron. Set aside.

2. Meanwhile, cook sausage in large paella pan or 3-inch deep 12-inch ovenproof skillet over medium heat about 5 minutes, stirring occasionally, until brown. Move sausage to one side of pan. Add bell peppers and onion to pan. Cook about 5 minutes, stirring occasionally, until crisp-tender. Stir in garlic and tomatoes; heat to boiling. Stir in rice, wine and heated broth mixture; heat to boiling. Reduce heat. Cover and simmer 15 minutes; remove from heat.

3. Stir in shrimp and peas. Cover and simmer about 10 minutes or until rice is tender. Sprinkle with parsley.

8 servings.
1 Serving: Calories 540 (Calories from Fat 205); Fat 23g (Saturated 9g); Cholesterol 105mg; Sodium 1,280mg; Carbohydrate 55g (Dietary Fiber 3g); Protein 28g
% Daily Value: Vitamin A 42%; Vitamin C 44%; Calcium 6%; Iron 26%
Exchanges: 3 Starch, 2 Vegetable, 2 Medium-Fat Meat, 2 Fat
Carbohydrate Choices: 3$^1/_2$

BETTY'S TIPS

⊛ **Success Hint**
If a paella pan or deep skillet is not available, use a Dutch oven to cook this recipe.

⊛ **Serve-With**
This all-in-one meal needs only crusty bread and assorted olives to complete it. Serve a Spanish red wine for toasting.

⊛ **Did You Know?**
White and red wines are available in small single-serving bottles, which are perfect for using in recipes where small amounts of wine are needed.

Sausage and Shrimp Paella

Shrimp Kabobs with Orange Spinach Salad

Prep: 20 min Marinate: 15 min Grill: 8 min
(Photo on page 123)

4   navel oranges
    Orange Marinade and Dressing (right)
1   pound uncooked, peeled and deveined large shrimp, thawed if frozen
1   small red onion, cut in half
1   package (10 ounces) fresh spinach

1. Cut two of the oranges into 8 wedges each. Peel and section remaining 2 oranges; reserve. Make Orange Marinade and Dressing; reserve half for dressing. Place shrimp and remaining marinade in shallow glass or plastic dish or heavy-duty resealable plastic food-storage bag. Cover dish or seal bag and refrigerate 15 minutes.

2. Heat coals or gas grill for direct heat. Cut one onion half into wedges; separate into pieces. Thinly slice remaining onion half; separate into pieces and set aside. Remove shrimp from marinade; reserve marinade for basting. Thread shrimp, orange wedges and onion wedges alternately on each of eight 8-inch or four 15-inch metal skewers, leaving space between each piece.

3. Grill kabobs uncovered 4 to 6 inches from medium heat 6 to 8 minutes, turning frequently and brushing with reserved basting marinade, until shrimp are pink and firm. Discard any remaining basting marinade.

4. Gently toss spinach, reserved orange sections, reserved thinly sliced onion and reserved dressing in large bowl. Serve with kabobs.

4 servings (2 kabobs each).

Orange Marinade and Dressing

¾   cup orange juice
⅓   cup light sesame or olive oil
½   teaspoon ground ginger
1   teaspoon garlic salt
¼   teaspoon pepper
4   medium green onions, chopped (¼ cup)

Mix all ingredients.

1 Serving: Calories 330 (Calories from Fat 180); Fat 30g (Saturated 3g); Cholesterol 160mg; Sodium 490mg; Carbohydrate 21g (Dietary Fiber 5g); Protein 21g
% Daily Value: Vitamin A 100%; Vitamin C 78%; Calcium 16%; Iron 28%
Exchanges: 3 Lean Meat, 1 Vegetable, 1 Fruit, 1 Fat
Carbohydrate Choices: 1½

BETTY'S TIPS

❂ **Success Hint**
To peel an orange, use a small sharp knife to peel around the orange, starting at the top; be sure to remove all the white pith from the fruit. To section an orange, gently slice on both sides of the orange section membrane.

❂ **Serve-With**
To round out this meal, serve warm garlic breadsticks. Sherbet and Melon (page 261) would be a perfect ending.

❂ **Variation**
The shrimp, orange wedges and onion wedges can be grilled in a grill basket instead of on skewers.

❂ **Do-Ahead**
The Orange Marinade and Dressing can be prepared one day ahead; cover and refrigerate.

Dilled Salmon and Vegetable Packet

Prep: 17 min Grill: 20 min

1¹/₄ pound salmon fillet, ¹/₂- to ³/₄-inch thick

2 tablespoons olive or vegetable oil

2 teaspoons chopped fresh or ¹/₂ teaspoon dried dill weed

2 teaspoons chopped parsley

1 teaspoon garlic salt

2 medium tomatoes, seeded and coarsely chopped (1¹/₂ cups)

1 medium yellow summer squash, sliced (1¹/₂ cups)

1 cup fresh snap pea pods, strings removed

1. Heat coals or gas grill for direct heat. Cut fillet into 4 serving-size pieces.

2. Mix oil, dill weed, parsley and garlic salt. Place fish and vegetables in heavy-duty aluminum foil bag. Brush oil mixture over fish and vegetables. Double-fold open end of bag.

3. Cover and grill bag 5 to 6 inches from medium heat 15 to 20 minutes or until fish flakes easily with fork. Place bag on serving plate; unfold.

4 servings.
1 Serving: Calories 285 (Calories from Fat 135); Fat 15g (Saturated 2g); Cholesterol 95mg; Sodium 220mg; Carbohydrate 6g (Dietary Fiber 2g); Protein 32g
% Daily Value: Vitamin A 16%; Vitamin C 24%; Calcium 10%; Iron 10%
Exchanges: 1 Vegetable, 4¹/₂ Lean Meat
Carbohydrate Choices: ¹/₂

BETTY'S TIPS

⚙ **Substitution**
For variety, try this packet using halibut, tuna or swordfish instead of the salmon. You can use zucchini in place of the yellow squash, or try a little bit of both for a colorful summer splash to this recipe.

⚙ **Did You Know?**
Although both snap pea pods and snow (Chinese) pea pods can be eaten pod and all, they do have some differences. A hybrid, snap peas are a cross between the English pea and snow peas. Their plump pods contain tiny tender peas that are sweet and delicious. Snow peas, an essential in Chinese cooking, are flat, thin pods with tiny seeds inside.

Dilled Salmon and Vegetable Packet

Halibut Packets Vera Cruz

Easy Salmon Strata

Quick
Halibut Packets Vera Cruz

Prep: 10 min Grill: 15 min

4	small halibut steaks, $^3/_4$ inch thick (about $1^1/_2$ pounds)
1	tablespoon vegetable oil
$^1/_2$	teaspoon salt
$^1/_2$	teaspoon ground cumin
1	cup green salsa (salsa verde)
$^1/_2$	cup fresh corn kernels or Green Giant Niblets frozen corn
1	small tomato, seeded and chopped ($^1/_2$ cup)
1	ripe avocado, pitted, peeled and chopped

1. Heat coals or gas grill for direct heat. Spray half of one side of four 18 × 12-inch sheets of heavy-duty aluminum foil with cooking spray.

2. Brush fish lightly with oil. Sprinkle with salt and cumin. Place fish on sprayed side of foil sheets. Mix salsa, corn and tomato; spoon onto fish. Fold foil over fish so edges meet. Seal edges, making tight $^1/_2$-inch fold; fold again. Allow space on sides for circulation and expansion.

3. Cover and grill packets 4 to 5 inches from medium heat 10 to 15 minutes or until fish flakes easily with fork. Place packets on plates; unfold foil. Sprinkle with avocado.

4 servings.
1 Serving: Calories 290 (Calories from Fat 110); Fat 12g (Saturated 2g); Cholesterol 90mg; Sodium 720mg; Carbohydrate 12g (Dietary Fiber 4g); Protein 34g
% Daily Value: Vitamin A 14%; Vitamin C 14%; Calcium 4%; Iron 8%
Exchanges: 1 Starch, 4 Lean Meat
Carbohydrate Choices: 1

BETTY'S TIPS

❂ **Success Hint**
If you can purchase only large fish steaks, cut them in half before cooking. You may want to check the different brands of green salsa. Some may be spicier than others. Choose to your liking.

❂ **Did You Know?**
Once avocados are cut and exposed to air, they begin to turn brown, as do apples or pears. So chop the avocado shortly before serving.

Easy Salmon Strata

Prep: 15 min Bake: 45 min

6	slices white bread, cubed
6	eggs
1	cup shredded Havarti cheese (4 ounces)
1	cup milk
$1^1/_4$	teaspoons dried dill weed
$^1/_2$	teaspoon salt
1	package ($4^1/_2$ ounces) smoked salmon, chopped
1	jar (2 ounces) diced pimientos, drained
2	medium green onions, sliced (2 tablespoons)

1. Heat oven to 350°. Spray baking dish, 8 × 8 × 2 inches, with cooking spray. Place bread cubes in dish.

2. Beat remaining ingredients in large bowl with fork or wire whisk until well mixed. Slowly pour over bread.

3. Bake uncovered 40 to 45 minutes or until knife inserted in center comes out clean.

6 servings.
1 Serving: Calories 270 (Calories from Fat 135); Fat 15g (Saturated 7g); Cholesterol 240mg; Sodium 720mg; Carbohydrate 16g (Dietary Fiber 1g); Protein 18g
% Daily Value: Vitamin A 18%; Vitamin C 8%; Calcium 22%; Iron 10%
Exchanges: 1 Starch, 2 Lean Meat, 1 Fat
Carbohydrate Choices: 1

BETTY'S TIPS

❂ **Success Hint**
Smoked salmon is available in a variety of flavors. Use the plain, not flavored, salmon for this casserole.

❂ **Serve-With**
Serve this casserole with a fresh fruit salad and cooked asparagus or broccoli spears.

❂ **Did You Know?**
Pimientos, a type of sweet pepper that is more fragrant and juicy than bell peppers, are used for their mild, sweet flavor and vivid color. Pimientos may be found fresh in specialty markets during the late summer months, but they are most commonly found in jars (and in green olives).

Thai Chicken and Shrimp

Prep: 15 min Cook: 10 hr + 10 min

1 package (1 pound 4 ounces) bone-in skinless chicken thighs

1 can (14 ounces) coconut milk (not cream of coconut)

1 package (3.5 ounces) Thai peanut sauce mix (2 envelopes)

2 medium carrots, sliced (1 cup)

1 medium onion, chopped ($^1/_2$ cup)

3 cups water

3 cups uncooked instant rice

1 pound uncooked, peeled and deveined medium shrimp, thawed if frozen and tails removed

1 cup Green Giant frozen sweet peas (from 1-pound bag)

1 tablespoon cornstarch

$^1/_3$ cup chopped peanuts, if desired

3 tablespoons chopped fresh cilantro, if desired

Thai Chicken and Shrimp

1. Place chicken in $3^1/_2$- to 4-quart slow cooker. Add coconut milk. Stir in both envelopes of sauce mix, carrots and onion.

2. Cover and cook on Low heat setting 8 to 10 hours.

3. About 30 minutes before serving, heat water to boiling in 2-quart saucepan over high heat. Remove from heat and stir in rice; cover and let stand about 5 minutes or until water is absorbed. Fluff rice with fork before serving.

4. Remove chicken from cooker; keep warm. Add shrimp and peas to cooker. Increase heat setting to High. Mix $^1/_4$ cup sauce from cooker and the cornstarch in small bowl; stir into mixture in cooker. Cover and cook 5 to 10 minutes, stirring frequently, until shrimp are pink and firm and sauce has thickened slightly.

5. Meanwhile, remove chicken from bones; coarsely chop chicken and return to cooker. Serve chicken mixture over rice. Garnish with peanuts and cilantro.

6 servings.
1 Serving: Calories 580 (Calories from Fat 200); Fat 22g (Saturated 13g); Cholesterol 145mg; Sodium 260mg; Carbohydrate 62g (Dietary Fiber 5g); Protein 34g
% Daily Value: Vitamin A 80%; Vitamin C 6%; Calcium 6%; Iron 32%
Exchanges: 4 Starch, 3 Lean Meat, 2 Fat
Carbohydrate Choices: 4

BETTY'S TIPS

⊗ **Success Hint**
Look for Thai peanut sauce mix in the ethnic-foods section of your grocery store. Bone-in chicken is used because the bones help keep the chicken from shredding during the long cooking time.

⊗ **Health Twist**
Reduced-fat ("lite") coconut milk can be used in place of the regular coconut milk.

⊗ **Variation**
If you're not a shrimp lover, just omit it for tasty **Thai Chicken.**

⊗ **Special Touch**
For a change of pace, serve over cooked jasmine rice.

Baked Fish with Confetti Stuffing

Prep: 15 min

1¼ cups chicken broth

3 tablespoons butter or margarine

2 cups Green Giant Select frozen broccoli, carrots and cauliflower (from 1-pound bag)

1 package (6 ounces) stuffing mix with five savory herbs

1 pound fish fillets, about ³⁄₄-inch thick

1 tablespoon chopped parsley

½ teaspoon seasoned salt

1. Heat oven to 350°. Spray rectangular baking dish, 11 × 7 × 1½ inches, with cooking spray.

2. Heat broth and 2 tablespoons butter to boiling in 3-quart saucepan over high heat. Stir in frozen vegetables; cook 2 minutes.

3. Stir in stuffing mix until evenly moistened. Spoon into baking dish. Arrange fish fillets on stuffing mixture. Melt remaining 1 tablespoon butter; stir in parsley and seasoned salt. Brush butter mixture over fish.

4. Cover with aluminum foil and bake about 35 minutes or until fish flakes easily with fork.

4 servings.
1 Serving: Calories 365 (Calories from Fat 110); Fat 12g (Saturated 6g); Cholesterol 85mg; Sodium 1,390mg; Carbohydrate 35g (Dietary Fiber 3g); Protein 29g
% Daily Value: Vitamin A 36%; Vitamin C 14%; Calcium 8%; Iron 14%
Exchanges: 2 Starch, 1 Vegetable, 4 Very Lean Meat, 1 Fat
Carbohydrate Choices: 2

BETTY'S TIPS

✿ **Success Hint**
Use a mild white fish in this casserole, such as cod, walleye or pike. If the pieces are large, cut them into smaller serving-size pieces. Also, make sure the fillets are a similar thickness so they cook evenly.

✿ **Serve-With**
Great for fish Fridays, this casserole can be served with warm rolls and a gelatin salad for a super, simple meal.

✿ **Did You Know?**
Seasoned salt is a mixture of salt and spices, such as paprika, garlic, turmeric and onion, that jazzes up foods with a couple of shakes.

Baked Fish with Confetti Stuffing

Mediterranean Tuna Steaks

Prep: 15 min Grill: 20 min

1 medium tomato, chopped (³/₄ cup)

¹/₄ cup crumbled feta cheese (1 ounce)

2 tablespoons chopped Kalamata or ripe olives

3 tablespoons chopped fresh basil or oregano leaves

¹/₄ cup olive or vegetable oil

¹/₂ teaspoon garlic salt

¹/₄ teaspoon pepper

4 tuna steaks, 1 inch thick (about 2 pounds)

1. Gently toss tomato, cheese, olives and 1 tablespoon basil in medium bowl. Cover and refrigerate until serving.

2. Spray grill rack with cooking spray. Heat coals or gas grill for direct heat.

3. Mix remaining 2 tablespoons basil, oil, garlic salt and pepper in small bowl. Brush mixture over tuna.

4. Grill tuna uncovered 4 inches from medium-high heat 5 minutes. Turn carefully; brush with any remaining oil mixture. Grill 10 to 15 minutes longer or until tuna flakes easily with a fork. Serve topped with tomato mixture.

4 servings.
1 Serving: Calories 470 (Calories from Fat 245); Fat 27g (Saturated 6g); Cholesterol 95mg; Sodium 350mg; Carbohydrate 2g (Dietary Fiber 0g); Protein 55g
% Daily Value: Vitamin A 8%; Vitamin C 4%; Calcium 6%; Iron 14%
Exchanges: 8 Lean Meat, ¹/₂ Fat
Carbohydrate Choices: 0

BETTY'S TIPS

❂ **Success Hint**
For a colorful presentation, use a mix of red and yellow tomatoes with the feta and olives.

❂ **Serve-With**
Serve with a mixed-greens salad and warm pita bread.

❂ **Did You Know?**
Kalamata olives are Greek olives with a dark eggplant color and a rich fruity flavor. They come packed in either olive oil or vinegar.

Mediterranean Tuna Steaks

Poultry Dishes
Something for Everyone

Plum-Glazed Turkey Tenderloins (page 172)

Creamy Chicken Lasagna (page 165)

Tuscan Rosemary Chicken and White Beans

Prep: 11 min Cook: 19 min

1/3 cup Italian dressing

4 boneless, skinless chicken breast halves (about 1¼ pounds)

1/4 cup water

2 medium carrots, sliced (1 cup)

2 medium ribs celery, sliced (1 cup)

1/4 cup coarsely chopped drained sun-dried tomatoes in oil

1 teaspoon dried rosemary leaves, crumbled

1 can (19 ounces) cannellini (white kidney) beans, rinsed and drained

1. Heat dressing in 12-inch skillet over medium-high heat. Cook chicken in dressing 2 to 3 minutes on each side or until lightly browned.

2. Reduce heat to medium-low. Add water, carrots, celery, tomatoes and rosemary to skillet. Cover and simmer about 10 minutes, or until juice of chicken is no longer pink when centers of thickest pieces are cut and carrots are crisp-tender.

3. Stir in beans. Cover and cook 5 to 6 minutes or until beans are thoroughly heated.

4 servings.
1 Serving: Calories 400 (Calories from Fat 115); Fat 13g (Saturated 2g); Cholesterol 75mg; Sodium 300mg; Carbohydrate 41g (Dietary Fiber 10g); Protein 40g
% Daily Value: Vitamin A 100%; Vitamin C 8%; Calcium 18%; Iron 34%
Exchanges: 3 Starch, 4½ Very Lean Meat
Carbohydrate Choices: 3

BETTY'S TIPS

⊕ **Substitution**
If you prefer dark meat, substitute 8 boneless, skinless chicken thighs for the chicken breasts.

⊕ **Success Hint**
Keep chicken as moist and tender as possible by not overcooking it. Check chicken for doneness at the minimum cooking time by cutting into the thickest part of the chicken with a knife to see if the juices are no longer pink.

⊕ **Health Twist**
Italian dressing comes in reduced-fat and fat-free varieties in addition to regular dressing. Using the reduced-fat version will save you 45 calories and 5 grams of fat per serving.

Tuscan Rosemary Chicken and White Beans

Quick

Fettuccine with Chicken and Vegetables

Prep: 10 min Cook: 15 min

1	package (9 ounces) refrigerated fettuccine
2	cups small fresh broccoli florets
1/3	cup Italian dressing
1	pound chicken breast strips for stir-fry
1	medium red onion, cut into thin wedges
1/4	teaspoon garlic pepper
1/2	cup sliced drained roasted red bell peppers (from 7-ounce jar)
	Shredded Parmesan cheese, if desired

4 servings.
1 Serving: Calories 470 (Calories from Fat 135); Fat 15g (Saturated 2g); Cholesterol 125mg; Sodium 260mg; Carbohydrate 49g (Dietary Fiber 4g); Protein 35g
% Daily Value: Vitamin A 32%; Vitamin C 58%; Calcium 8%; Iron 22%
Exchanges: 3 Starch, 3 1/2 Lean Meat, 1 Vegetable
Carbohydrate Choices: 3

1. Cook and drain fettuccine and broccoli as directed on fettuccine package. Toss with 2 tablespoons of the dressing. Cover to keep warm.

2. Meanwhile, spray 12-inch nonstick skillet with cooking spray; heat over medium-high heat. Add chicken and onion to skillet; sprinkle with garlic pepper. Cook 4 to 6 minutes, stirring occasionally, until chicken is no longer pink in center.

3. Stir in bell peppers and remaining dressing. Cook 2 to 3 minutes, stirring occasionally, until warm. Serve chicken mixture over fettuccine and broccoli. Serve with cheese.

BETTY'S TIPS

⊘ **Substitution**
Refrigerated linguine can be used instead of the fettuccine.

⊘ **Variation**
Omit the broccoli, and add 4 cups fresh baby spinach leaves after warming the roasted peppers and dressing in step 3. Cook 1 to 2 minutes or just until the spinach wilts.

⊘ **Did You Know?**
The garlic pepper we call for in this recipe is a favorite of many of our editors. Look for it in the spice aisle of the grocery store. You can use a combination of coarsely ground pepper and garlic powder if you don't have it on hand.

Fettuccine with Chicken and Vegetables

Southwest Chicken and Couscous

Prep: 10 min Cook: 15 min

- 1 cup frozen stir-fry bell peppers and onions (from 1-pound bag)
- 1 can (15 ounces) black beans with cumin and chili spices, undrained
- ½ cup Old El Paso Thick 'n Chunky salsa
- 1 package (9 ounces) frozen cooked Southwest-seasoned chicken breast strips
- ½ cup Green Giant Niblets frozen corn (from 1-pound bag)
- 2 cups water
- 1½ cups uncooked couscous
- ¼ cup chopped fresh cilantro

1. Spray 12-inch nonstick skillet with cooking spray; heat over medium-high heat. Cook stir-fry vegetables in skillet 2 to 3 minutes, stirring frequently, until crisp-tender.

2. Stir in beans, salsa, frozen chicken and corn. Heat to boiling; reduce heat to low. Cover and simmer about 5 minutes, stirring occasionally, until chicken is thoroughly heated (break up large pieces of chicken with stirring spoon as mixture cooks).

3. Meanwhile, heat water to boiling. Stir in couscous; remove from heat. Cover and let stand 5 minutes. Fluff with fork.

4. Spoon couscous onto serving plates. Top with chicken mixture. Sprinkle with cilantro.

4 servings.
1 Serving: Calories 505 (Calories from Fat 35); Fat 4g (Saturated 1g); Cholesterol 55mg; Sodium 610mg; Carbohydrate 90g (Dietary Fiber 12g); Protein 39g
% Daily Value: Vitamin A 10%; Vitamin C 34%; Calcium 12%; Iron 26%
Exchanges: 6 Starch, 2 Very Lean Meat
Carbohydrate Choices: 5

BETTY'S TIPS

⊛ **Substitution**
Use your choice of mild, medium or hot salsa to make this dish as mild or spicy as you like. If you don't have the stir-fry vegetables, use a combination of one or more colors of chopped bell peppers and onion to equal 1 cup.

⊛ **Variation**
For delicious handheld sandwiches, omit the couscous, spoon the chicken mixture onto flour tortillas and roll up.

Southwest Chicken and Couscous

Quick & Low Fat

Lemon Chicken Stir-Fry

Prep: 15 min Cook: 13 min

8 ounces uncooked capellini (angel hair) pasta

1 tablespoon vegetable oil

1 pound boneless, skinless chicken tenders (not breaded), cut into 1-inch pieces

1 medium onion, cut into 8 wedges

2 cups small broccoli florets

1/2 cup sugar snap peas

1 cup chicken broth

1 tablespoon chopped fresh or 1 teaspoon dried thyme leaves

1 teaspoon grated lemon peel

4 teaspoons cornstarch

1 1/2 teaspoons lemon pepper

1 cup cherry or grape tomatoes, cut in half

1. Cook and drain pasta as directed on package.

2. While pasta is cooking, heat oil in 12-inch skillet over medium-high heat. Add chicken and onion; stir-fry 5 to 6 minutes or until chicken is brown.

3. Add broccoli and peas to chicken mixture. Cook over medium-high heat 4 to 5 minutes, stirring frequently, until vegetables are crisp-tender.

4. Stir together broth, thyme, lemon peel, cornstarch and lemon pepper in small bowl; stir into chicken mixture. Cook over medium-high heat 1 to 2 minutes or until sauce is thickened and vegetables are coated.

5. Stir in tomatoes; cook until thoroughly heated. Serve over pasta.

4 servings.
1 Serving: Calories 425 (Calories from Fat 80); Fat 9g (Saturated 2g); Cholesterol 70mg; Sodium 340mg; Carbohydrate 55g (Dietary Fiber 5g); Protein 36g
% Daily Value: Vitamin A 20%; Vitamin C 46%; Calcium 6%; Iron 22%
Exchanges: 3 Starch, 2 Vegetable, 3 Very Lean Meat, 1/2 Fat
Carbohydrate Choices: 3 1/2

BETTY'S TIPS

❂ **Serve-With**
Serve this lemony stir-fry over cooked Chinese noodles, vermicelli or rice instead of the angel hair pasta.

❂ **Special Touch**
Cherry tomatoes come in a variety of shapes and colors. Try pear-shaped, round, red, yellow or orange tomatoes.

Lemon Chicken Stir-Fry

Quick
Chicken Lo Mein

Prep: 4 min Cook: 16 min

2 ounces uncooked Oriental noodles

2 tablespoons light sesame or vegetable oil

1 teaspoon finely chopped garlic

1 pound chicken breast strips for stir-fry

$1/3$ cup chopped green onions

4 cups coleslaw mix (from 1-pound bag)

1 bag (1 pound) Green Giant Create a Meal! frozen teriyaki stir-fry meal starter

1. Cook and drain noodles as directed on package.

2. While noodles are cooking, heat oil in 4- to 6-quart Dutch oven over medium-high heat. Cook garlic and chicken in oil 4 to 5 minutes, stirring frequently, just until chicken is no longer pink in center.

3. Stir in onions, coleslaw mix and meal starter vegetables and sauce. Cover and cook 7 to 9 minutes, stirring frequently, until vegetables are hot. Stir in noodles. Cook 1 to 2 minutes, stirring constantly, until noodles are well mixed.

4 servings.
1 Serving: Calories 425 (Calories from Fat 135); Fat 15g (Saturated 3g); Cholesterol 70mg; Sodium 1,080mg; Carbohydrate 37g (Dietary Fiber 6g); Protein 3g
% Daily Value: Vitamin A 2%; Vitamin C 24%; Calcium 6%; Iron 12%
Exchanges: 2 Starch, 1 Vegetable, 4 Lean Meat, $1/2$ Fat
Carbohydrate Choices: $2^1/2$

BETTY'S TIPS

⊙ **Substitution**
Ground pork for chow mein can be substituted for the chicken, and 2 ounces uncooked spaghetti can be substituted for the Oriental noodles.

⊙ **Success Hint**
Garnish noodles with extra chopped green onions, chopped peanuts or toasted sesame seed.

⊙ **Serve-With**
A salad of chilled pineapple chunks and mandarin orange segments served in a lettuce cup is an easy addition to this quick meal.

Scalloped Chicken and Potatoes

Prep: 15 min Cook: 40 min

1 package (4.8 ounces) Betty Crocker sour cream 'n chives potato mix

$2^1/4$ cups boiling water

$3/4$ cup half-and-half or whole milk

3 cups cubed cooked chicken

1 cup Green Giant frozen sweet peas (from 1-pound bag)

1 can (8 ounces) Green Giant mushroom pieces and stems, drained

$1/2$ cup Progresso plain bread crumbs

$1/4$ cup butter or margarine, melted

1 tablespoon chopped parsley

1. Heat oven to 450°. Mix potatoes, sauce mix, water, half-and-half, chicken, peas and mushrooms in ungreased 2-quart casserole.

2. Bake uncovered 30 to 35 minutes, stirring once, until potatoes are tender.

3. Mix remaining ingredients in small bowl; sprinkle over potato mixture. Bake uncovered about 5 minutes or until light golden brown.

5 servings.
1 Serving: Calories 450 (Calories from Fat 200); Fat 22g (Saturated 11g); Cholesterol 110mg; Sodium 800mg; Carbohydrate 34g (Dietary Fiber 4g); Protein 29g
% Daily Value: Vitamin A 14%; Vitamin C 2%; Calcium 8%; Iron 14%
Exchanges: 2 Starch, 1 Vegetable, 3 Medium-Fat Meat, 1 Fat
Carbohydrate Choices: 2

BETTY'S TIPS

⊙ **Substitution**
A 12-ounce can of tuna, drained, can be substituted for the chicken.

⊙ **Serve-With**
Cooked baby carrots will add color to this creamy comfort meal.

Scalloped Chicken and Potatoes

Chicken Lo Mein

Chipotle Chicken and Pintos with Spanish Rice

Prep: 15 min Cook: 10 hr

1¼ pounds boneless, skinless chicken thighs

2 cans (15.5 ounces each) pinto beans, rinsed and drained

2 cans (4.5 ounces each) Old El Paso chopped green chiles

2 chipotle chiles (from 6-ounce can), seeded and chopped

1 envelope (0.87 ounce) chicken gravy mix

1 package (6.8 ounces) Spanish rice mix

2 cups water

2 tablespoons olive oil or butter

1 medium tomato, seeded and chopped (¾ cup)

Chopped fresh cilantro, if desired

1. Place chicken, pinto beans, green chiles, chipotle chiles and gravy mix (dry) in order listed in 3- to 3½-quart slow cooker.

2. Cover and cook on Low heat setting 8 to 10 hours.

3. About 30 minutes before serving, make Spanish rice mix as directed on package, using water and oil.

4. Meanwhile, gently stir tomato into chicken mixture.

5. To serve, spoon about 1¼ cups chicken mixture over ½ cup rice. Sprinkle with cilantro.

4 servings (1¾ cups each).
1 Serving: Calories 610 (Calories from Fat 180); Fat 20g (Saturated 5g); Cholesterol 90mg; Sodium 1,420mg; Carbohydrate 77g (Dietary Fiber 21g); Protein 51g
% Daily Value: Vitamin A 18%; Vitamin C 28%; Calcium 18%; Iron 54%
Exchanges: 5 Starch, 5 Very Lean Meat, 1 Fat
Carbohydrate Choices: 5

BETTY'S TIPS

⊛ **Substitution**
Use plain white rice for a milder meal.

⊛ **Success Hint**
If you want a hotter dish, leave the seeds in the chipotle chiles. Stirring in the tomato at the end gives this dish a fresh taste.

Chipotle Chicken and Pintos with Spanish Rice

Chicken and Rice Cordon Bleu

Prep: 20 min Cook: 1 hr 5 min

2 packages (6.2 ounces each) quick-cooking long-grain and wild rice

4 cups water

4 thin slices baked ham, cut into 1-inch strips

1 1/2 pounds chicken breast tenders (not breaded)

1 jar (16 ounces) Parmesan and mozzarella cheese pasta sauce

1/2 teaspoon ground paprika

1 cup finely shredded Swiss cheese (4 ounces)

1 tablespoon chopped parsley

1. Heat oven to 350°. Spray rectangular baking dish, 13 × 9 × 2 inches, with cooking spray. Mix rice, contents of seasoning packets and water in baking dish. Place ham over rice. Place chicken tenders over ham. Spoon pasta sauce over each chicken tender; sprinkle with paprika.

2. Cover with aluminum foil and bake 40 minutes. Uncover and bake about 20 minutes longer or until rice is tender and chicken is no longer pink in center. Sprinkle with cheese. Bake uncovered about 5 minutes or until cheese is melted. Sprinkle with parsley.

8 servings.
1 Serving: Calories 350 (Calories from Fat 155); Fat 17g (Saturated 9g); Cholesterol 90mg; Sodium 580mg; Carbohydrate 16g (Dietary Fiber 0g); Protein 33g
% Daily Value: Vitamin A 12%; Vitamin C 0%; Calcium 30%; Iron 8%
Exchanges: 1 Starch, 4 Lean Meat, 1 Fat
Carbohydrate Choices: 1

BETTY'S TIPS

✿ **Substitution**
If fresh chicken breast tenders are not available, frozen (thawed) chicken tenders (not breaded) may be used. Or substitute boneless, skinless chicken breast halves that have been cut lengthwise into thirds. Leftover ham from a holiday meal can be used in this recipe. Slice it thin, and cut enough strips to cover the rice.

✿ **Serve-With**
A salad of mixed greens or fresh arugula and sliced red pears complete this easy chicken casserole meal.

Chicken and Rice Cordon Bleu

Quick

Chicken and Broccoli Pasta Alfredo

Prep: 25 min

1   tablespoon olive or vegetable oil
1   pound boneless, skinless chicken breast strips
$^1/_3$ cup water
1   bag (1 pound) Green Giant Pasta Accents® frozen garlic vegetables with pasta
$^1/_3$ cup whipping (heavy) cream
$^1/_2$ cup shredded Parmesan cheese
   Chopped fresh basil leaves, if desired

1. Heat oil in 12-inch skillet over medium-high heat. Cook chicken in oil 6 to 7 minutes, stirring frequently, just until chicken is no longer pink in center.

2. Stir in water and frozen pasta-vegetable mixture. Cover and cook 4 to 5 minutes, stirring occasionally, until vegetables are hot. Stir in whipping cream. Cook 2 to 3 minutes or until hot.

3. Turn off heat. Stir in cheese. Let stand 2 to 3 minutes or until cheese is melted. Sprinkle with basil. Serve with additional shredded Parmesan cheese if desired.

4 servings.
1 Serving: Calories 385 (Calories from Fat 170); Fat 19g (Saturated 8g); Cholesterol 100mg; Sodium 470mg; Carbohydrate 24g (Dietary Fiber 2g); Protein 30g
% Daily Value: Vitamin A 24%; Vitamin C 12%; Calcium 4%; Iron 10%
Exchanges: $1^1/_2$ Starch, $3^1/_2$ Lean Meat, $1^1/_2$ Fat
Carbohydrate Choices: $1^1/_2$

BETTY'S TIPS

⊛ **Substitution**
Shrimp or scallops can be substituted for the chicken in this recipe. Reduce the cooking time in step 1 to 4 to 5 minutes.

⊛ **Success Hint**
Boneless, skinless chicken breast strips can be found in the meat department of the supermarket.

⊛ **Serve-With**
A tossed green salad with tomatoes and crusty bread go well with this "comfort food" meal.

⊛ **Special Touch**
Chopped fresh basil adds color and flavor to this pleasing meal. Strips of red bell pepper or chopped red bell pepper can also be used to garnish this recipe.

Chicken and Broccoli Pasta Alfredo

Curried Country Chicken

Prep: 15 min Cook: 30 min

1¼   pounds boneless, skinless chicken breasts, cut into 1-inch pieces

1   medium onion, chopped (½ cup)

1   small green bell pepper, chopped (½ cup)

1   can (28 ounces) diced tomatoes, undrained

½   cup golden raisins

1 to 2   teaspoons curry powder

¼   teaspoon ground nutmeg

¼   teaspoon salt

1⅓   cups Reduced Fat Bisquick mix

⅓   cup cornmeal

⅔   cup fat-free (skim) milk

Curried Country Chicken

1. Cook chicken in 4-quart nonstick Dutch oven over medium-high heat 5 minutes, stirring occasionally, until no longer pink. Stir in onion and bell pepper. Cook about 5 minutes, stirring occasionally, until vegetables are tender. Stir in tomatoes, raisins, curry powder, nutmeg and salt. Heat to boiling; reduce heat to simmer.

2. Stir Bisquick mix, cornmeal and milk until soft dough forms. Drop dough by tablespoonfuls onto hot chicken mixture.

3. Cook uncovered over low heat 10 minutes. Cover and cook 10 minutes longer.

4 servings.
1 Serving: Calories 470 (Calories from Fat 70); Fat 8g (Saturated 2g); Cholesterol 85mg; Sodium 980mg; Carbohydrate 65g (Dietary Fiber 5g); Protein 40g
% Daily Value: Vitamin A 18%; Vitamin C 38%; Calcium 18%; Iron 26%
Exchanges: 4 Starch, 4 Very Lean Meat, 1 Vegetable
Carbohydrate Choices: 4

BETTY'S TIPS

❂ **Variation**
Give this country chicken dish a whole new flavor! For a southwestern taste, omit the raisins, curry powder and nutmeg, and add 1 to 2 teaspoons chili powder. For a Cajun taste, omit the raisins, curry powder and nutmeg, and add 1 teaspoon Cajun seasoning and ¼ teaspoon dried oregano leaves.

❂ **Did You Know?**
Golden raisins come from the same grape as regular raisins, but golden raisins are treated to prevent darkening and then dried with artificial heat to give a plumper, moister raisin with a pale gold color.

Sesame Ginger Chicken

Basil and Prosciutto Chicken

Quick & Low Fat
Sesame Ginger Chicken

Prep: 5 min Grill: 20 min

2 tablespoons teriyaki sauce
1 tablespoon sesame seed, toasted*
1 teaspoon ground ginger
4 boneless, skinless chicken breast halves (about 1¼ pounds)
    Hot cooked Japanese curly noodles, if desired

1. Brush grill rack with vegetable oil. Heat coals or gas grill for direct heat. Mix teriyaki sauce, sesame seed and ginger.

2. Cover and grill chicken 4 to 6 inches from medium heat 15 to 20 minutes, brushing frequently with sauce mixture and turning after 10 minutes, until juice is no longer pink when centers of thickest pieces are cut. Discard any remaining sauce mixture.

3. Serve chicken with noodles.

*To toast sesame seed, heat in ungreased skillet over medium heat about 2 minutes, stirring occasionally, until golden brown.

4 servings.
1 Serving: Calories 165 (Calories from Fat 45); Fat 5g (Saturated 1g); Cholesterol 75mg; Sodium 410mg; Carbohydrate 2g (Dietary Fiber 0g); Protein 28g
% Daily Value: Vitamin A 0%; Vitamin C 0%; Calcium 2%; Iron 6%
Exchanges: 4 Very Lean Meat, ½ Fat
Carbohydrate Choices: 0

BETTY'S TIPS

⚙ **Success Hint**
To retain food juices, turn chicken with tongs instead of piercing it with a fork.

⚙ **Serve-With**
For a really easy meal, add warm egg rolls and an Asian salad from the deli. Any flavor of sherbet would be the perfect refreshing dessert.

Low Fat
Basil and Prosciutto Chicken

Prep: 15 min Cook: 16 min

1 tablespoon vegetable oil
4 boneless, skinless chicken breast halves (about 1¼ pounds)
4 teaspoons Dijon mustard
4 thin slices prosciutto or fully cooked ham
¼ cup shredded mozzarella cheese (1 ounce)
4 fresh basil leaves

1. Heat oil in 10-inch skillet over medium heat. Cook chicken in oil 6 minutes. Turn chicken; brush with mustard and top with prosciutto. Cook 6 to 8 minutes longer or until juice of chicken is no longer pink when centers of thickest pieces are cut.

2. Sprinkle cheese over chicken. Cook about 2 minutes or until cheese is melted. Garnish with basil.

4 servings.
1 Serving: Calories 225 (Calories from Fat 90); Fat 10g (Saturated 3g); Cholesterol 85mg; Sodium 440mg; Carbohydrate 1g (Dietary Fiber 0g); Protein 32g
% Daily Value: Vitamin A 2%; Vitamin C 0%; Calcium 6%; Iron 6%
Exchanges: 4 Lean Meat
Carbohydrate Choices: 0

BETTY'S TIPS

⚙ **Success Hint**
Boneless, skinless chicken breast halves vary considerably in size. For this recipe, select ones that are about 5 ounces each. Be sure that they are all the same size so they cook in the same amount of time.

⚙ **Serve-With**
Serve this Italian-style dish with steamed green beans and warm breadsticks. Italian gelato and biscotti for dessert keep with the Italian theme.

Grilled Whole Chicken with Herbs

Prep: 15 min Grill: 1 hr 10 min

8 medium green onions, chopped ($^1/_2$ cup)
2 tablespoons chopped fresh rosemary leaves
2 tablespoons chopped flat-leaf parsley
2 tablespoons lemon juice
1 teaspoon salt
$^1/_2$ teaspoon pepper
1 clove garlic, finely chopped
2$^1/_2$- to 3-pound whole broiler-fryer chicken

1. If using charcoal grill, place drip pan directly under grilling area, and arrange coals around edge of firebox. Heat coals or gas grill for indirect heat.

2. Mix all ingredients except chicken in small bowl. Rub mixture over skin of chicken, and place 2 tablespoons mixture in cavity of chicken. Insert barbecue meat thermometer so tip is in thickest part of inside thigh muscle and does not touch bone.

3. Cover and grill chicken, breast side up, over drip pan or over unheated side of gas grill and 4 to 6 inches from medium-high heat 1 hour to 1 hour 10 minutes. Rotate chicken one-half turn once, until thermometer reads 180° and juice of chicken is no longer pink when center of thigh is cut. Garnish as desired.

4 servings.
1 Serving: Calories 295 (Calories from Fat 155); Fat 17g (Saturated 5g); Cholesterol 105mg; Sodium 400mg; Carbohydrate 2g (Dietary Fiber 0g); Protein 34g
% Daily Value: Vitamin A 6%; Vitamin C 4%; Calcium 2%; Iron 10%
Exchanges: 5 Lean Meat, $^1/_2$ Fat
Carbohydrate Choices: 0

Grilled Whole Chicken with Herbs

BETTY'S TIPS

⚙ **Substitution**
If fresh herbs are not available, use 1 teaspoon dried rosemary leaves and 2 tablespoons dried parsley flakes.

⚙ **Success Hint**
Indirect grilling makes chicken tender and juicy without having to monitor the grill constantly. Arrange coals around edge of firebox. For gas grills, heat both sides of grill, and turn off one side when placing chicken on the grill.

⚙ **Serve-With**
For an easy summer dinner, serve with warm linguine tossed with halved cherry tomatoes and freshly grated Parmesan cheese. For dessert, try Peach and Raspberry Cobbler (page 268).

Quick & Low Fat

Chicken Breasts with Cucumber Peach Salsa

Prep: 15 min Grill: 15 min

$^1/_2$ cup chopped cucumber

$^1/_3$ cup peach preserves

  1   tablespoon chopped fresh mint or
      1 teaspoon dried mint flakes

$^1/_4$ teaspoon salt

  2   tablespoons chopped red onion

  1   peach or nectarine, peeled and chopped
      ($^3/_4$ cup)

  4   boneless, skinless chicken breast halves
      (about 1$^1/_4$ pounds)

1. Spray grill rack with cooking spray. Heat coals or gas grill for direct heat.

2. Mix cucumber, 2 tablespoons preserves, mint, salt, onion and peach; set aside.

3. Cover and grill chicken 4 to 6 inches from medium heat 10 to 15 minutes, turning and brushing 2 or 3 times with remaining peach preserves, until chicken is no longer pink when centers of thickest pieces are cut. Discard any remaining preserves. Serve chicken with salsa.

4 servings.
1 Serving: Calories 230 (Calories from Fat 35); Fat 4g (Saturated 1g); Cholesterol 75mg; Sodium 220mg; Carbohydrate 22g (Dietary Fiber 1g); Protein 27g
% Daily Value: Vitamin A 2%; Vitamin C 10%; Calcium 2%; Iron 6%
Exchanges: 1 Fruit, 1 Vegetable, 4 Very Lean Meat
Carbohydrate Choices: 1$^1/_2$

BETTY'S TIPS

⊕ **Success Hint**
If you're using a charcoal grill, plan on about 40 minutes to prep the grill and heat the charcoal to the correct temperature. Gas and electric grills will take about 10 minutes.

⊕ **Serve-With**
Serve this fruity chicken dish with steamed broccoli, sliced garden-fresh tomatoes and seasoned rice.

⊕ **Do-Ahead**
The salsa can be made up to 24 hours in advance and refrigerated. Making it ahead will actually allow the flavors to blend.

Chicken Breasts with Cucumber Peach Salsa

Antipasto Chicken

Prep: 10 min Cook: 18 min

1 tablespoon olive or vegetable oil

1 teaspoon garlic pepper

4 boneless, skinless chicken breast halves (about 1¼ pounds)

1 jar (6 ounces) marinated artichoke hearts, undrained

1 small green bell pepper, chopped (½ cup)

2 medium tomatoes, chopped (1½ cups)

1 can (2¼ ounces) sliced ripe olives, drained

1 tablespoon chopped fresh or 1 teaspoon dried basil leaves

Crumbled feta cheese, if desired

1. Heat oil in 12-inch skillet over medium heat. Sprinkle garlic pepper over chicken. Cook chicken in oil about 8 minutes, turning once, until brown on both sides.

2. Mix undrained artichokes and remaining ingredients except cheese in medium bowl. Cut large artichoke pieces in half if necessary. Spoon mixture over chicken. Cook about 10 minutes or until chicken is no longer pink when centers of thickest pieces are cut. Sprinkle with cheese.

4 servings.
1 Serving: Calories 245 (Calories from Fat 90); Fat 10g (Saturated 2g); Cholesterol 75mg; Sodium 340mg; Carbohydrate 10g (Dietary Fiber 4g); Protein 29g
% Daily Value: Vitamin A 14%; Vitamin C 26%; Calcium 4%; Iron 12%
Exchanges: 2 Vegetable, 3½ Lean Meat
Carbohydrate Choices: ½

Antipasto Chicken

BETTY'S TIPS

⚙ **Substitution**
If you prefer the dark meat of the bird, use 8 boneless, skinless chicken-thighs instead of the chicken breasts.

⚙ **Serve-With**
Serve this hearty chicken dinner over a plate of hot spaghetti. Add warm focaccia and cooked zucchini slices for dinner with an authentic Italian feel.

⚙ **Did You Know?**
Garlic pepper is an all-purpose seasoning that contains garlic, black pepper and bits of bell pepper and onion.

Low Fat

Oven-Fried Picnic Chicken

Prep: 10 min Stand: 5 min Bake: 50 min

2/3 cup buttermilk

8 boneless, skinless chicken breast halves
(2 1/2 pounds)

1 cup Country® Corn Flakes cereal

1 cup Original Bisquick mix

2 envelopes (1 ounce each) ranch dressing mix
Cooking spray

1. Heat oven to 400°. Spray cookie sheet with cooking spray.

2. Pour buttermilk into shallow glass or plastic bowl. Add chicken; turn to coat. Let stand 5 minutes.

3. Place cereal in 2-quart resealable plastic food-storage bag; crush with rolling pin. Add Bisquick mix and dressing mix (dry) to cereal in plastic bag. Remove chicken from buttermilk; discard buttermilk. Add chicken to cereal mixture. Seal bag; shake to coat.

4. Place chicken on cookie sheet. Spray with cooking spray. Bake 45 to 50 minutes or until juice of chicken is no longer pink when centers of thickest pieces are cut.

8 servings.
1 Serving: Calories 220 (Calories from Fat 55); Fat 6g (Saturated 2g); Cholesterol 75mg; Sodium 650mg; Carbohydrate 13g (Dietary Fiber 0g); Protein 29g
% Daily Value: Vitamin A 2%; Vitamin C 0%; Calcium 8%; Iron 10%
Exchanges: 1 Starch, 4 Very Lean Meat
Carbohydrate Choices: 1

BETTY'S TIPS

⊘ **Do-Ahead**
You can enjoy this chicken hot or cold! If you'd like to make and take, bake it the night before, and then pack it up for a picnic in the park the next day!

⊘ **Serve-With**
Serve with traditional picnic fare such as coleslaw, baked beans, frosted brownies and lemonade. Don't forget the napkins!

⊘ **Did You Know?**
Buttermilk, with its thick consistency and slightly tangy flavor, has long been a cook's "secret" for making fried chicken. Once found only at the bottom of the churn after churning butter, buttermilk is now found with the regular milk in the grocery store.

Oven-Fried Picnic Chicken

Pizza Chicken Kabobs

Prep: 20 min Grill: 11 min

1½ pounds chicken breast tenders (not breaded)
1 medium red bell pepper, cut into 1-inch pieces (1 cup)
1 package (8 ounces) whole mushrooms
⅓ cup Italian dressing
2 teaspoons pizza seasoning
¼ cup grated Parmesan cheese
½ cup pizza sauce (from 14-ounce jar)

1. Heat coals or gas grill for direct heat. Thread chicken, bell pepper and mushrooms alternately on each of six 11-inch metal skewers, leaving ½-inch space between each piece. Brush kabobs with dressing; sprinkle with pizza seasoning.

2. Cover and grill kabobs 4 to 6 inches from medium heat 9 to 11 minutes, turning once, until chicken is no longer pink in center. Sprinkle immediately with cheese.

3. Meanwhile, heat pizza sauce in small saucepan over low heat. Serve kabobs with warm sauce.

6 servings.
1 Serving: Calories 245 (Calories from Fat 100); Fat 11g (Saturated 2g); Cholesterol 75mg; Sodium 400mg; Carbohydrate 7g (Dietary Fiber 1g); Protein 29g
% Daily Value: Vitamin A 28%; Vitamin C 36%; Calcium 10%; Iron 8%
Exchanges: ½ Starch, 4 Lean Meat
Carbohydrate Choices: ½

BETTY'S TIPS

⊗ **Substitution**
If the chicken tenders are not available, just cut boneless skinless chicken breasts into 3 × 1-inch strips and follow the recipe as directed. Pizza seasoning can be found in the spice aisle of the supermarket. If it's not available, use 1 teaspoon Italian seasoning instead.

⊗ **Serve-With**
For an easy summer meal, serve the kabobs with pasta salad from the deli and Italian hard rolls. Spumoni or chocolate ice cream for dessert would be perfect.

Pizza Chicken Kabobs

Home-Style Chicken and Corn

Prep: 20 min Total: 40 min

1 tablespoon butter or margarine

8 chicken legs (about 2 pounds)

1 large onion, cut in half and sliced

1 teaspoon seasoned salt

$1/4$ teaspoon pepper

$1/3$ cup water

8 half-ears Green Giant Nibblers® frozen corn on the cob (from 12-count package)

1 bag (1 pound 4 ounces) refrigerated new potato wedges

Chopped fresh parsley, if desired

1. Melt butter in 4-quart nonstick Dutch oven over high heat. Cook chicken, onion, $1/2$ teaspoon seasoned salt and pepper in butter 10 to 15 minutes, turning chicken occasionally, until chicken is light golden brown. Stir onions to side of Dutch oven if they start to burn.

2. Reduce heat to medium-high. Add water, corn and potatoes to Dutch oven; sprinkle remaining $1/2$ teaspoon seasoned salt evenly over top. Cover and cook 15 to 20 minutes or until juice of chicken is no longer pink when centers of thickest pieces are cut.

3. Remove chicken and corn to serving platter, using tongs. Gently stir potatoes with onions and pan juices; spoon onto serving platter. Sprinkle with parsley.

4 servings.
1 Serving: Calories 480 (Calories from Fat 135); Fat 15g (Saturated 5g); Cholesterol 95mg; Sodium 460mg; Carbohydrate 57g (Dietary Fiber 6g); Protein 35g
% Daily Value: Vitamin A 8%; Vitamin C 18%; Calcium 4%; Iron 26%
Exchanges: 4 Starch, 3 Lean Meat
Carbohydrate Choices: 4

BETTY'S TIPS

⊕ **Substitution**
Chicken thighs can be used in place of the chicken legs.

⊕ **Serve-With**
Serve this family-pleasing chicken dinner with warm biscuits, butter and honey.

⊕ **Variation**
Sprinkle the cooked chicken with chopped fresh thyme and parsley for a fresh herb flavor.

Home-Style Chicken and Corn

Maple Mustard Glazed Chicken

Prep: 10 min Grill: 55 min

> ³⁄₄ cup maple-flavored syrup
> ¹⁄₂ cup Dijon mustard
> 2 tablespoons chopped fresh chives
> 3- to 3¹⁄₂-pound cut-up broiler-fryer chicken
> 1 teaspoon seasoned salt
> ¹⁄₄ teaspoon coarse pepper

1. Heat coals or gas grill for direct heat. Mix maple syrup, mustard and chives in 1-quart saucepan.

2. Sprinkle both sides of chicken pieces with seasoned salt and pepper. Cover and grill chicken, skin sides up, 4 to 6 inches from medium heat 15 minutes; turn chicken. Cover and grill 20 to 40 minutes longer, turning occasionally and brushing 2 or 3 times with mustard mixture, until juice of chicken is no longer pink when centers of thickest pieces are cut.

3. Heat remaining mustard mixture to boiling; boil 1 minute. Serve sauce with chicken.

4 servings.
1 Serving: Calories 555 (Calories from Fat 200); Fat 22g (Saturated 6g); Cholesterol 130mg; Sodium 1,280mg; Carbohydrate 48g (Dietary Fiber 0g); Protein 41g
% Daily Value: Vitamin A 2%; Vitamin C 0%; Calcium 4%; Iron 12%
Exchanges: 3 Starch, 4¹⁄₂ Medium-Fat Meat
Carbohydrate Choices: 3

BETTY'S TIPS

⊛ **Substitution**
If you have real maple syrup, use it instead of the maple-flavored syrup. It's easy to double this recipe for larger groups.

⊛ **Success Hint**
Brushing with the sauce during the last part of the cooking time helps to keep it from burning. Remember this any time you have a sauce with sugar in it.

⊛ **Serve-With**
Coleslaw, baked beans, buttermilk biscuits and strawberry shortcake are perfect accompaniments to this tasty chicken. Don't forget the lemonade!

Maple Mustard Glazed Chicken

Creamy Chicken Lasagna

Prep: 40 min Bake: 55 min Stand: 15 min
(Photo on page 145)

12 uncooked lasagna noodles (12 ounces)
1 tablespoon butter or margarine
³/₄ cup chopped green bell pepper
³/₄ cup chopped onion
¹/₃ cup milk
2 cans (10³/₄ ounces each) condensed cream of chicken soup
¹/₂ teaspoon dried basil leaves
¹/₄ teaspoon pepper
1 container (12 ounces) small curd creamed cottage cheese
3 cups diced cooked chicken
2 cups shredded mozzarella cheese (8 ounces)
1 cup shredded Cheddar cheese (4 ounces)
¹/₂ cup grated Parmesan cheese

1. Heat oven to 350°. Spray bottom and sides of rectangular baking dish, 13 × 9 × 2 inches, with cooking spray. Cook and drain noodles as directed on package.

2. While noodles are cooking, melt butter in 2-quart saucepan over medium-high heat. Cook bell pepper and onion in butter, stirring occasionally, until crisp-tender; remove from heat. Stir in milk, soup, basil and pepper.

3. Place 4 noodles in baking dish. Top with about 1 cup of the soup mixture, half of the cottage cheese, 1¹/₂ cups of the chicken, ²/₃ cup mozzarella cheese and ¹/₃ cup Cheddar cheese. Repeat layers once, starting with noodles. Place remaining 4 noodles over top. Top with remaining soup mixture, mozzarella cheese and Cheddar cheese. Sprinkle Parmesan cheese over top.

4. Bake uncovered 50 to 55 minutes or until bubbly and hot in center. Let stand 15 minutes before cutting.

8 servings.
1 Serving: Calories 490 (Calories from Fat 205); Fat 23g (Saturated 12g); Cholesterol 80mg; Sodium 1,120mg; Carbohydrate 35g (Dietary Fiber 2g); Protein 36g
% Daily Value: Vitamin A 18%; Vitamin C 10%; Calcium 42%; Iron 12%
Exchanges: 2 Starch, 4 Medium-Fat Meat, 1 Fat
Carbohydrate Choices: 2

BETTY'S TIPS

✿ **Substitution**
Ricotta cheese can be substituted for the cottage cheese.

✿ **Time-Saver**
If you don't want to cook chicken for this recipe, your supermarket offers these options: deli roasted chicken, frozen diced precooked chicken and canned chicken breast chunks.

Betty Crocker
ON BASICS

Cooked Chicken

Prep: 5 min Cook: 16 min Stand: 5 min

1$^1/_2$ pounds boneless, skinless chicken breast halves

1. Arrange chicken, thickest parts to outside edges in glass pie plate, 10 × 1$^1/_2$ or 9 × 1$^1/_4$ inches (sides of chicken will touch).

2. Cover dish with plastic wrap, folding back one corner or edge $^1/_4$ inch to vent steam. Microwave on Medium (50%) 14 to 16 minutes or until juice of chicken is no longer pink when center of thickest pieces are cut and temperature reaches 170°. Let stand 5 minutes.

3. Cool slightly; cut into desired size of pieces.

3$^1/_2$ cups cooked chicken.
1 Cup: Calories 265 (Calories from Fat 65); Fat 7g (Saturated 2g); Cholesterol 135mg; Sodium 125mg; Carbohydrate 0g (Dietary Fiber 0g); Protein 50g
% Daily Value: Vitamin A 0%; Vitamin C 0%; Calcium 2%; Iron 8%
Exchanges: 7 Very Lean Meat, $^1/_2$ Fat
Carbohydrate Choices: 0

Quick

Chicken-Cashew Casserole

Prep: 15 min Bake: 1 hr 5 min

3 cups chow mein noodles

1 can (28 ounces) chicken chow mein mix

3 cups diced Cooked Chicken (opposite page)

2 cups snow (Chinese) pea pods

1 can (10³/₄ ounces) condensed 98% fat-free cream of chicken soup

1 can (8 ounces) sliced water chestnuts, drained

¹/₄ cup reduced-sodium soy sauce

1 cup cashew pieces

1. Heat oven to 350°. Spray 3-quart casserole with cooking spray. Place 1¹/₂ cups of the chow mein noodles in bottom of casserole.

2. Separate cans of chow mein mix. Drain large can of vegetables. Stir together both cans of chow mein mix, chicken, pea pods, soup, water chestnuts, soy sauce and ³/₄ cup of the cashews in large bowl. Spoon over chow mein noodles.

3. Cover with aluminum foil and bake about 1 hour or until hot. Mix remaining 1¹/₂ cups noodles and ¹/₄ cup cashews; sprinkle over casserole. Bake uncovered 5 minutes.

6 servings (1¹/₂ cups each).
1 Serving: Calories 515 (Calories from Fat 235); Fat 26g (Saturated 6g); Cholesterol 75mg; Sodium 1,590mg; Carbohydrate 37g (Dietary Fiber 4g); Protein 33g
% Daily Value: Vitamin A 8%; Vitamin C 14%; Calcium 4%; Iron 22%
Exchanges: 2 Starch, 1 Vegetable, 3¹/₂ Lean Meat, 3 Fat
Carbohydrate Choices: 2¹/₂

BETTY'S TIPS

⊘ Serve-With
This all-in-one casserole needs very little served alongside it. Serve with apple wedges, fortune cookies and hot tea.

⊘ Potluck Pointer
If you're transporting this casserole to a potluck, bake it for 1 hour, but do not top with the noodle-cashew mixture. Transport the covered casserole in an insulated carrier, and sprinkle the noodle-cashew mixture over the top just before serving.

Chicken-Cashew Casserole

Creamy Pesto-Chicken Casserole

Prep: 20 min Bake: 35 min

2 cups uncooked radiatore (nugget) pasta (6 ounces)

1/2 cup chopped drained roasted red bell peppers (from 7-ounce jar)

1/3 cup basil pesto

1/4 cup fat-free (skim) milk

1 container (10 ounces) refrigerated reduced-fat Alfredo sauce

2 packages (6 ounces each) refrigerated grilled chicken breast strips, chopped

1/4 cup shredded Parmesan cheese (1 ounce)

1. Heat oven to 350°. Spray square baking dish, 8 × 8 × 2 inches, with cooking spray.

2. Cook pasta 9 minutes as directed on package. Return to saucepan. Stir in remaining ingredients except cheese. Spoon into baking dish.

3. Cover with aluminum foil and bake 35 minutes. Sprinkle with cheese.

4 servings (1 1/2 cups each).
1 Serving: Calories 520 (Calories from Fat 235); Fat 26g (Saturated 10g); Cholesterol 110mg; Sodium 720mg; Carbohydrate 43g (Dietary Fiber 2g); Protein 42g
% Daily Value: Vitamin A 36%; Vitamin C 34%; Calcium 38%; Iron 18%
Exchanges: 3 Starch, 4 1/2 Medium-Fat Meat
Carbohydrate Choices: 3

BETTY'S TIPS

⊛ **Substitution**
Although using the refrigerated chicken strips is convenient, you can also use 2 1/2 cups of any cooked chicken. Look for the recipe on page 166 to help you.

⊛ **Serve-With**
This creamy casserole is delicious served with cooked baby carrots, focaccia and sherbet for dessert.

⊛ **Do-Ahead**
Go ahead and cook the pasta the night (or morning) before dinner as directed in step 2. Drain and rinse with cold water. Drizzle with a teaspoon of olive oil, and refrigerate in a large plastic food-storage bag or container. You can assemble the casserole in 5 minutes!

Creamy Pesto-Chicken Casserole

Chicken Pot Pie with Herb Crust

Prep: 15 min Bake: 40 min Stand: 5 min

4 cups cut-up cooked chicken

1 bag (1 pound) Green Giant frozen mixed vegetables, thawed

2 cans (10^3/$_4$ ounces each) condensed cream of chicken soup

1 can (10^1/$_2$ ounces) condensed chicken broth

2 cups Original Bisquick mix

1^1/$_2$ cups milk

^{1}/$_2$ teaspoon dried thyme leaves

^{1}/$_4$ teaspoon dried sage leaves

   Chopped parsley, if desired

1. Heat oven to 350°. Heat chicken, vegetables, soup and broth to boiling in 4-quart saucepan or Dutch oven, stirring occasionally. Boil and stir 1 minute. Spread in ungreased rectangular baking dish, 13 × 9 × 2 inches.

2. Stir together remaining ingredients except parsley in medium bowl; pour evenly over soup mixture (crust will rise during baking).

3. Bake uncovered 30 to 40 minutes or until golden brown. Sprinkle with parsley. Let stand 5 minutes before serving.

8 servings.
1 Serving: Calories 365 (Calories from Fat 135); Fat 15g (Saturated 5g); Cholesterol 70mg; Sodium 1,230mg; Carbohydrate 30g (Dietary Fiber 2g); Protein 27g
% Daily Value: Vitamin A 40%; Vitamin C 14%; Calcium 14%; Iron 14%
Exchanges: 2 Starch, 3 Lean Meat, 1 Fat
Carbohydrate Choices: 2

Chicken Pot Pie with Herb Crust

BETTY'S TIPS

⚙ **Substitution**
This family-favorite pot pie can be made slightly different by substituting leftover turkey or pork in place of the chicken.

⚙ **Time-Saver**
Instead of cooking your own chicken, you can save time by purchasing cut-up cooked chicken from the deli or buying a roasted chicken and cutting it up.

⚙ **Health Twist**
For 10 grams of fat and 310 calories per serving, prepare this recipe using reduced-fat cream of chicken soup, Reduced Fat Bisquick mix and fat-free (skim) milk.

Salsa-Turkey Corn Bread Casserole

Prep: 25 min Cook: 24 min

1	tablespoon olive or vegetable oil
1¼	pounds ground turkey
1	cup Old El Paso Thick 'n Chunky salsa
2	tablespoons Gold Medal all-purpose flour
2	cans (15 ounces each) Green Giant cream style sweet corn
2	cans (15 ounces each) black beans, rinsed and drained
1	tablespoon chili powder
2	teaspoons ground cumin
½	teaspoon salt
⅛	teaspoon pepper
	Corn Bread Topping (right)

1. Heat oven to 450°. Spray rectangular baking dish, 13 × 9 × 2 inches, with cooking spray. Heat oil in 4-quart Dutch oven over medium-high heat. Cook turkey in oil 4 to 6 minutes, stirring frequently, until no longer pink. Stir in salsa and flour. Cook 2 to 3 minutes, stirring constantly, until slightly thickened.

2. Stir in remaining ingredients except Corn Bread Topping. Heat to boiling. Spread turkey mixture in baking dish.

3. Make Corn Bread Topping. Pour topping over turkey mixture; gently spread to sides of baking dish. Bake uncovered 12 to 15 minutes or until topping is golden brown.

8 servings.

Corn Bread Topping

1	pouch (6.5 ounces) Betty Crocker golden corn muffin and bread mix
⅓	cup milk
2	tablespoons margarine or butter, melted
1	egg

Stir all ingredients in medium bowl just until moistened (batter will be lumpy).

1 Serving: Calories 485 (Calories from Fat 125); Fat 14g (Saturated 3g); Cholesterol 75mg; Sodium 1,230mg; Carbohydrate 70g (Dietary Fiber 11g); Protein 31g
% Daily Value: Vitamin A 16%; Vitamin C 12%; Calcium 16%; Iron 32%
Exchanges: 4 Starch, ½ Other Carbohydrate, 3 Very Lean Meat, 1 Fat
Carbohydrate Choices: 4½

BETTY'S TIPS

⊘ **Substitution**
Ground beef or pork can be substituted for the ground turkey in this recipe.

⊘ **Success Hint**
For a fun fiesta feel to dinnertime, set the table with colorful napkins, plates and glassware.

⊘ **Serve-With**
Serve crispy coleslaw and orange wedges with this tasty casserole.

Salsa-Turkey Corn Bread Casserole

Plum-Glazed Turkey Tenderloins

Prep: 10 min Marinate: 30 min Grill: 30 min
(Photo on page 145)

1	cup plum jam
1/4	cup dry sherry or chicken broth
2	tablespoons olive or vegetable oil
2	teaspoons chopped fresh rosemary leaves
1 1/2	teaspoons garlic salt
1/4	teaspoon pepper
1	medium onion, finely chopped (1/2 cup)
2	pounds turkey tenderloins (3 to 4 tenderloins)

1. Mix all ingredients except turkey. Place turkey in shallow glass or plastic dish or heavy-duty resealable plastic food-storage bag. Pour half of the plum mixture over turkey; turn turkey to coat. Reserve remaining half of plum mixture. Cover dish or seal bag and refrigerate 30 minutes, turning once.

2. If using charcoal grill, place drip pan directly under grilling area, and arrange coals around edge of firebox. Heat coals or gas grill for indirect heat.

3. Remove turkey from marinade; reserve marinade for basting. Cover and grill turkey over drip pan or over unheated side of gas grill and 4 to 6 inches from medium-high heat 25 to 30 minutes, turning and brushing with reserved basting marinade occasionally, until turkey is no longer pink when center of thickest part is cut. Discard any remaining basting marinade.

4. Heat reserved plum mixture. Serve with sliced turkey.

6 servings.
1 Serving: Calories 350 (Calories from Fat 20); Fat 2g (Saturated 1g); Cholesterol 150mg; Sodium 270mg; Carbohydrate 30g (Dietary Fiber 1g); Protein 53g
% Daily Value: Vitamin A 0%; Vitamin C 2%; Calcium 2%; Iron 16%
Exchanges: 7 Very Lean Meat, 2 Fruit
Carbohydrate Choices: 2

BETTY'S TIPS

⚙ **Substitution**
If turkey tenderloins are not available, use half of a boneless, skinless turkey breast. If plum jam is not available, try your favorite fruit jam in this recipe.

⚙ **Serve-With**
For a lovely evening on the porch with friends, serve Caramelized-Onion Bruschetta (page 43) for an appetizer and hot basmati rice tossed with chopped fresh parsley with the turkey. Serve ice cream and fresh berries for dessert.

⚙ **Do-Ahead**
Prepare the plum mixture ahead; cover and refrigerate up to one day.

Pork Dishes
Savory and Satisfying Meals

Orange-Glazed Pork Chops with Herb Stuffing (page 175)

Red Beans and Rice (page 190)

Brown Sugar–Topped Pork with Sweet Potatoes

Prep: 10 min Cook: 10 hr

4 medium sweet potatoes (about 2¹/₂ pounds), peeled and cut into ¹/₂-inch slices

2¹/₂- pound pork boneless shoulder roast (tied or in netting)

¹/₂ cup packed brown sugar

¹/₄ teaspoon ground red pepper (cayenne)

2 teaspoons salt

¹/₄ teaspoon pepper

1 clove garlic, finely chopped

1. Place sweet potato slices in 5- to 6-quart slow cooker. Place pork on sweet potatoes. Mix remaining ingredients in small bowl; sprinkle over pork and potatoes.

2. Cover and cook on Low heat setting 8 to 10 hours.

3. Remove pork from cooker; place on cutting board. Remove strings or netting from pork. Cut pork into slices, or pull pork into serving pieces using 2 forks. Serve with sweet potatoes, spooning juices over pork.

8 servings.
1 Serving: Calories 410 (Calories from Fat 155); Fat 17g (Saturated 6g); Cholesterol 90mg; Sodium 660mg; Carbohydrate 32g (Dietary Fiber 2g); Protein 32g
% Daily Value: Vitamin A 100%; Vitamin C 16%; Calcium 4%; Iron 8%
Exchanges: 2 Starch, 4 Lean Meat, ¹/₂ Fat
Carbohydrate Choices: 2

BETTY'S TIPS

✿ **Substitution**
For something different, try the super-sweet red sweet potatoes.

✿ **Success Hint**
When a pork shoulder is boned, the butcher uses kitchen string or an elastic net to shape the meat into a tidy roast. Leave the string or netting on while the roast cooks, insuring neat slices at serving time.

✿ **Serve-With**
Add a fresh spinach salad and a basket of warm biscuits to round out the meal.

Brown Sugar–Topped Pork with Sweet Potatoes

Orange-Glazed Pork Chops with Herb Stuffing

Prep: 20 min Bake: 2 hr
(Photo on page 173)

1	loaf (1 pound) sliced bakery white bread
1/2	cup butter or margarine
3	medium ribs celery, diced (1 1/4 cups)
3/4	cup finely chopped onion
2	teaspoons dried sage leaves
1/2	teaspoon dried thyme leaves
1/2	teaspoon salt
1/4	teaspoon pepper
1	cup chicken broth
8	pork boneless center-cut loin chops (about 4 ounces each)
3	tablespoons orange marmalade
1	teaspoon lemon juice

1. Heat oven to 200°. Place bread slices in single layer on cookie sheet. Bake about 1 hour or until dry. Coarsely crumble enough dry bread to measure 10 cups. Place in large bowl.

2. Heat oven to 350°. Melt butter in 8-inch skillet over medium heat. Cook celery and onion in butter 6 to 8 minutes, stirring occasionally, until tender. Stir in sage, thyme, salt and pepper. Pour over bread crumbs; toss to mix. Pour broth over bread crumbs; toss to mix (mixture will be dry). Spoon into ungreased rectangular baking dish, 13 × 9 × 2 inches.

3. Place pork chops on stuffing. Mix marmalade and lemon juice in small bowl; brush over pork. Bake 45 to 60 minutes or until pork is no longer pink in center.

8 servings.
1 Serving: Calories 450 (Calories from Fat 200); Fat 22g (Saturated 10g); Cholesterol 95mg; Sodium 710mg; Carbohydrate 35g (Dietary Fiber 2g); Protein 28g
% Daily Value: Vitamin A 10%; Vitamin C 2%; Calcium 8%; Iron 14%
Exchanges: 2 Starch, 1 Vegetable, 3 Lean Meat, 2 Fat
Carbohydrate Choices: 2

BETTY'S TIPS

✿ **Success Hint**
The stuffing will be dry when you put it in the baking dish, but the juices from the pork add lots of moisture. If you wish to bake the stuffing separately, use a 14-ounce can of broth instead of 1 cup.

✿ **Time-Saver**
Cut the prep time in this recipe by using purchased stuffing. Melt 1/2 cup butter or margarine, and heat 1 cup chicken broth. In a large bowl, toss butter and broth with 8 cups herb-seasoned bread stuffing cubes (from 14-ounce package). Spoon into ungreased rectangular baking dish, 13 × 9 × 2 inches. Continue with step 3.

✿ **Do-Ahead**
To make the bread crumbs a day ahead, place bread slices in a single layer on wire rack, and let dry at room temperature.

Almond- and Peach-Crusted Pork Chops

Prep: 10 min Cook: 18 min

1 egg
2 tablespoons peach preserves
1/2 cup Original Bisquick mix
1/2 cup coarsely chopped sliced almonds
1 tablespoon cornmeal
1/2 teaspoon salt
6 pork boneless loin chops, 1/2-inch thick (1 1/2 pounds)
1 tablespoon vegetable oil
Chopped parsley, if desired

1. Beat egg and preserves in shallow dish with fork, breaking apart any large pieces of preserves. Mix Bisquick mix, almonds, cornmeal and salt in another shallow dish. Dip pork into egg mixture, then coat with Bisquick mixture.

2. Heat oil in 12-inch nonstick skillet over medium-low heat. Cook pork in oil 15 to 18 minutes, turning once, until crust is golden brown and pork is slightly pink in center. Sprinkle with parsley. Serve immediately.

6 servings.
1 Serving: Calories 315 (Calories from Fat 155); Fat 17g (Saturated 4g); Cholesterol 90mg; Sodium 390mg; Carbohydrate 14g (Dietary Fiber 2g); Protein 27g
% Daily Value: Vitamin A 0%; Vitamin C 0%; Calcium 4%; Iron 10%
Exchanges: 1 Starch, 3 1/2 Lean Meat, 1 Fat
Carbohydrate Choices: 1

BETTY'S TIPS

⊗ **Substitution**
Apricot preserves can be substituted for the peach preserves.

⊗ **Special Touch**
An extra-easy dress-up for these moist chops is to heat additional peach preserves until melted and drizzle over them.

Italian Pork Chops

Prep: 5 min Cook: 20 min

4 pork boneless loin chops, 1/2-inch thick (1 1/2 pounds)
1/2 cup Original Bisquick mix
1/3 cup Italian dressing
1/2 cup Progresso garlic herb bread crumbs
2 tablespoons vegetable oil

1. Coat pork chops with Bisquick mix. Dip coated pork chops in Italian dressing, then coat with bread crumbs.

2. Heat oil in 12-inch nonstick skillet over medium-high heat. Cook pork in oil about 5 minutes or until golden brown; reduce heat to low. Carefully turn pork. Cook 10 to 15 minutes longer or until pork is slightly pink in center. Serve immediately.

4 servings.
1 Serving: Calories 370 (Calories from Fat 200); Fat 22g (Saturated 5g); Cholesterol 68mg; Sodium 470mg; Carbohydrate 18g (Dietary Fiber 0g); Protein 25g
% Daily Value: Vitamin A 0%; Vitamin C 0%; Calcium 6%; Iron 10%
Exchanges: 1 Starch, 3 High-Fat Meat
Carbohydrate Choices: 1

BETTY'S TIPS

⊗ **Success Hint**
Be sure to use regular Italian dressing, not fat free. You'll get more flavor and a better coating.

⊗ **Serve-With**
Make it super simple. Serve these savory pork chops with cooked broccoli, carrot sticks and whole-grain rolls. Dessert? Cookies or ice cream!

⊗ **Special Touch**
Sprinkle with chopped parsley just before serving.

Italian Pork Chops

Almond- and Peach-Crusted Pork Chops

Betty Crocker
ON BASICS

Quick & Low Fat
Apple Cider Gravy

Prep: 5 min Cook: 5 min

$^1/_4$ cup Gold Medal all-purpose flour

1 to 1$^1/_2$ cups chicken broth

Pan juices from pork roast

1. Mix flour and $^1/_4$ cup of the broth in a small bowl.

2. Pour pan juices into 2-cup measuring cup; add enough broth to measure 2 cups. Return mixture to pan; heat to boiling. Stir in flour mixture. Boil and stir 1 minute.

Heat mixture to boiling, stirring constantly.

8 servings ($^1/_4$ cup each).
1 Serving: Calories 20 (Calories from Fat 0); Fat 0g (Saturated 0g); Cholesterol 0mg; Sodium 250mg; Carbohydrate 4g (Dietary Fiber 0g); Protein 1g
% Daily Value: Vitamin A 0%; Vitamin C 0%; Calcium 0%; Iron 2%
Exchanges: 1 Serving is Free
Carbohydrate Choices: 0

Fruit-Stuffed Pork Roast

Fruit-Stuffed Pork Roast

Prep: 35 min Bake: 2 hr

3- pound pork boneless center-cut loin roast (not tied)

1 cup mixed dried fruits (apples, apricots, figs)

2 tablespoons finely chopped onion

1 teaspoon kosher salt

1 teaspoon dried thyme leaves

$1/2$ teaspoon ground cinnamon

$1/2$ teaspoon coarsely ground pepper

2 tablespoons vegetable oil

1 cup apple cider

Apple Cider Gravy (opposite page) or 2 cups purchased pork gravy

1. Heat oven to 350°. Place pork, fat side up, on cutting board. Cut horizontally through center of pork almost to opposite side. Open pork like a book. Layer dried fruits and onion in opening. Bring halves of pork together; tie at 1-inch intervals with kitchen twine. Turn pork so fat is on bottom. Mix salt, thyme, cinnamon and pepper in small bowl; rub into pork.

2. Heat oil in roaster over medium-high heat. Cook pork in oil until brown on all sides. Add 2 tablespoons of the apple cider. Cook pork, turning frequently, until cider caramelizes and surface of pork turns dark brown. Repeat browning with additional 2 tablespoons cider. Add remaining cider. Insert meat thermometer so tip is in thickest part of pork.

3. Cover and bake 1 hour 30 minutes to 2 hours or until pork is no longer pink in center and thermometer reads 155°. Remove pork from pan, cover with aluminum foil and let stand about 15 minutes until temperature rises to 160°. Serve pork with Apple Cider Gravy.

8 servings.
1 Serving: Calories 390 (Calories from Fat 155); Fat 17g (Saturated 5g); Cholesterol 110mg; Sodium 620mg; Carbohydrate 19g (Dietary Fiber 2g); Protein 40g
% Daily Value: Vitamin A 8%; Vitamin C 0%; Calcium 2%; Iron 12%
Exchanges: 1 Fruit, 6 Lean Meat
Carbohydrate Choices: 1

BETTY'S TIPS

⊛ **Do-Ahead**
This roast can be stuffed and rubbed with herbs several hours ahead. Wrap tightly in plastic wrap and refrigerate.

⊛ **Did You Know?**
Butchers often tie 2 pieces of center-cut pork loin together to make a thicker roast. Be sure to ask for a single muscle so the roast can be "butterflied," as directed in this recipe.

Honey-Orange Ham

Prep: 15 min Marinate: 2 hr Bake: 2 hr 30 min

1   orange
¹⁄₃   cup honey
1   teaspoon ground mustard
1   fully cooked bone-in half-ham
    (6 to 9 pounds)
    Whole cloves, if desired

12 servings.
1 Serving: Calories 170 (Calories from Fat 55); Fat 6g (Saturated 2g); Cholesterol 60mg; Sodium 1,310mg; Carbohydrate 6g (Dietary Fiber 0g); Protein 23g
% Daily Value: Vitamin A 0%; Vitamin C 0%; Calcium 0%; Iron 8%
Exchanges: 3 Lean Meat
Carbohydrate Choices: ¹⁄₂

1. Grate 1 tablespoon peel from orange; squeeze juice. Mix peel and juice with honey and mustard in small bowl. Pierce surface of ham at 2-inch intervals with metal skewer; place in 2-gallon resealable plastic food-storage bag. Pour honey mixture over ham; seal bag. Refrigerate 2 hours.

2. Heat oven to 325°. Place ham, fat side up, on rack in shallow roasting pan. Discard marinade. Insert cloves in ham. Insert meat thermometer so tip is in thickest part of ham and does not touch bone or rest in fat.

3. Bake uncovered 1 hour. Cover loosely with aluminum foil so ham does not overbrown. Bake 1 hour to 1 hour 30 minutes longer or until thermometer reads 135° to 140°. Let ham stand loosely covered 10 to 15 minutes for easier carving.

BETTY'S TIPS

⊕ **Serve-With**
Baked potatoes with sour cream and Cheesy Broccoli (page 219) are good accompaniments for this heavenly ham.

⊕ **Special Touch**
Fresh orange slices or kumquats and sprigs of watercress make a simple yet elegant garnish for this holiday favorite.

⊕ **Did You Know?**
The honey marinade soaks into the ham, giving the ham great flavor and a deep golden brown glaze.

Honey-Orange Ham

Pork Tenderloins with Vegetable Medley

Prep: 20 min Marinate: 2 hr Grill: 20 min

1/2 cup Italian herb dressing

3 cloves garlic, finely chopped

2 pork tenderloins (about 1 pound each)

3 small onions, cut into quarters

2 medium zucchini, cut into 1/2-inch slices

1 cup baby carrots, cut lengthwise into quarters

1 large red bell pepper, cut into 1-inch pieces

2 cups whole mushrooms

2 tablespoons Italian herb dressing

Grated Parmesan cheese, if desired

1. Mix 1/2 cup dressing and garlic in shallow glass or plastic dish or resealable plastic food-storage bag. Add pork; turn to coat with marinade. Cover dish or seal bag and refrigerate at least 2 hours but no longer than 12 hours.

2. Heat coals or gas grill for direct heat. Mix remaining ingredients except cheese in square aluminum pan, 9 × 9 × 2 inches.

3. Remove pork from marinade; reserve marinade. Cover and grill pork and pan of vegetables 4 to 5 inches from medium heat 15 to 20 minutes, brushing pork occasionally with marinade and turning once, until pork is slightly pink in center and vegetables are crisp-tender. Stir vegetables 2 or 3 times during grilling. Discard any remaining marinade.

4. Cut pork into slices. Sprinkle cheese over vegetables.

6 servings.
1 Serving: Calories 345 (Calories from Fat 145); Fat 16g (Saturated 3g); Cholesterol 100mg; Sodium 300mg; Carbohydrate 13g (Dietary Fiber 3g); Protein 37g
% Daily Value: Vitamin A 100%; Vitamin C 48%; Calcium 6%; Iron 14%
Exchanges: 5 Lean Meat, 3 Vegetable
Carbohydrate Choices: 1

Pork Tenderloins with Vegetable Medley

BETTY'S TIPS

⚙ **Substitution**
Instead of Italian herb dressing, use other dressing you may have on hand, such as Caesar or any vinaigrette.

⚙ **Success Hint**
To easily remove the pan from the grill, carefully slide it onto a cookie sheet. For moist and juicy pork tenderloin, cook it just until slightly pink in the center. It will become dry and tough if overcooked.

⚙ **Serve-With**
Serve the pork with Bread Machine Potato-Rosemary Bread (page 15) and sliced cantaloupe and honeydew melon wedges.

Peppered Pork Pitas with Garlic Spread

Barbecued Pork Tenderloin

Peppered Pork Pitas with Garlic Spread

Prep: 20 min

- 1/3 cup mayonnaise or salad dressing
- 2 tablespoons milk
- 2 cloves garlic, finely chopped
- 1 pound pork boneless loin chops, cut into thin, bite-size strips
- 1 tablespoon olive or vegetable oil
- 1 teaspoon coarsely ground pepper
- 1 jar (7.25 ounces) roasted red bell peppers, drained and sliced
- 4 pita fold breads (7 inches in diameter)

1. Mix mayonnaise, milk and garlic in small bowl; set aside.

2. Mix pork, oil and ground pepper in medium bowl. Heat 12-inch skillet over medium-high heat. Cook pork in skillet 5 to 6 minutes, stirring occasionally, until pork is lightly browned and no longer pink in center. Stir in bell peppers; heat until warm.

3. Heat pita folds as directed on package. Lightly spread one side of each pita fold with garlic mixture. Spoon pork mixture over each; fold up.

4 servings.
1 Serving: Calories 555 (Calories from Fat 250); Fat 28g (Saturated 6g); Cholesterol 80mg; Sodium 630mg; Carbohydrate 44g (Dietary Fiber 2g); Protein 32g
% Daily Value: Vitamin A 58%; Vitamin C 74%; Calcium 8%; Iron 16%
Exchanges: 3 Starch, 3 Lean Meat, 3 1/2 Fat
Carbohydrate Choices: 3

BETTY'S TIPS

⚙ **Substitution**
Thinly sliced chicken can be substituted for the pork in this recipe. Cook 5 to 6 minutes or until the chicken is no longer pink in center.

⚙ **Serve-With**
Crispy carrot sticks, celery sticks and cucumber rounds go well with these filling pork sandwiches.

⚙ **Variation**
Look for flavored and whole wheat pita breads in the bakery section of the supermarket to use instead of the pita folds.

Barbecued Pork Tenderloin

Prep: 10 min Grill: 22 min

- 2 pork tenderloins (about 3/4 pound each)
- 1/4 teaspoon seasoned salt
- 1/3 cup barbecue sauce
- 1/4 cup teriyaki baste and glaze (from 12-ounce bottle)
- 2 tablespoons finely chopped onion
- 2 tablespoons finely chopped chipotle chile in adobo sauce (from 7-ounce can)

1. Heat coals or gas grill for direct heat. Sprinkle pork with seasoned salt. Mix remaining ingredients. Brush pork with barbecue sauce mixture.

2. Cover and grill pork 4 to 6 inches from medium-low heat 18 to 22 minutes, turning several times and basting generously with remaining sauce, until pork is slightly pink in center. Discard any remaining sauce.

6 servings.
1 Serving: Calories 175 (Calories from Fat 35); Fat 4g (Saturated 2g); Cholesterol 70mg; Sodium 770mg; Carbohydrate 9g (Dietary Fiber 0g); Protein 26g
% Daily Value: Vitamin A 2%; Vitamin C 0%; Calcium 0%; Iron 10%
Exchanges: 1/2 Starch, 3 1/2 Very Lean Meat
Carbohydrate Choices: 1/2

BETTY'S TIPS

⚙ **Serve-With**
Add corn on the cob and sliced fresh tomatoes sprinkled with cilantro for a super backyard meal.

⚙ **Variation**
For a great sandwich idea, slice the pork and serve it in toasted buns with shredded lettuce and sliced tomato.

⚙ **Did You Know?**
Chipotle chiles are dried jalapeños, and just a small amount adds lots of flavor. You can freeze any remaining chiles in the adobo sauce to use at a later time.

Low Fat

Caribbean Pork Tenderloin

Prep: 25 min Marinate: 15 min Grill: 20 min

2 cups cut-up assorted fresh fruit, such as cantaloupe, honeydew melon, grapes, papaya and mango

1 tablespoon chopped fresh cilantro

1 to 2 teaspoons lime juice

Spice Rub (below)

1 pork tenderloin, 1¼ pounds

1. Mix fruit, cilantro and lime juice. Cover and refrigerate until serving.

2. Make Spice Rub. Place pork in heavy-duty resealable plastic food-storage bag. Sprinkle with Spice Rub. Turn bag several times to coat pork. Seal bag; refrigerate 15 minutes.

3. Heat coals or gas grill for direct heat. Remove pork from bag. Cover and grill pork 4 to 6 inches from medium heat 15 to 20 minutes, turning frequently, until slightly pink in center. Serve with fruit mixture.

4 servings.

Spice Rub

1 tablespoon ground cinnamon

4 teaspoons ground nutmeg

4 teaspoons ground cumin

4 teaspoons garlic salt

¼ to ½ teaspoon ground red pepper (cayenne)

Mix all ingredients.

1 Serving: Calories 305 (Calories from Fat 70); Fat 8g (Saturated 3g); Cholesterol 125mg; Sodium 820mg; Carbohydrate 13g (Dietary Fiber 2g); Protein 45g
% Daily Value: Vitamin A 14%; Vitamin C 18%; Calcium 4%; Iron 18%
Exchanges: 6 Lean Meat, 1 Fruit, 1 Fat
Carbohydrate Choices: 1

BETTY'S TIPS

⊗ **Substitution**
You'll find a variety of Caribbean spice mixes in the spice section of the supermarket to use instead of making the Spice Rub.

⊗ **Time-Saver**
To make this recipe even easier, look for precut mixed fruit in the produce or deli sections of your supermarket.

⊗ **Serve-With**
Serve grilled corn on the cob with cilantro butter with this Caribbean island dinner. Sherbet with fresh fruit and coconut is a pleasing finale.

Caribbean Pork Tenderloin

Smoked Sausage and Cheddar Potato Packets

Prep: 10 min Grill: 25 min

³/₄ cup process Cheddar cheese sauce
(from 16-ounce jar)

¹/₂ cup shredded Cheddar cheese (2 ounces)

2 cups frozen stir-fry bell peppers and onions
(from 1-pound bag)

2 cups refrigerated diced potatoes with onions
(from 20-ounce bag)

1 pound fully cooked smoked sausage, cut
into 1¹/₂-inch pieces

1. Heat coals or gas grill for direct heat. Spray four
18 × 12-inch sheets of heavy-duty aluminum foil
with cooking spray.

2. Mix cheese sauce and cheese in medium bowl. Stir in
stir-fry vegetables and potatoes. Arrange 4 sausage
pieces and 1 cup potato mixture on center of each
foil piece. Fold foil over sausage and potatoes so
edges meet. Seal edges, making tight ¹/₂-inch fold;
fold again. Allow space on sides for circulation and
expansion.

3. Cover and grill packets 4 to 6 inches from medium-
low heat 20 to 25 minutes, rotating packets ¹/₂ turn
after 10 minutes, until potatoes are tender. Place
packets on plates. Cut large X across each packet;
fold back foil.

4 servings.
1 Serving: Calories 605 (Calories from Fat 395); Fat 44g (Saturated 19g);
Cholesterol 100mg; Sodium 1,510mg; Carbohydrate 29g (Dietary Fiber
3g); Protein 24g
% Daily Value: Vitamin A 14%; Vitamin C 34%; Calcium 22%; Iron 10%
Diet Exchanges: 2 Starch, 2¹/₂ High-Fat Meat, 4 Fat
Carbohydrate Choices: 2

BETTY'S TIPS

⊗ **Health Twist**
Use smoked turkey sausage and reduced-fat cheese to
reduce the fat to 19 grams and the calories to 390 per
serving.

⊗ **Serve-With**
Although these packets contain the major portion of
your meal, go ahead and add crusty French bread and
fresh fruit to complete your picnic.

Smoked Sausage and Cheddar Potato Packets

Pork Chop and Green Bean Casserole

Prep: 20 min Bake: 55 min

4   pork boneless loin or rib chops, about
    $3/4$-inch thick (about $1^1/4$ pounds)

$1/4$ teaspoon salt

$1/4$ teaspoon pepper

3   cups Green Giant frozen cut green beans
    (from 1-pound bag), thawed

1   can ($10^3/4$ ounces) condensed cream of
    celery soup

1   cup shredded Swiss cheese (4 ounces)

$1/3$ cup milk

2   tablespoons chopped pimientos

1   can (2.8 ounces) French-fried onions

1. Heat oven to 350°. Spray square baking dish,
8 × 8 × 2 inches, with cooking spray. Trim fat from
pork if necessary. Sprinkle both sides of pork with
salt and pepper.

2. Spray 10-inch nonstick skillet with cooking spray;
heat over medium-high heat. Cook pork in skillet
about 10 minutes, turning once, until brown. Place
in baking dish.

3. Mix remaining ingredients except onions in medium
bowl. Spread over pork chops.

4. Bake uncovered about 50 minutes or until mixture is
bubbly. Sprinkle onions over casserole. Bake uncovered 5 minutes.

4 servings.
1 Serving: Calories 510 (Calories from Fat 280); Fat 31g (Saturated 11g);
Cholesterol 95mg; Sodium 1,000mg; Carbohydrate 23g (Dietary Fiber
4g); Protein 35g
% Daily Value: Vitamin A 26%; Vitamin C 10%; Calcium 40%; Iron 14%
Exchanges: 1 Starch, 1 Vegetable, 4 Medium-Fat Meat, 2 Fat
Carbohydrate Choices: $1^1/2$

BETTY'S TIPS

⚙ **Success Hint**
Browning the pork chops before adding them to the
casserole adds flavor and provides a jump start on the
cooking.

⚙ **Health Twist**
We've browned the pork chops without oil to create a
leaner casserole. You can slightly reduce the fat further
by using reduced-fat soup and fat-free (skim) milk.

⚙ **Did You Know?**
We've adapted family-favorite green bean casserole by
putting pork chops on the bottom and adding Swiss
cheese for a subtle twist. "Hiding" the pork chops keeps
them moist and juicy and gives the top a pretty look.

Pork Chop and Green Bean Casserole

Ham and Three-Bean Bake

Prep: 15 min Bake: 20 min

2 cups diced fully cooked ham

1 cup barbecue sauce

1 medium onion, chopped ($^1/_2$ cup)

1 can (15 to 16 ounces) great Northern beans, rinsed and drained

1 can (15 to 16 ounces) kidney beans, rinsed and drained

1 can (15 ounces) black beans, rinsed and drained

2 pouches (6.5 ounces each) Betty Crocker golden corn muffin and bread mix

$^2/_3$ cup milk

$^1/_4$ cup butter or margarine, melted

2 eggs

1. Heat oven to 400°. Spray rectangular baking dish, 13 × 9 × 2 inches, with cooking spray.

2. Heat ham, barbecue sauce, onion and beans in 3-quart saucepan over medium-high heat, stirring occasionally, until thoroughly heated. Pour into baking dish.

3. Stir muffin mix, milk, butter and eggs in large bowl just until moistened (batter will be lumpy). Spread over ham and bean mixture to edges of dish.

4. Bake uncovered about 20 minutes or until toothpick inserted in center comes out clean and corn bread is golden brown.

8 servings.
1 Serving: Calories 550 (Calories from Fat 145); Fat 16g (Saturated 7g); Cholesterol 90mg; Sodium 1,600mg; Carbohydrate 87g (Dietary Fiber 12g); Protein 27g
% Daily Value: Vitamin A 8%; Vitamin C 2%; Calcium 22%; Iron 38%
Exchanges: 6 Starch, 1 Lean Meat
Carbohydrate Choices: 6

Ham and Three-Bean Bake

BETTY'S TIPS

⊙ **Time-Saver**
You can purchase diced cooked ham in 1-pound packages. Refrigerate or freeze the rest of the ham for another meal.

⊙ **Serve-With**
Complete the meal with creamy coleslaw, carrot sticks and your favorite cookies.

⊙ **Special Touch**
If you like, sprinkle your favorite shredded cheese over the top of the baked casserole and bake 2 to 3 minutes longer until the cheese is melted. Try Cheddar or Colby-Monterey Jack cheese.

Taco Shortcakes

Prep: 25 min Cook: 10 hr

2 pound pork boneless shoulder roast, trimmed of fat

1 envelope (1.25 ounces) Old El Paso taco seasoning mix

1 can (16 ounces) Old El Paso refried beans

8 ounces mild Mexican-style process cheese spread loaf, cubed

12 prepared corn muffins

¾ cup shredded lettuce

¾ cup chopped tomato

¾ cup sour cream

¼ cup chopped fresh cilantro

1. If pork is tied, remove strings or netting. Place pork in 3- to 4-quart slow cooker. Sprinkle with taco seasoning mix. Top with beans.

2. Cover and cook on Low heat setting 8 to 10 hours.

3. Remove pork from cooker; place on cutting board. Shred pork, using 2 forks. Return pork to cooker and mix well. Stir in cheese.

4. To serve, cut muffins crosswise in half. Place each bottom half on plate; top with ½ cup pork mixture, 1 tablespoon lettuce, 1 tablespoon tomato and muffin top. Serve with sour cream; sprinkle with cilantro.

12 servings.
1 Serving: Calories 480 (Calories from Fat 225); Fat 25g (Saturated 12g); Cholesterol 105mg; Sodium 1,000mg; Carbohydrate 37g (Dietary Fiber 4g); Protein 27g
% Daily Value: Vitamin A 16%; Vitamin C 4%; Calcium 22%; Iron 14%
Exchanges: 2½ Starch, 3 Medium-Fat Meat, 1 Fat
Carbohydrate Choices: 2½

BETTY'S TIPS

⊕ **Substitution**
If you like it really hot, use hot Mexican-style process cheese in place of the mild.

⊕ **Variation**
This recipe also tastes delicious served in hard or soft taco shells. Just omit the corn muffins.

⊕ **Do-Ahead**
Make your evening meal a success by baking corn muffins the night before or purchasing them ahead of time.

Taco Shortcakes

Quick

Kung Pao Pork over Sesame Noodles

Prep: 15 min Cook: 15 min

1 tablespoon vegetable oil

1 bag (1 pound) broccoli slaw mix

1 pound pork boneless loin, cut into $1/2$-inch pieces

1 medium red bell pepper, cut into $1/2$-inch pieces

$1/2$ cup water

$1/2$ cup spicy Sichuan (Szechuan) stir-fry sauce

1 tablespoon honey

1 package (7 ounces) rice stick noodles

2 teaspoons sesame or vegetable oil

2 tablespoons salted peanuts

1. Heat 12-inch nonstick skillet over medium-high heat. Add vegetable oil; rotate skillet to coat bottom. Add broccoli slaw; stir-fry 2 to 3 minutes or until crisp-tender. Remove broccoli slaw from skillet; keep warm.

2. Add pork to same skillet; stir-fry over medium-high heat 5 to 6 minutes or until brown. Stir in bell pepper and water. Cover and cook 3 to 4 minutes, stirring occasionally, until pork is tender. Stir in stir-fry sauce and honey; reduce heat. Simmer uncovered 1 to 2 minutes.

3. Meanwhile, heat 3 quarts water to boiling. Add noodles. Boil 3 minutes; drain. Toss noodles and sesame oil. Divide noodles among bowls. Top with broccoli slaw and pork mixture. Sprinkle with peanuts.

4 servings.
1 Serving: Calories 60 (Calories from Fat 160); Fat 18g (Saturated 4g); Cholesterol 70mg; Sodium 1,240mg; Carbohydrate 68g (Dietary Fiber 7g); Protein 34g
% Daily Value: Vitamin A 74%; Vitamin C 100%; Calcium 10%; Iron 18%
Exchanges: 3 Starch, 2 Lean Meat, 4 Vegetable, 2 Fat
Carbohydrate Choices: 4

BETTY'S TIPS

⊙ **Substitution**
Can't find broccoli slaw mix at your grocery store? Use a 16-ounce bag of coleslaw mix instead.

⊙ **Did You Know?**
"Kung Pao" refers to stir-fries seasoned with garlic, chili puree and peanuts. The flavor for this Kung Pao dish is easily achieved with a stir-fry sauce. Chinese rice stick noodles are very thin and white and can be found in most large grocery stores in the Asian foods area.

Kung Pao Pork over Sesame Noodles

Red Beans and Rice

Prep: 10 min Cook: 9 hr + 15 min
(Photo on page 173)

2   smoked pork hocks (about 1¼ pounds)
1   small onion, chopped (¼ cup)
1   can (15 ounces) red beans, rinsed and drained
1   dried bay leaf
1   can (15 ounces) tomato sauce
1   tablespoon red pepper sauce
1   medium bell pepper, coarsely chopped (¾ cup)
3   cups water
3   cups uncooked instant rice
2   teaspoons Cajun seasoning
1   pound fully cooked smoked sausage, cut lengthwise in half, then cut crosswise into 1-inch pieces

1. Place pork hocks in 3- to 4-quart slow cooker. Top with onion, beans, bay leaf, tomato sauce, pepper sauce and bell pepper in order listed.

2. Cover and cook on Low heat setting 8 to 9 hours.

3. About 30 minutes before serving, heat water to boiling in 2-quart saucepan over high heat. Remove from heat and stir in rice. Cover and let stand about 5 minutes or until water is absorbed. Fluff rice with fork and remove bay leaf before serving.

4. Meanwhile, remove pork from cooker; place on cutting board. Pull meat from bones, using 2 forks; discard bones and skin. Return pork to cooker. Stir in Cajun seasoning and sausage. Increase heat setting to high. Cover and cook 15 minutes or until sausage is heated through.

5. For each serving, place ½ cup rice in soup bowl and top with ¾ cup red bean mixture.

8 servings.
1 Serving: Calories 475 (Calories from Fat 190); Fat 21g (Saturated 7g); Cholesterol 55mg; Sodium 1,420mg; Carbohydrate 54g (Dietary Fiber 5g); Protein 22g
% Daily Value: Vitamin A 10%; Vitamin C 20%; Calcium 6%; Iron 24%
Exchanges: 3½ Starch, 1½ Medium-Fat Meat, 2 Fat
Carbohydrate Choices: 3½

BETTY'S TIPS

⚙ **Substitution**
If you can't find smoked pork hocks, you may substitute 1 cup cubed fully cooked ham.

✴ **Success Hint**
Use Louisiana-style hot sauce for a more authentic flavor. Long cooking can leach out the flavor from smoked sausage, so we added it at the end to keep the flavor in the sausage where it belongs.

Italian Sausage with Tomatoes and Penne

Prep: 25 min

3 cups uncooked penne pasta (9 ounces)

1 pound uncooked Italian sausage links, cut crosswise into $1/4$-inch slices

$1/2$ cup beef broth

1 medium yellow summer squash, cut lengthwise in half, then cut crosswise into $1/4$-inch slices

2 cups grape or cherry tomatoes, cut lengthwise in half

$1/4$ cup chopped fresh or 1 tablespoon dried basil leaves

6 green onions, cut into $1/2$-inch pieces ($1/2$ cup)

2 tablespoons olive or vegetable oil

1. Cook and drain pasta as directed on package.

2. While pasta is cooking, spray 12-inch nonstick skillet with cooking spray; heat over medium-high heat. Cook sausage in skillet 4 to 6 minutes, stirring frequently, until brown. Stir in broth; reduce heat to medium. Cover and cook 5 minutes.

3. Stir in squash, tomatoes and 2 tablespoons of the basil. Heat to boiling; reduce heat to low. Cover and simmer 5 minutes, stirring occasionally. Stir in onions. Simmer uncovered 1 minute.

4. Toss pasta, oil and remaining 2 tablespoons basil. Divide pasta among individual bowls. Top with sausage mixture.

4 servings.
1 Serving: Calories 590 (Calories from Fat 280); Fat 31g (Saturated 9g); Cholesterol 120mg; Sodium 920mg; Carbohydrate 51g (Dietary Fiber 4g); Protein 27g
% Daily Value: Vitamin A 24%; Vitamin C 22%; Calcium 8%; Iron 28%
Exchanges: 3 Starch, 1 Vegetable, 2 High-Fat Meat, 5 Fat
Carbohydrate Choices: $3^1/2$

BETTY'S TIPS

⊗ **Substitution**
One pound fully cooked mild Italian sausages can be used instead of the uncooked links. Just omit the cooking in step 2, and heat the broth and sausage with the squash, tomato and basil in a 12-inch skillet as directed in step 3.

⊗ **Success Hint**
Cut meat and vegetables into pieces of uniform size to ensure even cooking. Meat and poultry will be easier to slice if you freeze them slightly before cutting.

⊗ **Special Touch**
Shave fresh Parmesan cheese over this Italian dish. Or if you are in a hurry, use purchased shredded or grated Parmesan cheese.

Italian Sausage with Tomatoes and Penne

Szechuan Pork with Orzo

Prep: 20 min Cook: 8 min

$^3/_4$ cup uncooked orzo or rosamarina pasta (5 ounces)

1 tablespoon light sesame or vegetable oil

1 pound coarsely ground pork (chow mein meat)

1 bag (1 pound) Green Giant Create a Meal! frozen Szechuan stir-fry meal starter

Peanuts, if desired

Chopped green onion, if desired

1. Cook and drain pasta as directed on package.

2. While pasta is cooking, heat oil in 12-inch skillet over medium-high heat. Cook pork in oil 4 to 6 minutes, stirring frequently, until brown.

3. Stir in meal starter vegetables and sauce. Cook 5 to 6 minutes, stirring frequently, until vegetables are crisp-tender and sauce block is melted. Stir in pasta. Cook 1 to 2 minutes, stirring frequently, until well mixed and hot. Garnish with peanuts and onion.

4 servings.
1 Serving: Calories 480 (Calories from Fat 215); Fat 24g (Saturated 7g); Cholesterol 70mg; Sodium 1,050mg; Carbohydrate 34g (Dietary Fiber 4g); Protein 32g
% Daily Value: Vitamin A 44%; Vitamin C 14%; Calcium 4%; Iron 12%
Exchanges: 2 Starch, 1 Vegetable, 3$^1/_2$ Medium-Fat Meat, 1 Fat
Carbohydrate Choices: 2

BETTY'S TIPS

⊗ **Substitution**
Ground beef can be substituted for the ground pork in this recipe. Cooked rice can be used in place of the pasta. Stir in 2 cups cold cooked rice instead of the pasta in step 3.

⊗ **Serve-With**
Serve with a salad of sliced cucumbers, chopped green onions and sliced celery tossed with vinaigrette. Add a light dessert of lime sherbet with fresh fruit to round out this meal.

Szechuan Pork with Orzo

Beef Dishes

Beef Dishes

Hearty Home-Style Meals

Skillet Beef, Veggies and Brown Rice (page 204)

Beef and Potatoes with Rosemary (page 196)

Easy Steak Kabobs

Prep: 15 min Grill: 18 min

1 pound beef boneless top sirloin steak

1 medium bell pepper, cut into 16 one-inch wedges

16 medium mushrooms

1 tablespoon chopped fresh or 1 teaspoon dried dill weed

1 tablespoon lemon juice

1 tablespoon olive or vegetable oil

1 tablespoon honey mustard

¹⁄₄ teaspoon salt

¹⁄₄ teaspoon pepper

1. Heat coals or gas grill for direct heat.

2. Cut beef into 24 one-inch pieces. Thread beef, bell pepper and mushrooms alternately on each of eight 10- to 12-inch metal skewers, leaving space between each piece. Mix remaining ingredients.

3. Cover and grill kabobs 4 to 6 inches from medium heat 15 to 18 minutes, turning and brushing kabobs 3 or 4 times with oil mixture, until beef is desired doneness and vegetables are tender.

4 servings.
1 Serving: Calories 185 (Calories from Fat 65); Fat 7g (Saturated 2g); Cholesterol 60mg; Sodium 240mg; Carbohydrate 5g (Dietary Fiber 2g); Protein 25g
% Daily Value: Vitamin A 4%; Vitamin C 24%; Calcium 0%; Iron 16%
Exchanges: 1 Vegetable, 3 Very Lean Meat, 1 Fat
Carbohydrate Choices: 0

BETTY'S TIPS

⊗ **Success Hint**
Leaving about a ¹⁄₄-inch space between pieces of food on the skewers allows for even cooking.

⊗ **Serve-With**
These kabobs are so easy! Make the rest of the meal just as easy by serving deli coleslaw, Parmesan Potatoes (page 224) and herb breadsticks.

⊗ **Variation**
If you prefer chicken, use boneless, skinless chicken breasts or chicken thighs, cut into 1-inch pieces, for the steak. Grill until no longer pink in center.

Easy Steak Kabobs

Quick

Lemon Pepper Steaks

Prep: 5 min Grill: 15 min

4 beef sirloin or rib eye steaks, 1-inch thick
 (about 2 pounds)
1/2 teaspoon garlic salt
1/4 cup butter or margarine, melted
2 tablespoons chopped fresh or 1 tablespoon
 dried basil leaves
2 teaspoons lemon pepper
2 medium bell peppers (any color), cut
 lengthwise in half and seeded

1. Spray grill rack with cooking spray. Heat coals or gas grill for direct heat.

2. Trim fat on beef steaks to 1/2-inch thickness if necessary. Sprinkle garlic salt over beef. Mix butter, basil and lemon pepper; brush over beef and bell pepper halves.

3. Cover and grill beef and bell peppers 4 to 5 inches from medium heat 10 to 15 minutes for medium beef doneness, turning once. Brush tops of steaks with butter mixture. Cut bell peppers into strips. Serve over beef.

4 servings.
1 Serving: Calories 345 (Calories from Fat 160); Fat 18g (Saturated 9g); Cholesterol 135mg; Sodium 450mg; Carbohydrate 5g (Dietary Fiber 1g); Protein 41g
% Daily Value: Vitamin A 82%; Vitamin C 94%; Calcium 2%; Iron 22%
Exchanges: 1 Vegetable, 5 1/2 Lean Meat
Carbohydrate Choices: 0

BETTY'S TIPS

⊛ **Substitution**
 If you like, use lemon basil instead of regular basil. This variety of basil has a subtle lemon fragrance and flavor.

⊛ **Success Hint**
 One of the best ways to make sure your steaks stay moist and juicy is to be sure the grill is hot before adding the steaks. A hot grill quickly sears the outside of the meat, sealing in the juices.

⊛ **Serve-With**
 Make this a classic summer meal by serving these steaks with corn on the cob, baked potatoes and grilled buttered Texas toast slices.

Lemon Pepper Steaks

Herb-Crusted
Top Loin Steaks

Prep: 5 min Marinate: 2 hr Grill: 12 min
(Photo on page iii)

1 tablespoon olive or vegetable oil
1 tablespoon chopped fresh or 1 teaspoon dried oregano leaves
1 tablespoon chopped fresh or 1 teaspoon dried thyme leaves
1 tablespoon chopped fresh parsley or parsley flakes
2 cloves garlic, finely chopped
2 beef boneless top loin steaks, 1 inch thick (about 1 pound)

1. Mix all ingredients except beef in small bowl. Rub and press mixture into all surfaces of beef. Cover and refrigerate at least 2 hours but no longer than 24 hours.

2. Heat coals or gas grill for direct heat. Grill beef uncovered 4 to 5 inches from medium heat 1 minute on each side to seal in juices. Cover and grill 6 to 10 minutes longer for medium doneness, turning once.

2 to 4 servings.
1 Serving: Calories 295 (Calories from Fat 110); Fat 12g (Saturated 3g); Cholesterol 120mg; Sodium 90mg; Carbohydrate 1g (Dietary Fiber 0g); Protein 46g
% Daily Value: Vitamin A 6%; Vitamin C 2%; Calcium 2%; Iron 24%
Exchanges: 6½ Very Lean Meat, 1½ Fat
Carbohydrate Choices: 0

BETTY'S TIPS

⊗ **Substitution**
The herb mixture from this recipe can also be used to coat boneless chicken breasts or pork chops before grilling.

⊗ **Did You Know?**
Top loin is one of the lower-fat cuts of meat. Other "skinny" cuts include eye round, top round, round tip, tenderloin and sirloin.

Beef and Potatoes
with Rosemary

Prep: 20 min Cook: 9 hr
(Photo on page 193)

1 pound medium red potatoes, cut into quarters
1 cup baby-cut carrots
3 tablespoons Dijon mustard
2 tablespoons chopped fresh or 1½ teaspoons dried rosemary leaves, crumbled
1 teaspoon chopped fresh or ½ teaspoon dried thyme leaves
1 teaspoon salt
½ teaspoon pepper
3 pound beef boneless chuck roast, trimmed of fat
1 small onion, finely chopped (¼ cup)
1½ cups beef broth

1. Arrange potatoes and carrots around edge in 4- to 5-quart slow cooker.

2. Mix mustard, rosemary, thyme, salt and pepper; spread evenly over beef. Place beef in cooker (it will overlap vegetables slightly). Sprinkle onion over beef. Pour broth evenly over beef and vegetables.

3. Cover and cook on Low heat setting 8 to 9 hours.

4. Remove beef from cooker; place on cutting board. Cut beef into slices. Remove vegetables from cooker with slotted spoon. To serve, spoon beef juices from cooker over beef and vegetables.

6 to 8 servings.
1 Serving: Calories 520 (Calories from Fat 245); Fat 27g (Saturated 10g); Cholesterol 140mg; Sodium 960mg; Carbohydrate 20g (Dietary Fiber 3g); Protein 49g
% Daily Value: Vitamin A 98%; Vitamin C 8%; Calcium 4%; Iron 34%
Exchanges: 1 Starch, 1 Vegetable, 6 Lean Meat, 2 Fat
Carbohydrate Choices: 1

BETTY'S TIPS

⊗ **Success Hint**
If you use the small variety of red potatoes, it's better to cut them just in half so they won't overcook.

⊗ **Special Touch**
If your family likes gravy, you may want to thicken the beef juices with 2 tablespoons cornstarch mixed with ¼ cup cold water.

Bacon and Herb-Crusted Beef Tenderloin Roast

Prep: 20 min

2 pound beef tenderloin roast
Salt and pepper to taste
1/4 cup chopped parsley
1/4 cup chopped fresh oregano leaves
2 teaspoons chopped fresh rosemary leaves
1 clove garlic, crushed
2 teaspoons vegetable oil
6 slices bacon

6 servings.
1 Serving: Calories 280 (Calories from Fat 135); Fat 15g (Saturated 5g); Cholesterol 90mg; Sodium 180mg; Carbohydrate 1g (Dietary Fiber 0g); Protein 35g
% Daily Value: Vitamin A 6%; Vitamin C 2%; Calcium 2%; Iron 16%
Exchanges: 5 Lean Meat
Carbohydrate Choices: 0

1. Heat oven to 425°. Rub beef roast with salt and pepper. Mix parsley, oregano, rosemary, garlic and oil in medium bowl. Press mixture onto top and sides of beef.

2. Place beef on rack in shallow roasting pan. Place bacon strips over top of beef, tucking ends under bottom. Insert meat thermometer so tip is in thickest part of beef.

3. Bake uncovered 35 to 50 minutes or until thermometer reads 140° for medium-rare or 155° for medium doneness. Remove beef from oven, cover with aluminum foil and let stand about 15 minutes until temperature rises 5°.

BETTY'S TIPS

⊕ **Success Hint**
Use thin or regular slices of bacon instead of a thick-sliced variety so the bacon cooks in the time the roast cooks.

⊕ **Do-Ahead**
The roast can be coated with the herb mixture and covered with the bacon several hours ahead of time; cover and refrigerate. Add a few extra minutes to the baking time.

⊕ **Special Touch**
Adorn the serving platter with fresh herbs and crabapples.

Bacon and Herb-Crusted Beef Tenderloin Roast

Quick

Flank Steak with Smoky Honey Mustard Sauce

Prep: 10 min Grill: 20 min

Smoky Honey Mustard Sauce (below)
1   beef flank steak (about 1¹/₂ pounds)
6   flour tortillas (8 to 10 inches in diameter)

1. Heat coals or gas grill for direct heat. Make Smoky Honey Mustard Sauce. Make cuts about ¹/₂-inch apart and ¹/₈-inch deep in diamond pattern in both sides of beef. Brush 2 tablespoons sauce on both sides of beef.

2. Cover and grill beef 4 to 5 inches from medium heat 17 to 20 minutes, turning once, until desired doneness. Cut beef across grain into thin slices. Serve with remaining sauce and tortillas.

6 servings.

Smoky Honey Mustard Sauce

¹/₄   cup honey mustard dressing
1   tablespoon frozen orange juice concentrate (thawed)
1   tablespoon water
1   small clove garlic, finely chopped
1   chipotle chile in adobo sauce (from 7-ounce can), finely chopped

Mix all ingredients.

1 Serving: Calories 345 (Calories from Fat 125); Fat 14g (Saturated 4g); Cholesterol 65mg; Sodium 360mg; Carbohydrate 27g (Dietary Fiber 1g); Protein 28g
% Daily Value: Vitamin A 2%; Vitamin C 4%; Calcium 6%; Iron 20%
Exchanges: 2 Starch, 3 Lean Meat, ¹/₂ Fat
Carbohydrate Choices: 2

BETTY'S TIPS

Serve-With
To make this dish more like fajitas, add ingredients such as chopped tomatoes, shredded lettuce, diced avocado, shredded cheese, sliced olives, sliced green onions and diced bell pepper to the menu.

Did You Know?
Flank steak is a long, thin piece of boneless beef cut from the lower hindquarters. Flank steak is known to be a less-tender cut and should be very thinly sliced across the grain for serving. It is typically used for fajitas or London broil.

Flank Steak with Smoky Honey Mustard Sauce

Garlic Braised Beef and Potatoes

Prep: 15 min Cook: 9 hr + 15 min

8 small red potatoes (about 1¹/₂ pounds), cut in half

8 cloves garlic, peeled

3 pound beef boneless bottom round roast, trimmed of fat

1 envelope garlic-and-herb dry soup mix (from 1.4-ounce package)

1 can (10³/₄ ounces) condensed beefy mushroom soup

2 cups frozen broccoli florets (from 1-pound bag)

8 servings.
1 Serving: Calories 335 (Calories from Fat 70); Fat 8g (Saturated 2g); Cholesterol 90mg; Sodium 500mg; Carbohydrate 28g (Dietary Fiber 3g); Protein 38g
% Daily Value: Vitamin A 10%; Vitamin C 18%; Calcium 4%; Iron 26%
Exchanges: 1¹/₂ Starch, 1 Vegetable, 4¹/₂ Very Lean Meat, 1 Fat
Carbohydrate Choices: 2

1. Place potatoes and garlic in 4- to 5-quart slow cooker. Place beef on potatoes. Sprinkle dry soup mix over beef; pour beefy mushroom soup over all.

2. Cover and cook on Low heat setting 8 to 9 hours.

3. Remove beef from cooker; place on cutting board. Cut beef into slices; place on serving platter with potatoes and garlic. Cover to keep warm.

4. Meanwhile, place frozen broccoli in slow cooker with remaining sauce. Increase heat setting to High. Cover and cook about 15 minutes or until broccoli is tender. Serve with beef and potatoes.

BETTY'S TIPS

⚙ **Substitution**
Not broccoli fans? Substitute your family's favorite frozen veggie for the broccoli.

⚙ **Serve-With**
The long-roasted garlic cloves are soft and sweet and will taste great spread on buttered rolls.

⚙ **Variation**
Serve any leftover beef on crusty French rolls for a nice sandwich.

Garlic Braised Beef and Potatoes

Parmesan Orzo and Meatballs

Glazed Peppered Steak

Glazed Peppered Steak

Prep: 10 min Grill: 12 minutes

1/2 cup orange marmalade
1/4 cup white balsamic vinegar
2 teaspoons coarsely ground pepper
1/2 teaspoon salt
4 beef boneless top loin steaks, about 3/4-inch thick

1. Heat coals or gas grill for direct heat. Mix marmalade and vinegar in small saucepan. Cook over low heat, stirring constantly, until marmalade is melted.

2. Rub pepper and salt on both sides of each beef steak. Cover and grill beef 4 to 5 inches from medium-high heat 8 to 12 minutes, turning once or twice, until desired doneness. Brush with marmalade glaze during last 2 minutes of grilling.

3. To serve, heat any remaining glaze to boiling. Boil and stir 1 minute. Serve glaze with beef.

4 servings.
1 Serving: Calories 300 (Calories from Fat 80); Fat 9g (Saturated 3g); Cholesterol 70mg; Sodium 370mg; Carbohydrate 28g (Dietary Fiber 0g); Protein 26g
% Daily Value: Vitamin A 2%; Vitamin C 2%; Calcium 2%; Iron 14%
Exchanges: 1 Starch, 3 Lean Meat, 1 Fruit
Carbohydrate Choices: 2

BETTY'S TIPS

✪ **Substitution**
White wine vinegar can be used instead of the balsamic vinegar.

✪ **Success Hint**
Sweet glazes can burn quickly on the grill, so it's important to brush the steaks with the glaze during only the last few minutes of grilling.

✪ **Variation**
To broil the steaks, broil on rack in broiler pan with tops of steaks 4 to 6 inches from heat for 8 to 12 minutes, turning once and brushing with the glaze during last 2 minutes of broiling.

Parmesan Orzo and Meatballs

Prep: 10 min Cook: 20 min

1 1/2 cups frozen stir-fry bell peppers and onions (from 1-pound bag)
2 tablespoons Italian dressing
1 can (14 ounces) beef broth
1 cup uncooked orzo or rosamarina pasta (6 ounces)
1 bag (10 1/2 ounces) frozen cooked Italian meatballs (16 meatballs)
1 large tomato, chopped (1 cup)
2 tablespoons chopped parsley
1/4 cup shredded Parmesan cheese

1. Cook stir-fry vegetables and dressing in 12-inch non-stick skillet over medium-high heat 2 minutes. Stir in broth; heat to boiling. Stir in pasta and meatballs. Heat to boiling; reduce heat to low. Cover and cook 10 minutes, stirring occasionally.

2. Stir in tomato. Cover and cook 3 to 5 minutes or until most of the liquid has been absorbed and pasta is tender. Stir in parsley. Sprinkle with cheese.

4 servings.
1 Serving: Calories 425 (Calories from Fat 165); Fat 18g (Saturated 6g); Cholesterol 80mg; Sodium 1,060mg; Carbohydrate 41g (Dietary Fiber 3g); Protein 25g
% Daily Value: Vitamin A 16%; Vitamin C 32%; Calcium 16%; Iron 22%
Exchanges: 2 1/2 Starch, 2 Medium-Fat Meat, 1 Vegetable, 1 Fat
Carbohydrate Choices: 3

BETTY'S TIPS

✪ **Health Twist**
To reduce the calories to 350 and fat to 10 grams per serving, use reduced-fat frozen meatballs and Italian dressing.

✪ **Did You Know?**
Orzo is a rice-shaped pasta that cooks fairly quickly. It's a great pasta to serve to kids because it is easier to eat than long spaghetti.

Cheesy Meatballs and Vegetables

Prep: 25 min

1¹/₂ cups uncooked regular long-grain rice

1 package (16 ounces) frozen cooked meatballs

²/₃ cup half-and-half

2 packages (10 ounces each) Green Giant frozen broccoli, cauliflower, carrots and cheese-flavored sauce

1. Cook rice as directed on package.

2. Meanwhile, cover and cook frozen meatballs in 12-inch skillet over medium-high heat 4 minutes, stirring once. Stir in half-and-half, scraping skillet to remove any browned bits of meat.

3. Add blocks of frozen vegetables and sauce, placing vegetable sides down. Cover and cook 10 to 12 minutes, stirring occasionally, until vegetables and meatballs are hot. Serve over rice.

6 servings.
1 Serving: Calories 465 (Calories from Fat 155); Fat 17g (Saturated 8g); Cholesterol 90mg; Sodium 520mg; Carbohydrate 54g (Dietary Fiber 3g); Protein 24g
% Daily Value: Vitamin A 52%; Vitamin C 24%; Calcium 14%; Iron 22%
Exchanges: 3 Starch, 2 Vegetable, 1¹/₂ Medium-Fat Meat, 1¹/₂ Fat
Carbohydrate Choices: 3¹/₂

BETTY'S TIPS

⚘ **Success Hint**
If the cheese sauce becomes too thick, stir in a couple of tablespoons of water or milk.

⚘ **Variation**
Serve spaghetti with these cheesy meatballs and vegetables to soak up the tasty cheese sauce. Cooked chicken pieces or frozen salad shrimp can be used in place of the meatballs.

⚘ **Special Touch**
Garnish with fresh parsley or thyme.

Cheesy Meatballs and Vegetables

Quick

Bow-Tie Pasta with Beef and Tomatoes

Prep: 20 min

2 cups uncooked farfalle (bow-tie) pasta (5 ounces)

1 tablespoon olive or vegetable oil

1 cup frozen stir-fry bell peppers and onions (from 1-pound bag)

1 pound thinly sliced beef for stir-fry or flank steak, thinly sliced

1 can (14.5 ounces) Italian-style stewed tomatoes, undrained

1 teaspoon garlic salt

$1/4$ teaspoon pepper

Fresh basil leaves, if desired

Freshly shredded Parmesan cheese, if desired

Bow-Tie Pasta with Beef and Tomatoes

1. Cook and drain pasta as directed on package.

2. While pasta is cooking, heat oil in 12-inch skillet over medium-high heat. Cook frozen stir-fry vegetables in oil 3 minutes, stirring frequently. Stir in beef. Cook 5 to 6 minutes, stirring frequently, until no longer pink.

3. Stir in tomatoes, garlic salt and pepper. Cook 2 to 3 minutes, stirring frequently and breaking up tomatoes slightly with spoon, until mixture is hot. Stir in pasta. Cook 1 to 2 minutes, stirring constantly, until pasta is well coated and hot. Garnish with basil. Serve with cheese.

4 servings.
1 Serving: Calories 350 (Calories from Fat 110); Fat 12g (Saturated 4g); Cholesterol 125mg; Sodium 300mg; Carbohydrate 31g (Dietary Fiber 2g); Protein 29g
% Daily Value: Vitamin A 2%; Vitamin C 14%; Calcium 2%; Iron 20%
Exchanges: 2 Starch, 3 Lean Meat, $1/2$ Fat
Carbohydrate Choices: 2

BETTY'S TIPS

✪ **Substitution**
Thinly sliced chicken can be used in this recipe instead of the beef.

✪ **Time-Saver**
Buy beef already sliced from the meat department, or ask the butcher to slice it for you.

✪ **Serve-With**
Serve with crusty dinner rolls and cooked fresh green beans.

Skillet Beef, Veggies and Brown Rice

Prep: 12 min Cook: 19 min
(Photo on page 193)

2 cups chicken broth

1¹/₂ cups uncooked instant brown rice

2 medium carrots, sliced (1 cup)

2 teaspoons vegetable oil

¹/₂ pound beef top round steak, trimmed of fat and cut into thin strips

¹/₄ cup chopped onion

1 cup fresh snap pea pods, strings removed

1 teaspoon Italian seasoning

¹/₂ teaspoon salt

¹/₄ teaspoon pepper

1. Heat broth to boiling in 2-quart saucepan. Stir in rice and carrots. Heat to boiling; reduce heat. Cover and simmer 6 to 8 minutes or until carrots are crisp-tender; remove from heat. Let stand 5 minutes.

2. Meanwhile, heat oil in 12-inch skillet over medium-high heat. Cook beef and onion in oil about 8 minutes, stirring frequently, until beef is brown and onion is tender. Stir in cooked rice mixture, pea pods, Italian seasoning, salt and pepper.

3. Cover and cook about 3 minutes, stirring occasionally, just until pea pods are tender. (Add a small amount of water to mixture if it becomes dry before pea pods are tender.)

4 servings.
1 Serving: Calories 405 (Calories from Fat 65); Fat 7g (Saturated 2g); Cholesterol 30mg; Sodium 880mg; Carbohydrate 63g (Dietary Fiber 7g); Protein 22g
% Daily Value: Vitamin A 100%; Vitamin C 14%; Calcium 4%; Iron 16%
Exchanges: 4 Starch, 2 Very Lean Meat
Carbohydrate Choices: 4

BETTY'S TIPS

⚙ **Substitution**
You can use fresh or frozen peas instead of snap peas.

⚙ **Do-Ahead**
All the prep work can be done ahead of time and the ingredients wrapped in plastic and refrigerated. Cut carrots and wrap separately. Cut and wrap beef and onion together.

⚙ **Special Touch**
Add slices of provolone cheese over the top of the skillet combination after the pea pods are done. Remove skillet from the heat, and cover and let stand 1 to 2 minutes or until the cheese is melted.

Quick

Stove-Top Lasagna

Prep: 30 min

1 pound bulk Italian sausage

1 medium onion, cut in half and sliced
   ($^1/_2$ cup)

1 jar (26 to 30 ounces) chunky tomato pasta
   sauce (any variety)

1 jar (4.5 ounces) Green Giant sliced
   mushrooms, drained

1 medium green bell pepper, cut into thin
   bite-size strips

3 cups uncooked mafalda (mini-lasagna
   noodle) pasta or medium egg noodles
   (6 ounces)

$2^1/_2$ cups water

$^1/_2$ teaspoon Italian seasoning

1 cup shredded Italian-style cheese blend or
   mozzarella cheese (4 ounces)

   Chopped fresh basil, if desired

1. Cook sausage and onion in 12-inch skillet or 4-quart
   Dutch oven over medium-high heat, stirring occasionally, until sausage is no longer pink; drain.

2. Stir remaining ingredients except cheese and basil
   into sausage. Heat to boiling, stirring occasionally;
   reduce heat to medium.

3. Simmer uncovered about 10 minutes or until pasta is
   tender. Sprinkle with cheese. Let stand 2 minutes.
   Garnish with basil.

6 servings.
1 Serving: Calories 510 (Calories from Fat 205); Fat 23g (Saturated 8g);
Cholesterol 35mg; Sodium 1,420mg; Carbohydrate 54g (Dietary Fiber
2g); Protein 23g
% Daily Value: Vitamin A 22%; Vitamin C 34%; Calcium 20%; Iron 18%
Exchanges: 3 Starch, 1 Vegetable, $1^1/_2$ High-Fat Meat, 2 Fat
Carbohydrate Choices: $3^1/_2$

BETTY'S TIPS

⊕ **Substitution**
Ground beef is a quick substitute for the sausage in this
easy lasagna.

⊕ **Serve-With**
Add garlic toast and a Caesar salad for an easy, tasty
dinner in minutes!

Stove-Top Lasagna

Hamburger Steaks with Roasted Onions

Prep: 10 min Grill: 15 min

4   lean ground beef patties (4 to 6 ounces each)

2   tablespoons steak sauce

1   envelope (1 ounce) onion soup mix (from 2-ounce package)

2   large Bermuda or other sweet onions, cut in half, then thinly sliced and separated (6 cups)

2   tablespoons packed brown sugar

1   tablespoon balsamic vinegar

4 servings.
1 Serving: Calories 295 (Calories from Fat 145); Fat 16g (Saturated 6g); Cholesterol 65mg; Sodium 780mg; Carbohydrate 15g (Dietary Fiber 2g); Protein 22g
% Daily Value: Vitamin A 4%; Vitamin C 6%; Calcium 4%; Iron 12%
Exchanges: 1 Starch, 2 High-Fat Meat
Carbohydrate Choices: 1

1. Heat coals or gas grill for direct heat. Spray two 18 × 12-inch sheets of heavy-duty aluminum foil with cooking spray.

2. Brush beef patties with steak sauce; sprinkle with half of the soup mix (dry). Place half of the onions on center of each foil piece. Sprinkle with remaining soup mix, brown sugar and vinegar. Fold foil over onions so edges meet. Seal edges, making tight 1/2-inch fold; fold again. Allow space on sides for circulation and expansion.

3. Cover and grill packets and beef patties 4 to 6 inches from medium heat 10 to 15 minutes, turning patties and rotating packets 1/2 turn once or twice, until patties are no longer pink in center and juice from beef is clear. Place packets and patties on plates. Cut large X across top of each packet; fold back foil.

BETTY'S TIPS

✪ **Substitution**
If you can't find the ground beef patties at your market, you can make your own with 1 pound of lean ground beef. Shape into 4 patties, each about 1/2-inch thick.

✪ **Variation**
These patties and onions can be served in sandwich buns. Just add your favorite condiments such as additional steak sauce, mustard, pickles, tomatoes, shredded lettuce and cheese.

Hamburger Steaks with Roasted Onions

Tex-Mex Tortilla Torte

Prep: 10 min Bake: 30 min Stand: 5 min

4	flour tortillas (6 to 8 inches in diameter)
1	can (15 to 16 ounces) chili
2	cups shredded Cheddar cheese (8 ounces)
1/4	cup sour cream, if desired

1. Heat oven to 350°. Spray bottom of pie plate, 9 × 1 1/4 inches, with cooking spray.

2. Place 1 tortilla on bottom of pie plate; spread evenly with 1/2 cup of the chili and sprinkle with 1/2 cup of the cheese. Repeat layers twice, starting each layer with tortilla. Top with remaining tortilla.

3. Cover with aluminum foil and bake 20 minutes. Sprinkle with remaining 1/2 cup cheese. Bake uncovered about 10 minutes or until heated through and cheese is melted. Let stand 5 minutes before cutting. To serve, cut into 4 wedges. Top each serving with 1 tablespoon sour cream.

4 servings.
1 Serving: Calories 450 (Calories from Fat 245); Fat 27g (Saturated 16g); Cholesterol 80mg; Sodium 1,000mg; Carbohydrate 29g (Dietary Fiber 4g); Protein 23g
% Daily Value: Vitamin A 22%; Vitamin C 4%; Calcium 36%; Iron 16%
Exchanges: 2 Starch, 2 1/2 High-Fat Meat, 1 Fat
Carbohydrate Choices: 2

BETTY'S TIPS

✪ **Substitution**
Do you have leftover chili or a stash of homemade chili in the freezer? Go ahead and use 1 1/2 cups leftover chili instead of the canned chili. Use a thicker chili instead of a watery one for best results.

✪ **Health Twist**
Fat-free flour tortillas, reduced-fat Cheddar cheese and reduced-fat or fat-free sour cream all help lower the fat in this family-pleasing meal.

✪ **Special Touch**
Sprinkle each wedge with shredded lettuce and chopped tomatoes; then top with the sour cream.

Easy Beef and Bean Enchiladas

Prep: 15 min Bake: 20 min

1	can (10 ounces) Old El Paso enchilada sauce
1 1/2	cups Old El Paso refrigerated taco sauce with seasoned ground beef (from 20-ounce tub)
1	can (16 ounces) chili beans in sauce, undrained
6	flour tortillas (8 inches in diameter)
1	cup shredded Colby-Monterey Jack cheese (4 ounces)
2	medium green onions, sliced (2 tablespoons)

1. Heat oven to 375°. Spray rectangular baking dish, 13 × 9 × 2 inches, with cooking spray. Spread 1/2 cup of the enchilada sauce in baking dish.

2. Mix beef and chili beans in medium bowl. Spoon 1/2 cup beef mixture down center of each tortilla. Roll up each tortilla; place seam side down on enchilada sauce in dish. Spoon remaining enchilada sauce over filled tortillas. Sprinkle with cheese.

3. Bake uncovered about 20 minutes or until sauce is bubbly and cheese is melted. Sprinkle with onions.

6 servings.
1 Serving: Calories 350 (Calories from Fat 15); Fat 15g (Saturated 7g); Cholesterol 40mg; Sodium 1,160mg; Carbohydrate 40g (Dietary Fiber 6g); Protein 20g
% Daily Value: Vitamin A 18%; Vitamin C 14%; Calcium 24%; Iron 24%
Exchanges: 2 1/2 Starch, 2 Medium-Fat Meat
Carbohydrate Choices: 2 1/2

BETTY'S TIPS

✪ **Substitution**
Marbled Colby-Monterey Jack cheese makes a pretty topping for these enchiladas, but Cheddar, Monterey Jack and taco cheese blend all work well, too.

✪ **Special Touch**
Serve with dollops of sour cream and chopped avocado for a picture-pretty presentation.

✪ **Did You Know?**
Canned chili beans, which are cooked pinto beans in a spice-rich sauce, are a high-fiber convenience food and boost the flavor of these enchiladas.

Easy Beef and Bean Enchiladas

Tex-Mex Tortilla Torte

Italian Spinach and Meatball Biscuit Bake

Prep: 20 min Bake: 25 min

1 bag (18 ounces) frozen cooked Italian meatballs

1 jar (14 ounces) tomato pasta sauce (any variety)

1 package (9 ounces) Green Giant frozen spinach, thawed and squeezed to drain

1 package (8 ounces) cream cheese, softened

1½ cups shredded Italian-style six-cheese blend or mozzarella cheese (6 ounces)

2¼ cups Original Bisquick mix

1 cup milk

1. Heat oven to 400°. Spray rectangular baking dish, 13 × 9 × 2 inches, with cooking spray. Thaw meatballs by microwaving them in microwavable bowl on High 3 to 5 minutes or until warm. Add pasta sauce; stir to coat.

2. Place half of the meatballs in baking dish. Mix spinach, cream cheese and ½ cup of the Italian-style cheese. Spoon half of the spinach mixture by tablespoonfuls randomly over meatballs.

3. Stir Bisquick mix and milk until soft dough forms. Spoon half of the dough by tablespoonfuls randomly over meatballs. Repeat layers with remaining meatballs, spinach mixture and Bisquick mixture.

4. Bake uncovered about 20 minutes or until biscuits are golden brown. Sprinkle with remaining 1 cup Italian-style cheese. Bake about 5 minutes or until cheese is melted.

6 to 8 servings.
1 Serving: Calories 725 (Calories from Fat 370); Fat 41g (Saturated 19g); Cholesterol 145mg; Sodium 1,760mg; Carbohydrate 54g (Dietary Fiber 3g); Protein 35g
% Daily Value: Vitamin A 82%; Vitamin C 12%; Calcium 48%; Iron 28%
Exchanges: 3½ Starch, 3½ High-Fat Meat, 2 Fat
Carbohydrate Choices: 3½

Italian Spinach and Meatball Biscuit Bake

BETTY'S TIPS

✿ **Do-Ahead**
Bake this casserole about 20 minutes as directed, but do not add the remaining 1 cup cheese. Cover and freeze. For an easy solution to weeknight hungries, bake frozen casserole in a 350° oven for 45 to 55 minutes or until hot. Sprinkle with 1 cup cheese, and bake about 5 minutes or until cheese is melted.

✿ **Did You Know?**
This casserole is great for toting to potlucks, sharing with a neighbor or thanking the teachers at school. With only seven ingredients, it's a snap to assemble.

Low Fat

Easy Beef and Broccoli

Prep: 10 min Cook: 10 hr + 30 min

1 pound beef boneless top round steak, trimmed of fat and cut into 1-inch cubes

1 jar (4.5 ounces) Green Giant sliced mushrooms, drained

1 medium onion, cut into wedges

1/2 cup condensed beef broth (from 10 1/2-ounce can)

3 tablespoons teriyaki baste and glaze (from 12-ounce bottle)

1 tablespoon sesame seed

1 teaspoon dark sesame oil, if desired

2/3 cup uncooked regular long-grain rice

1 1/3 cups water

2 tablespoons water

1 tablespoon cornstarch

2 cups Green Giant Select frozen broccoli florets (from 1-pound bag)

1. Mix beef, mushrooms, onion, broth, teriyaki baste and glaze, sesame seed and sesame oil in 3 1/2- to 4-quart slow cooker.

2. Cover and cook on Low heat setting 8 to 10 hours.

3. About 35 minutes before serving, cook rice in 1 1/3 cups water as directed on package. Meanwhile, mix 2 tablespoons water and the cornstarch in small bowl. Stir cornstarch mixture and broccoli into beef mixture. Cover and cook on Low heat setting 30 minutes or until broccoli is crisp-tender. Serve over rice.

4 servings (1 3/4 cups each).
1 Serving: Calories 335 (Calories from Fat 45); Fat 5g (Saturated 2g); Cholesterol 60mg; Sodium 880mg; Carbohydrate 40g (Dietary Fiber 5g); Protein 32g
% Daily Value: Vitamin A 32%; Vitamin C 32%; Calcium 8%; Iron 26%
Exchanges: 2 Starch, 2 Vegetable, 3 Very Lean Meat, 1/2 Fat
Carbohydrate Choices: 2 1/2

BETTY'S TIPS

⊗ **Success Hint**

Be sure to cut the beef into pieces of the same size to ensure that all the beef cooks evenly and is tender.

When using a slow cooker, don't lift the lid during cooking unless necessary; removing the lid allows steam that is vital to the cooking process to escape.

Easy Beef and Broccoli

Impossibly Easy Lasagna Pie

Prep: 15 min Bake: 44 min Stand: 5 min

2 pounds ground beef

1 cup small curd creamed cottage cheese

$^1/_2$ cup grated Parmesan cheese

3 cups shredded mozzarella cheese (12 ounces)

$1^1/_2$ teaspoons Italian seasoning

1 can (15 ounces) tomato paste

1 cup Original or Reduced Fat Bisquick mix

2 cups milk

$^1/_2$ teaspoon pepper

3 eggs

Chopped fresh parsley, if desired

1. Heat oven to 400°. Spray rectangular baking dish, 13 × 9 × 2 inches, with cooking spray. Cook beef in 12-inch skillet over medium-high heat, stirring occasionally, until brown; drain.

2. Layer cottage cheese and Parmesan cheese in baking dish. Mix beef, $1^1/_2$ cups of the mozzarella cheese, the Italian seasoning and tomato paste; spoon evenly over cheese in baking dish. Stir Bisquick mix, milk, pepper and eggs until blended. Pour over beef mixture.

3. Bake uncovered 40 to 42 minutes or until knife inserted in center comes out clean. Sprinkle with remaining $1^1/_2$ cups mozzarella cheese. Bake 1 to 2 minutes or until cheese is melted. Let stand 5 minutes before cutting. Sprinkle with parsley.

12 to 15 servings.
1 Serving: Calories 390 (Calories from Fat 190); Fat 21g (Saturated 10g); Cholesterol 120mg; Sodium 800mg; Carbohydrate 18g (Dietary Fiber 2g); Protein 31g
% Daily Value: Vitamin A 26%; Vitamin C 14%; Calcium 36%; Iron 14%
Exchanges: 1 Starch, 4 Medium-Fat Meat
Carbohydrate Choices: 1

BETTY'S TIPS

☺ **Health Twist**
Lighten up this lasagna by using Reduced Fat Bisquick mix, fat-free (skim) milk, fat-free cottage cheese and reduced-fat mozzarella cheese for a savings of 4 grams of fat and 30 calories per serving.

☺ **Serve-With**
This is a contemporary twist to traditional lasagna. We recommend serving with garlic bread, cooked zucchini, tossed green salad and rainbow sherbet for dessert.

Impossibly Easy Lasagna Pie

Something on the Side

Sides to Complement Any Dish

Stir-Fry Broccoli and Carrots (page 221)

Squash and Cranberry Gratin (page 216)

Nutty Veggie Combo

Prep: 12 min Grill: 15 min

2 tablespoons butter or margarine, melted
2 tablespoons chopped parsley
¼ teaspoon salt
1 cup small cauliflowerets
8 Brussels sprouts, cut in half
8 baby yellow pattypan squash
½ cup walnut halves

1. Heat coals or gas grill for direct heat.

2. Mix butter, parsley and salt. Place vegetables and walnuts in grill basket.

3. Cover and grill vegetables 4 to 5 inches from medium heat 10 to 15 minutes, turning and brushing with butter mixture 2 or 3 times, until crisp-tender.

6 servings.
1 Serving: Calories 145 (Calories from Fat 100); Fat 11g (Saturated 3g); Cholesterol 10mg; Sodium 135mg; Carbohydrate 8g (Dietary Fiber 3g); Protein 4g
% Daily Value: Vitamin A 12%; Vitamin C 28%; Calcium 4%; Iron 4%
Exchanges: 2 Vegetable, 2 Fat
Carbohydrate Choices: ½

BETTY'S TIPS

✿ **Substitution**
You can really use almost any of your favorite vegetables; just make sure they are similar in size. You'll need a total of about 4 cups of vegetables. If walnuts aren't your favorite nuts, try cashews, almonds or pecans.

✿ **Did You Know?**
Farmers' markets and local gardens may offer varieties of cauliflower and squash in a rainbow of colors, such as green squash and orange or purple cauliflower.

Nutty Veggie Combo

Quick

Peas and Onions Alfredo

Prep: 15 min

2 packages (9 ounces each) Green Giant frozen sweet peas and pearl onions

1 jar (2 ounces) diced pimientos, drained

1/2 cup Alfredo pasta sauce (from 1-pound jar)

2 tablespoons shredded fresh Parmesan cheese

1. Cook peas and onions as directed on package.

2. Place peas and onions in serving bowl. Stir in pimientos and Alfredo sauce. Sprinkle with cheese.

6 servings.
1 Serving: Calories 125 (Calories from Fat 65); Fat 7g (Saturated 4g); Cholesterol 20mg; Sodium 160mg; Carbohydrate 10g (Dietary Fiber 3g); Protein 5g
% Daily Value: Vitamin A 14%; Vitamin C 10%; Calcium 8%; Iron 4%
Exchanges: 1/2 Starch, 1/2 High-Fat Meat, 1/2 Fat
Carbohydrate Choices: 1/2

BETTY'S TIPS

⚙ **Time-Saver**
Both packages of peas and onions can be microwaved at the same time. Simply follow the directions on the packages.

⚙ **Variation**
If your family doesn't care for onions, use two 9-ounce packages of Green Giant LeSueur® frozen baby sweet peas.

⚙ **Did You Know?**
Alfredo sauce is available in shelf-stable jars and in refrigerated containers. Either works in this recipe. If using refrigerated sauce, warm it before adding it to the peas and onions. Stir the remaining sauce into cooked pasta for a quick side dish with another meal.

Peas and Onions Alfredo

Squash and Cranberry Gratin

Prep: 25 min Cook: 15 min Stand: 5 min Bake: 30 min
(Photo on page 213)

4	pounds butternut or buttercup squash (2 medium)
1/4	cup sweetened dried cranberries
2	tablespoons packed brown sugar
1/2	cup whipping (heavy) cream
1/2	teaspoon salt
1	tablespoon butter or margarine, softened
2	slices sandwich bread
1/2	cup finely shredded Swiss cheese (2 ounces)
1/2	teaspoon ground nutmeg

1. Cut squash into halves or quarters; remove seeds and fibers. Place cut sides down in microwavable dish. Cover with plastic wrap, folding back one edge or corner 1/4 inch to vent steam. Microwave on High 13 to 15 minutes or until tender when pierced with fork. Let stand 5 minutes. Scoop flesh from shells and mash with fork.

2. Heat oven to 350°. Butter 1 1/2-quart shallow au gratin dish or casserole. Mix squash, cranberries, brown sugar, whipping cream and salt in medium bowl. Spoon into au gratin dish.

3. Spread butter on bread. Tear buttered bread into pieces. Place bread, cheese and nutmeg in food processor. Cover and process until fine crumbs form. Sprinkle over squash mixture.

4. Bake uncovered 25 to 30 minutes or until thoroughly heated and crumb topping is brown and crisp.

8 servings.
1 Serving: Calories 210 (Calories from Fat 70); Fat 8g (Saturated 5g); Cholesterol 25mg; Sodium 220mg; Carbohydrate 30g (Dietary Fiber 3g); Protein 5g
% Daily Value: Vitamin A 100%; Vitamin C 24%; Calcium 16%; Iron 8%
Exchanges: 2 Starch, 1 Fat
Carbohydrate Choices: 2

BETTY'S TIPS

⊗ **Substitution**

If you want to use leftover mashed cooked squash or purchased frozen (thawed) cooked squash, you'll need 4 cups.

⊗ **Success Hint**

To bake the squash instead of microwaving it, place the cut and seeded squash pieces cut sides down in a glass baking dish. Cover and bake at 350° for 50 to 60 minutes or until tender when pierced with a fork.

⊗ **Time-Saver**

Buttering the bread and processing it in a food processor is a quick way to make buttered bread crumbs. If a food processor is not available, tear the bread into small pieces and drizzle with melted butter.

Quick

Corn with Basil

Prep: 10 min Cook: 17 min

- 2 cups Green Giant Niblets frozen corn (from 1-pound bag)
- 2 tablespoons butter or margarine
- 1 medium onion, chopped ($^1/_2$ cup)
- 1 medium rib celery, thinly sliced ($^1/_2$ cup)
- 1 jar (2 ounces) diced pimientos, drained
- 1 teaspoon chopped fresh or $^1/_4$ teaspoon dried basil leaves
- $^1/_4$ teaspoon salt
- $^1/_8$ teaspoon garlic powder or $^1/_4$ teaspoon instant minced onion

1. Rinse frozen corn with cold water to separate; drain. Melt butter in 2-quart saucepan over medium heat. Cook corn, onion and celery in butter 10 to 12 minutes, stirring frequently, until onion is tender.

2. Stir in remaining ingredients; reduce heat. Cover and simmer 3 to 5 minutes or until corn is tender.

6 servings.
1 Serving: Calories 95 (Calories from Fat 35); Fat 4g (Saturated 2g); Cholesterol 10mg; Sodium 140mg; Carbohydrate 13g (Dietary Fiber 2g); Protein 2g
% Daily Value: Vitamin A 8%; Vitamin C 10%; Calcium 0%; Iron 2%
Exchanges: 1 Starch, $^1/_2$ Fat
Carbohydrate Choices: 1

BETTY'S TIPS

⊘ **Substitution**
You can use 2 tablespoons of dried instant minced onion in place of the fresh onion.

⊘ **Time-Saver**
Look in the frozen-food case for bags of frozen chopped onions. Keep it on hand for fuss-free chopped onion.

⊘ **Did You Know?**
Newer varieties of frozen corn are available. Look for extra-sweet Green Giant Select gold & white corn.

Corn with Basil

Cheesy Broccoli

Garden Patch Sauté

Garden Patch Sauté

Prep: 20 min

1 tablespoon olive or vegetable oil

1 medium zucchini, cut into ¼-inch slices (1 cup)

1 medium yellow summer squash, cut into ¼-inch slices (1 cup)

1 cup sliced mushrooms

1 cup grape tomatoes or cherry tomatoes, cut in half

2 tablespoons chopped fresh chives

½ teaspoon garlic salt

1. Heat oil in 10-inch nonstick skillet over medium-high heat. Cook zucchini, yellow squash and mushrooms in oil 4 to 5 minutes, stirring frequently, until vegetables are crisp-tender.

2. Stir in tomatoes. Sprinkle vegetables with chives and garlic salt. Cook 2 to 3 minutes, stirring frequently, just until tomatoes begin to soften.

6 servings (½ cup each).
1 Serving: Calories 45 (Calories from Fat 25); Fat 3g (Saturated 0g); Cholesterol 0mg; Sodium 200mg; Carbohydrate 4g (Dietary Fiber 1g); Protein 1g
% Daily Value: Vitamin A 10%; Vitamin C 12%; Calcium 2%; Iron 2%
Exchanges: 1 Vegetable, ½ Fat
Carbohydrate Choices: 0

BETTY'S TIPS

⚙ **Substitution**
Fresh basil, oregano, marjoram or even lemon balm can be substituted for the fresh chives.

⚙ **Serve-With**
Grilled chicken would pair nicely with this fresh-tasting vegetable combination.

⚙ **Do-Ahead**
All of the vegetables and the chives can be cut up one day ahead and kept covered in the refrigerator.

Cheesy Broccoli

Prep: 5 min Cook: 9 min

1 pound fresh broccoli florets (about 6 cups)

2 tablespoons water

2 cups shredded Cheddar Jack and American cheese blend (8 ounces)

½ cup crumbled cooked bacon or toasted sliced almonds

1. Place broccoli and water in rectangular microwavable dish, 11 × 7 × 1½ inches. Cover with plastic wrap, folding back one edge or corner ¼ inch to vent steam. Microwave on High about 5 minutes or until hot and crisp-tender.

2. Drain broccoli; return to dish. Sprinkle with cheese. Microwave uncovered on High 3 to 4 minutes or until cheese is melted. Sprinkle bacon over top.

12 servings.
1 Serving: Calories 110 (Calories from Fat 70); Fat 8g (Saturated 4g); Cholesterol 20mg; Sodium 170mg; Carbohydrate 2g (Dietary Fiber 1g); Protein 7g
% Daily Value: Vitamin A 14%; Vitamin C 28%; Calcium 14%; Iron 2%
Exchanges: 1 High-Fat Meat
Carbohydrate Choices: 0

BETTY'S TIPS

⚙ **Success Hint**
To assure a bright green color, be sure to not overcook the broccoli. Overcooked broccoli takes on an olive color. If using almonds instead of bacon, toast them quickly in the microwave. Place almonds and 1 tablespoon butter or margarine in 1-quart microwavable casserole. Microwave uncovered on High 2 to 3 minutes, stirring after 1 minute, until golden brown.

⚙ **Special Touch**
For a festive holiday garnish, sprinkle diced pimientos over the broccoli.

Quick

Green Beans with Browned Butter

Prep: 25 min

³/₄ pound green beans, cut in half
2 tablespoons butter*
2 tablespoons pine nuts
1 teaspoon grated lemon peel

1. Place beans in 1 inch water in 2¹/₂-quart saucepan. Heat to boiling; reduce heat. Simmer uncovered 8 to 10 minutes or until crisp-tender; drain. Keep warm.

2. Meanwhile, melt butter in 1-quart saucepan over low heat. Stir in pine nuts. Heat, stirring constantly, until butter is golden brown. Immediately remove from heat. Pour butter mixture over beans; toss to coat. Sprinkle with lemon peel.

*Do not use margarine or vegetable oil spreads.

6 servings (¹/₂ cup each).
1 Serving: Calories 70 (Calories from Fat 45); Fat 5g (Saturated 3g); Cholesterol 10mg; Sodium 30mg; Carbohydrate 4g (Dietary Fiber 2g); Protein 2g
% Daily Value: Vitamin A 10%; Vitamin C 2%; Calcium 2%; Iron 4%
Exchanges: 1 Vegetable, 1 Fat
Carbohydrate Choices: 0

BETTY'S TIPS

☻ **Substitution**
Sliced or slivered almonds or chopped pecans or walnuts can be substituted for the pine nuts.

☻ **Success Hint**
It is the proteins in butter that provide the rich and distinctive flavor of browned butter. Once the browning begins, it continues to brown very quickly and can burn, so low heat and a watchful eye are important. Margarine and vegetable oil spreads cannot be browned because they lack the necessary proteins and will burn.

Green Beans with Browned Butter

Stir-Fry Broccoli and Carrots

Prep: 20 min Cook: 8 min
(Photo on page 213)

2	teaspoons finely chopped fresh ginger
1	clove garlic, finely chopped
1½	cups small broccoli florets
2	medium carrots, thinly sliced (1 cup)
1	small onion, sliced and separated into rings
¾	cup fat-free chicken broth
¼	teaspoon salt
1	tablespoon cornstarch
1	tablespoon cold water
1	cup sliced mushrooms (about 3 ounces)
2	tablespoons oyster sauce

1. Spray wok or 12-inch skillet with cooking spray; heat over medium-high heat. Add ginger and garlic; stir-fry about 1 minute or until light brown. Add broccoli, carrots and onion; stir-fry 1 minute.

2. Stir in broth and salt; cover and cook about 3 minutes or until carrots are crisp-tender. Mix cornstarch and cold water; stir into vegetable mixture. Cook and stir about 10 seconds or until thickened.

3. Add remaining ingredients; cook and stir 30 seconds.

4 servings.
1 Serving: Calories 70 (Calories from Fat 10); Fat 1g (Saturated 0g); Cholesterol 0mg; Sodium 580mg; Carbohydrate 10g (Dietary Fiber 3g); Protein 3g
% Daily Value: Vitamin A 100%; Vitamin C 28%; Calcium 2%; Iron 4%
Exchanges: 2 Vegetable
Carbohydrate Choices: ½

BETTY'S TIPS

❂ **Substitution**
Oyster sauce is a thick, brown sauce made from oysters, salt and starch. If oyster sauce isn't available, you can substitute 1 tablespoon soy sauce for the 2 tablespoons oyster sauce.

❂ **Health Twist**
This stir-fry has a lean look. The veggies are cooked in fat-free chicken broth so you get lots of flavor and fiber but no fat.

❂ **Special Touch**
Instead of plain button mushrooms, think a little more exotic for this stir-fry. Try shitake, cremini or brown mushrooms for a different look.

Twice-Baked Potatoes

Prep: 30 min Bake: 1 hr 50 min

8	large baking potatoes
¹⁄₂ to 1	cup milk
¹⁄₂	cup butter or margarine, softened
¹⁄₂	teaspoon salt
	Dash of pepper
2	cups shredded Cheddar cheese (8 ounces)
2	tablespoons chopped fresh chives

1. Heat oven to 350°. Prick potatoes several times with fork to allow steam to escape. Bake 1 hour 15 minutes to 1 hour 30 minutes or until tender.

2. Cut thin slice from top of each potato; scoop out inside, leaving a thin shell. Mash potatoes in 4-quart bowl with potato masher or electric mixer until no lumps remain. Add small amounts of milk, mashing after each addition. (Amount of milk needed to make potatoes smooth and fluffy depends on kind of potatoes.) Add butter, salt and pepper; mash vigorously until potatoes are light and fluffy. Stir in cheese and chives. Fill potato shells with mashed potatoes. Place on ungreased cookie sheet.

3. Increase oven temperature to 400°. Bake about 20 minutes or until hot. Garnish with additional fresh chives if desired.

8 servings.
1 Serving: Calories 355 (Calories from Fat 190); Fat 21g (Saturated 13g); Cholesterol 60mg; Sodium 410mg; Carbohydrate 32g (Dietary Fiber 2g); Protein 11g
% Daily Value: Vitamin A 16%; Vitamin C 16%; Calcium 18%; Iron 4%
Exchanges: 2 Starch, 1 Medium-Fat Meat, 3 Fat
Carbohydrate Choices: 2

Twice-Baked Potatoes

BETTY'S TIPS

✪ **Do-Ahead**
Refrigerate filled potatoes tightly covered up to 48 hours or freeze up to 2 months. To reheat, place on ungreased cookie sheet and bake uncovered in 400° oven 35 to 40 minutes for refrigerated potatoes, or 45 to 50 minutes for frozen potatoes, until hot. To reheat in microwave, arrange potatoes in circle on 10-inch microwavable plate. Cover loosely with plastic wrap and microwave on High 12 to 15 minutes (a few minutes longer if potatoes are frozen), rotating plate one-half turn after 5 minutes, until hot.

Roasted Sweet Potatoes and Onions

Prep: 20 min Bake: 45 min

4 pounds sweet potatoes, peeled and cut into 1¹/₂-inch cubes

2 medium onions, cut into eighths

¹/₄ cup butter or margarine, melted

¹/₄ cup firmly packed brown sugar

¹/₄ cup coarsely chopped pecans

1 teaspoon dried sage leaves

1. Heat oven to 450°. Place sweet potatoes and onions in roasting pan or rectangular pan, 13 × 9 × 2 inches. Drizzle with butter; toss to coat.

2. Bake uncovered 25 to 30 minutes, stirring once, until almost tender. Stir in brown sugar, pecans and sage. Bake 10 to 15 minutes longer or until coated and tender.

16 servings.
1 Serving: Calories 150 (Calories from Fat 35); Fat 4g (Saturated 2g); Cholesterol 10mg; Sodium 30mg; Carbohydrate 26g (Dietary Fiber 3g); Protein 2g
% Daily Value: Vitamin A 100%; Vitamin C 18%; Calcium 2%; Iron 2%
Exchanges: ¹/₂ Starch, ¹/₂ Other Carbohydrate, 1 Fat
Carbohydrate Choices: 2

BETTY'S TIPS

❂ **Success Hint**
Sweet potatoes vary greatly in size. Purchasing them by weight assures the correct amount for this recipe.

❂ **Serve-With**
These toasty roasted sweet potatoes pair perfectly with your Thanksgiving turkey. Cranberry sauce and steamed asparagus make great accompaniments.

❂ **Did You Know?**
Sweet potatoes are usually available with pale or dark orange skin and flesh. The dark orange sweet potatoes are the moister, sweeter and more flavorful of the two, and they are often mistakenly labeled "yams."

Roasted Sweet Potatoes and Onions

Parmesan Potatoes

Prep: 20 min Grill: 23 min

4   medium potatoes, thinly sliced
$^1/_2$ teaspoon salt
$^1/_4$ cup Progresso Italian style bread crumbs
2   tablespoons grated Parmesan cheese
2   tablespoons butter or margarine, melted
1   tablespoon chopped fresh or 1 teaspoon dried basil leaves

1. Heat coals or gas grill for direct heat.

2. Divide potato slices between two 30 × 18-inch sheets of heavy-duty aluminum foil. Sprinkle with salt. Mix remaining ingredients; sprinkle over potatoes. Wrap foil securely around potatoes; pierce top of foil once or twice with fork to vent steam.

3. Cover and grill foil packets, seam side up, 4 to 6 inches from medium heat 18 to 23 minutes, rotating packets once, until potatoes are tender. Place packets on plates; unfold foil.

4 servings.
1 Serving: Calories 225 (Calories from Fat 65); Fat 7g (Saturated 4g); Cholesterol 20mg; Sodium 460mg; Carbohydrate 36g (Dietary Fiber 3g); Protein 5g
% Daily Value: Vitamin A 6%; Vitamin C 12%; Calcium 6%; Iron 12%
Exchanges: 2 Starch, $^1/_2$ Other Carbohydrate, 1 Fat
Carbohydrate Choices: $2^1/_2$

BETTY'S TIPS

✪ Serve-With
Because of their simple, fresh flavor, these potatoes are a perfect accompaniment to grilled steak, pork chops or chicken.

✪ Variation
If the rain drives you inside or you prefer to try these in the oven, simply prepare as directed and bake at 450° for 25 to 30 minutes or until potatoes are tender.

✪ Did You Know?
Italian style bread crumbs are a combination of plain bread crumbs and seasonings that give a subtle Italian flavor. If you want to use your own bread crumbs, add a little onion powder and garlic powder and a dash of dried Italian seasonings.

Parmesan Potatoes

Low Fat

Three-Potato Medley

Prep: 15 min Microwave: 10 min Grill: 15 min

4 small red potatoes, cut into ³/₄-inch pieces

4 small Yukon gold potatoes, cut into ³/₄-inch pieces

1 medium dark-orange sweet potato, peeled and cut into ³/₄-inch pieces

3 tablespoons honey mustard barbecue sauce

1 tablespoon fresh lemon juice

1 tablespoon vegetable oil

1 teaspoon chopped fresh sage, if desired

¹/₂ teaspoon salt

¹/₂ teaspoon green bell pepper, cut into 1-inch pieces

1 large onion, cut into thin wedges

1. Heat coals or gas grill for direct heat. Place all potato pieces in shallow microwavable dish. Cover with microwavable plastic wrap, folding back one edge or corner ¹/₄ inch to vent steam. Microwave on High 8 to 10 minutes, stirring once after 4 minutes, until tender. Cool slightly.

2. Meanwhile, mix barbecue sauce, lemon juice, oil, sage and salt in medium bowl. Stir in potatoes, bell pepper and onion. Place in grill basket.

3. Cover and grill vegetables 4 to 6 inches from medium heat 10 to 15 minutes, stirring 2 or 3 times, until potatoes are tender and lightly browned.

8 servings.
1 Serving: Calories 150 (Calories from Fat 20); Fat 2g (Saturated 0g); Cholesterol 0mg; Sodium 215mg; Carbohydrate 31g (Dietary Fiber 3g); Protein 3g
% Daily Value: Vitamin A 58%; Vitamin C 20%; Calcium 2%; Iron 8%
Exchanges: 1 Starch, 1 Other Carbohydrate
Carbohydrate Choices: 2

BETTY'S TIPS

✿ **Substitution**
The trio of colors and textures of the potatoes is a wonderful medley. Russet potatoes or other varieties may be substituted for the Yukon gold potatoes.

✿ **Serve-With**
The hearty flavor of this delicious side dish makes it a terrific choice for grilled steak or pork chops.

✿ **Did You Know?**
Sage has long been used for medicinal purposes as well as for cooking. This pungent herb with its musty aroma is a nice complement to the homey, earthy potatoes.

Three-Potato Medley

Bake Sale Favorites

Cookies, Brownies and Bars to Bake and Take

Lemon Fruit Squares (page 229)

Peanut Butter Cupcakes with Chocolate Frosting (page 240)

Grasshopper Dessert Squares

Prep: 15 min Refrigerate: 45 min Freeze: 4 hr

1¹⁄₂   cups chocolate cookie crumbs (from 15-ounce package)

¹⁄₄   cup sugar

6   tablespoons butter or margarine, melted

2   packages (8 ounces each) cream cheese, cubed and softened

¹⁄₃   cup green crème de menthe liqueur

¹⁄₄   cup white crème de cacao liqueur

1¹⁄₂   jars (7 ounces each) marshmallow creme

1¹⁄₂   cups whipping (heavy) cream

1. Line rectangular pan, 13 × 9 × 2 inches, with aluminum foil so edges of foil extend over sides of pan; spray with cooking spray. Mix cookie crumbs, sugar and butter in pan. Press evenly in bottom of pan.

2. Beat cream cheese, crème de menthe and crème de cacao in large bowl with electric mixer on medium speed until smooth. Add marshmallow creme; beat until smooth. Refrigerate about 45 minutes or until mixture mounds when dropped from a spoon.

3. Beat whipping cream in chilled large bowl on high speed until stiff peaks form. Fold whipped cream into marshmallow mixture until blended. Pour over crust. Freeze about 4 hours or until firm.

4. Remove from pan, using foil to lift. Let dessert stand at room temperature 10 minutes before cutting.

16 servings.
1 Serving: Calories 355 (Calories from Fat 235); Fat 26g (Saturated 16g); Cholesterol 75mg; Sodium 190mg; Carbohydrate 26g (Dietary Fiber 0g); Protein 4
% Daily Value: Vitamin A 18%; Vitamin C 0%; Calcium 4%; Iron 4%
Exchanges: 1 Starch, 1 Other Carbohydrate, 5 Fat
Carbohydrate Choices: 2

BETTY'S TIPS

⊗ **Substitution**
You can use ²⁄₃ cup crème de menthe syrup in place of the liqueurs in this recipe. The mint flavor will be slightly subtle but still very wonderful. You'll find the syrup in the ice cream toppings section of your local supermarket.

⊗ **Success Hint**
To easily scoop the marshmallow creme out of the jars, lightly spray a rubber scraper with cooking spray. The sticky marshmallow won't stick quite as much.

⊗ **Special Touch**
Top each serving of this minty dessert with a dollop of whipped cream and chopped chocolate mint candies.

Grasshopper Dessert Squares

Lemon Fruit Squares

Prep: 15 min Bake: 25 min Cool: 30 min
(Photo on page 227)

1 1/2 cups Gold Medal all-purpose flour

3/4 cup butter or margarine, cut into pieces

1/3 cup powdered sugar

2 tablespoons grated lemon peel

1 cup whipping (heavy) cream

3 tablespoons powdered sugar

2 containers (6 ounces each) Yoplait® Original lemon yogurt

2 nectarines, sliced

1 cup fresh blackberries

1. Heat oven to 350°. Mix flour, butter, 1/3 cup powdered sugar and 1 tablespoon lemon peel in medium bowl, using pastry blender or crisscrossing 2 knives, until coarse crumbs form. Press mixture evenly on bottom of rectangular pan, 13 × 9 × 2 inches.

2. Bake 20 to 25 minutes or until crust is dry and light golden brown. Cool completely, about 30 minutes.

3. Beat whipping cream, 3 tablespoons powdered sugar and remaining 1 tablespoon lemon peel in chilled medium bowl with electric mixer on high speed until stiff peaks form. Fold in yogurt. Spoon over crust. Top with nectarines and blackberries. Serve immediately, or cover and refrigerate until serving.

4. For serving pieces, cut into 5 rows by 4 rows. Store covered in refrigerator.

20 squares.
1 Square: Calories 175 (Calories from Fat 100); Fat 11g (Saturated 7g); Cholesterol 30mg; Sodium 60mg; Carbohydrate 17g (Dietary Fiber 1g); Protein 2g
% Daily Value: Vitamin A 8%; Vitamin C 2%; Calcium 4%; Iron 2%
Exchanges: 1/2 Starch, 1/2 Fruit, 2 Fat
Carbohydrate Choices: 1

BETTY'S TIPS

✤ Success Hint
Line pan with heavy-duty aluminum foil, leaving at least 3 inches around all edges. The foil serves as a handle for lifting the dessert out of the pan, so cutting and serving will be easier. Be sure to use butter or margarine, not a vegetable oil spread. Spreads contain less fat than butter or margarine and will not give the same results.

✤ Special Touch
Garnish each serving with a mint leaf or lemon balm leaf.

Chocolate Chunk Blondies

Prep: 10 min Bake: 22 min Cool: 1 hr Stand: 30 min

1 package Betty Crocker SuperMoist® French vanilla cake mix

$\frac{1}{2}$ cup butter or margarine, melted

2 eggs

1 cup semisweet chocolate chunks (from 11.5-ounce bag)

$\frac{1}{3}$ cup Betty Crocker Rich & Creamy® chocolate ready-to-spread frosting

1. Heat oven to 350° (325° for dark or nonstick pans). Grease bottom only of rectangular pan, 13 × 8 × 2 inches, with shortening, or spray bottom with cooking spray.

2. Mix cake mix, butter and eggs in large bowl with spoon. Stir in chocolate chunks. Spread evenly in pan.

3. Bake 20 to 22 minutes or until edges are golden brown. Cool completely, about 1 hour.

4. Microwave frosting in small microwavable bowl uncovered on High 20 to 25 seconds or until melted; stir. Drizzle over bars. Let stand about 30 minutes or until frosting is set. For bars, cut into 6 rows by 4 rows.

2 dozen bars.
1 Bar: Calories 185 (Calories from Fat 80); Fat 9g (Saturated 5g); Cholesterol 30mg; Sodium 180mg; Carbohydrate 24g (Dietary Fiber 1g); Protein 2g
% Daily Value: Vitamin A 2%; Vitamin C 0%; Calcium 2%; Iron 4%
Exchanges: 1 Starch, $\frac{1}{2}$ Other Carbohydrate, $1\frac{1}{2}$ Fat
Carbohydrate Choices: $1\frac{1}{2}$

BETTY'S TIPS

⊘ Substitution
Like chips instead of chunks? Semisweet chocolate chips can be substituted for the chocolate chunks.

⊘ Variation
Walnuts and chocolate taste great together, so why not add $\frac{1}{2}$ cup chopped walnuts with the chocolate chunks? Or instead of walnuts, try $\frac{1}{2}$ cup dried cherries.

⊘ Special Touch
For a different look, cut the bars into triangles. To make triangles, cut bars into 6 rows by 2 rows, then cut each bar diagonally in half to form triangles.

Chocolate Chunk Blondies

Low Fat
Graham and Fruit Bars

Prep: 15 min Bake: 25 min Cool: 15 min

$^2/_3$ cup Gold Medal all-purpose flour

2 cups Golden Grahams® cereal, crushed (1 cup)

$^1/_2$ cup packed brown sugar

$^1/_2$ teaspoon ground cinnamon

$^1/_3$ cup butter or margarine, melted

$^2/_3$ cup apricot jam or preserves

1. Heat oven to 350°. Mix flour, cereal, brown sugar and cinnamon in medium bowl. Stir in butter until well blended. Reserve $^3/_4$ cup of the cereal mixture. Press remaining cereal mixture in bottom of square pan, 8 × 8 × 2 inches.

2. Spread jam over cereal mixture. Sprinkle with reserved cereal mixture.

3. Bake 23 to 25 minutes or until top is light golden brown and jam is bubbling. Cool 15 minutes before cutting. For bars, cut into 6 rows by 4 rows.

24 bars.
1 Bar: Calories 95 (Calories from Fat 25); Fat 3g (Saturated 2g); Cholesterol 5mg; Sodium 50mg; Carbohydrate 16g (Dietary Fiber 0g); Protein 1g
% Daily Value: Vitamin A 4%; Vitamin C 2%; Calcium 0%; Iron 4%
Exchanges: $^1/_2$ Starch, $^1/_2$ Other Carbohydrate, $^1/_2$ Fat
Carbohydrate Choices: 1

BETTY'S TIPS

⊗ **Substitution**
For a different flavor, try $^1/_4$ teaspoon ground nutmeg in place of the $^1/_2$ teaspoon cinnamon.

⊗ **Success Hint**
Bars can be covered and stored in a cool place for 3 to 4 days.

Graham and Fruit Bars

Chocolate and Caramel Oatmeal Bars

Prep: 20 min Bake: 43 min Cool: 2 hr

1 package Betty Crocker SuperMoist yellow cake mix
1 cup butter or margarine, softened
1 egg
2 cups quick-cooking oats
1½ cups semisweet chocolate chips
1 cup chopped walnuts or pecans
1 jar (12.25 ounces) caramel topping (1 cup)
3 tablespoons Gold Medal all-purpose flour

1. Heat oven to 350°. Line bottom and sides of rectangular pan, 13 × 9 × 2 inches, with aluminum foil. Spray foil with cooking spray.

2. Beat cake mix, butter and egg in large bowl with electric mixer on low speed about 1 minute or just until crumbly. Stir in oats, using hands if necessary. Reserve 1½ cups oat mixture. Press remaining oat mixture in bottom of pan. Bake 14 to 18 minutes or until light golden brown.

3. Sprinkle chocolate chips and walnuts over hot crust. Mix caramel topping and flour in small bowl; drizzle evenly over chocolate chips and walnuts. Sprinkle reserved oat mixture over top.

4. Bake 20 to 25 minutes or until golden brown. Cool completely, about 2 hours. For bars, cut into 6 rows by 4 rows.

2 dozen bars.
1 Bar: Calories 345 (Calories from Fat 155); Fat 17g (Saturated 8g); Cholesterol 30mg; Sodium 280mg; Carbohydrate 44g (Dietary Fiber 2g); Protein 4g
% Daily Value: Vitamin A 6%; Vitamin C 0%; Calcium 4%; Iron 6%
Exchanges: 1 Starch, 2 Other Carbohydrate, 3 Fat
Carbohydrate Choices: 3

BETTY'S TIPS

⊙ **Success Hint**
Be sure to check your oats to see if they are the quick-cooking kind. Don't use instant oatmeal, which will become mushy when it's baked in dough. It's best to bake bars in the exact pan size called for in a recipe. Bars baked in a pan that is too large will overbake and be hard. Those baked in a pan that's too small can be doughy in the center and hard on the edges.

⊙ **Variation**
Not a nut lover? Go ahead and leave them out. The bars will be just as gooey and delicious.

Chocolate and Caramel Oatmeal Bars

Caramel Brownies

Prep: 30 min Bake: 40 min Cool: 2 hr
(Photo on page iii)

- 1 bag (14 ounces) caramels
- 1/4 cup milk
- 1 package Betty Crocker Original Supreme® brownie mix (with chocolate syrup pouch)
- 1/4 cup water
- 1/3 cup vegetable oil
- 2 eggs
- 1 bag (6 ounces) semisweet chocolate chips (1 cup)
- 1 cup coarsely chopped nuts

1. Heat oven to 350°. Grease bottom only of rectangular pan, 13 × 9 × 2 inches, with shortening, or spray bottom with cooking spray. Heat caramels and milk in 1 1/2-quart saucepan over low heat, stirring frequently, until melted and smooth.

2. Stir brownie mix, chocolate syrup, water, oil and eggs in medium bowl until well blended. Spread in pan. Drizzle caramel mixture evenly over batter. Sprinkle with chocolate chips and nuts.

3. Bake 35 to 40 minutes or until edges are set. Cool completely, about 2 hours. For brownies, cut into 8 rows by 6 rows. Store covered at room temperature.

48 brownies.
1 Brownie: Calories 205 (Calories from Fat 100); Fat 11g (Saturated 4g); Cholesterol 20mg; Sodium 30mg; Carbohydrate 24g (Dietary Fiber 1g); Protein 2g
% Daily Value: Vitamin A 0%; Vitamin C 0%; Calcium 2%; Iron 4%
Exchanges: 1 Starch, 1/2 Other Carbohydrate, 2 Fat
Carbohydrate Choices: 1 1/2

BETTY'S TIPS

⚙ **Success Hint**
Use your favorite type of nut for these decadent brownies. For a tropical twist, try macadamia nuts or a cashew-macadamia mix. Pecans will lend a hint of southern flavor. For super-easy cleanup, line your baking pan with aluminum foil that is longer than the pan. Spray the bottom of the foil as directed. When brownies are cool, lift them out of the pan by the foil "handles," peel back foil and cut.

Chex® and O's Snackin' Bars

Prep: 10 min Cook: 5 min Cool: 30 min
(Photo on page xii)

- 3 cups Corn Chex cereal
- 3 cups Cheerios® cereal
- 1 package (7 ounces) mixed dried fruit
- 1 cup dried pineapple, chopped
- 1/4 cup butter or margarine
- 3/4 cup packed brown sugar
- 2 tablespoons Gold Medal all-purpose flour
- 1/2 cup light corn syrup

1. Spray rectangular pan, 13 × 9 × 2 inches, with cooking spray. Mix cereals, dried fruit and pineapple in large heatproof bowl.

2. Melt butter in 2-quart saucepan over medium heat. Stir in brown sugar, flour and corn syrup. Heat to boiling, stirring constantly. Boil 1 minute over medium heat, stirring occasionally. Pour over cereal mixture; toss to mix well (mixture will be sticky).

3. Spoon cereal mixture into pan; spread evenly. Cool completely, about 30 minutes, before cutting. For bars, cut into 6 rows by 6 rows.

3 dozen bars.
1 Bar: Calories 95 (Calories from Fat 20); Fat 2g (Saturated 1g); Cholesterol 5mg; Sodium 65mg; Carbohydrate 18g (Dietary Fiber 1g); Protein 1g
% Daily Value: Vitamin A 4%; Vitamin C 2%; Calcium 2%; Iron 10%
Exchanges: 1/2 Starch, 1/2 Fruit, 1/2 Fat
Carbohydrate Choices: 1

Double-Chocolate Candy Cashew Bars

Prep: 10 min Bake: 35 min Cool: 2 hr

1 package (18 ounces) refrigerated chocolate chunk cookie dough
1 cup white baking chips
1¹/₂ cups cashew halves and pieces
¹/₂ cup caramel topping
1 tablespoon Gold Medal all-purpose flour
¹/₂ cup miniature candy-coated milk chocolate baking bits (from 12-ounce bag)

1. Heat oven to 350°. Spray rectangular pan, 13 × 9 × 2 inches, with cooking spray. Cut cookie dough into ¹/₂-inch slices. Arrange slices in bottom of pan. Press dough evenly to form crust. Bake 10 to 15 minutes or until light golden brown.

2. Sprinkle white baking chips and cashews over warm crust. Mix caramel topping and flour in small bowl until smooth; drizzle over baking chips and cashews. Sprinkle with candy-coated baking bits; press lightly.

3. Bake 15 to 20 minutes or until topping is bubbly. Cool completely, 1 hour 30 minutes to 2 hours, before cutting. For bars, cut into 6 rows by 6 rows.

3 dozen bars.
1 Bar: Calories 175 (Calories from Fat 80); Fat 9g (Saturated 3g); Cholesterol 5mg; Sodium 115mg; Carbohydrate 21g (Dietary Fiber 1g); Protein 3g
% Daily Value: Vitamin A 0%; Vitamin C 0%; Calcium 2%; Iron 4%
Exchanges: ¹/₂ Fruit, 1¹/₂ Fat
Carbohydrate Choices: 1¹/₂

Mocha-Toffee Chocolate Cookies

Prep: 15 min Bake: 10 min Cool: 1 min

4 teaspoons instant espresso coffee (dry)
2 teaspoons vanilla extract
1 package Betty Crocker SuperMoist butter recipe chocolate cake mix
¹/₂ cup butter or margarine, softened
2 eggs
1 cup miniature semisweet chocolate chips
¹/₂ cup English toffee bits

1. Heat oven to 350°. Stir together coffee and vanilla in small bowl until coffee is dissolved. Mix cake mix, coffee mixture, butter and eggs in large bowl with spoon until soft dough forms. Stir in chocolate chips and toffee bits.

2. Drop dough by rounded teaspoonfuls about 2 inches apart onto ungreased cookie sheet.

3. Bake 7 to 10 minutes or until surface appears dry. Cool 1 minute; remove from cookie sheet to wire rack.

About 5 dozen cookies.
1 Cookie: Calories 95 (Calories from Fat 45); Fat 5g (Saturated 2g); Cholesterol 15mg; Sodium 95mg; Carbohydrate 11g (Dietary Fiber 0g); Protein 1g
% Daily Value: Vitamin A 2%; Vitamin C 0%; Calcium 0%; Iron 2%
Exchanges: ¹/₂ Starch, ¹/₂ Other Carbohydrate, ¹/₂ Fat
Carbohydrate Choices: 1

BETTY'S TIPS

☺ **Substitution**
For a milder coffee flavor, substitute regular instant coffee granules for the instant espresso.

☺ **Special Touch**
Coffee lovers may enjoy a little extra jolt by gently pressing one chocolate-covered coffee bean into the center of dough for each cookie before baking.

☺ **Did You Know?**
English toffee bits can become rancid, so it's a great idea to taste a few before adding them to the cookie dough.

Double-Chocolate Candy Cashew Bars

Mocha-Toffee Chocolate Cookies

Cookies 'n Creme Brownies

Prep: 25 min Bake: 30 min Cool: 1 hr 30 min

1   package (1 pound 3.8 ounces) Betty Crocker fudge brownie mix

¹⁄₄ cup water

¹⁄₂ cup vegetable oil

2   eggs

1   cup coarsely chopped creme-filled chocolate sandwich cookies (about 7 cookies)

¹⁄₂ cup powdered sugar

2 to 4   teaspoons milk

1. Heat oven to 350°. Grease bottom only of rectangular pan, 13 × 9 × 2 inches, with shortening, or spray bottom with cooking spray. Stir brownie mix, water, oil and eggs in large bowl until well blended. Spread in pan. Sprinkle cookies over batter.

2. Bake 28 to 30 minutes or until toothpick inserted 2 inches from side of pan comes out almost clean. Cool completely, about 1 hour 30 minutes.

3. Stir together powdered sugar and milk in small bowl until smooth and thin enough to drizzle. Drizzle over brownies. For brownies, cut into 5 rows by 4 rows. Store covered at room temperature.

20 brownies.
1 Brownie: Calories 340 (Calories from Fat 160); Fat 18g (Saturated 5g); Cholesterol 45mg; Sodium 40mg; Carbohydrate 41g (Dietary Fiber 2g); Protein 4g
% Daily Value: Vitamin A 0%; Vitamin C 0%; Calcium 2%; Iron 6%
Exchanges: 1 Starch, 2 Other Carbohydrates, 3 Fat
Carbohydrate Choices: 3

BETTY'S TIPS

☺ **Substitution**
With the variety of cookies available, you can easily substitute mint-flavored chocolate sandwich cookies, peanut butter chocolate sandwich cookies or double chocolate cookies to suit your taste.

☺ **Variation**
If you'd like to make Cookies 'n Creme Brownie Sundaes, omit the glaze and top warm brownies with a scoop of vanilla ice cream (or your personal favorite) and drizzle with chocolate sauce or warm hot fudge sauce.

Cookies 'n Creme Brownies

Peanut Butter Swirl Brownies

Prep: 15 min Microwave: 30 sec Bake: 34 min Cool: 1 hr

1/2 cup peanut butter chips

1 package (3 ounces) cream cheese, softened

1/4 cup sugar

1 egg

1 package Betty Crocker Supreme® chocolate chunk brownie mix

3 tablespoons water

1/2 cup vegetable oil

2 eggs

1. Heat oven to 350°. Grease bottom only of rectangular pan, 13 × 9 × 2 inches, with shortening.

2. Place peanut butter chips in small microwavable bowl. Microwave uncovered on High 30 seconds, stir until chips are melted. Stir in cream cheese, sugar and 1 egg until smooth; set aside.

3. Stir brownie mix, water, oil and 2 eggs in medium bowl about 50 strokes or until well blended. Spread two-thirds batter in pan. Spread peanut butter mixture over batter in pan. Drop remaining batter by tablespoonfuls onto peanut butter mixture; swirl lightly with spatula for marbled design.

4. Bake 30 to 34 minutes or until edges begin to pull away from sides of pan. Cool completely, about 1 hour. For brownies, cut into 6 rows by 3 rows or 6 rows by 4 rows. Store tightly covered.

18 to 24 brownies.
1 Brownie: Calories 265 (Calories from Fat 125); Fat 14g (Saturated 5g); Cholesterol 40mg; Sodium 140mg; Carbohydrate 32g (Dietary Fiber 0g); Protein 3g
% Daily Value: Vitamin A 2%; Vitamin C 0%; Calcium 2%; Iron 6%
 Exchanges: 1 Starch, 1 Fruit, 3 Fat
Carbohydrate Choices: 2

BETTY'S TIPS

⚙ **Success Hint**
Be sure not to overbake brownies because the edges will become hard and dry. No peanut butter chips on hand? Butterscotch chips will work just as well and taste great, too.

⚙ **Serve-With**
A scoop of ice cream or frozen yogurt goes great with these decadent brownies.

Peanut Butter Swirl Brownies

Raspberry Cheesecake Bars

Raspberry Cheesecake Bars

Prep: 10 min Bake: 40 min Cool: 1 hr Chill: 4 hr

2 cups Gold Medal all-purpose flour

$^1/_2$ cup powdered sugar

$^2/_3$ cup firm butter or margarine

2 packages (8 ounces each) cream cheese, softened

$^1/_2$ cup granulated sugar

2 eggs

1 package (10 ounces) frozen raspberries in syrup, thawed and undrained

Fresh raspberries, if desired

1. Heat oven to 350°. Mix flour and powdered sugar in medium bowl. Cut in butter, using pastry blender or crisscrossing 2 knives, until mixture resembles fine crumbs. Press firmly and evenly in bottom of ungreased rectangular pan, 13 × 9 × 2 inches. Bake 15 minutes.

2. Beat cream cheese in medium bowl with electric mixer on medium-high speed until smooth and fluffy. Beat in granulated sugar and eggs. Stir in raspberries (with syrup). Spread cream cheese mixture over baked crust.

3. Bake 20 to 25 minutes or just until center is set. Cool completely, about 1 hour. Cover loosely and refrigerate about 4 hours or until firm. For bars, cut into 6 rows by 6 rows. Garnish with fresh raspberries. Store covered in refrigerator.

About 3 dozen bars.
1 Bar: Calories 130 (Calories from Fat 70); Fat 8g (Saturated 5g); Cholesterol 35mg; Sodium 65mg; Carbohydrate 12g (Dietary Fiber 1g); Protein 2g
% Daily Value: Vitamin A 6%; Vitamin C 0%; Calcium 0%; Iron 2%
Exchanges: $^1/_2$ Starch, $^1/_2$ Fruit, $1^1/_2$ Fat
Carbohydrate Choices: 1

BETTY'S TIPS

✿ **Substitution**
A package of frozen strawberries can be used instead of the raspberries.

✿ **Do-Ahead**
These rich bars can be made up to two days ahead of time. To transport, place the bars in a sturdy plastic container with a lid, then place in a cooler.

Peanut Butter Cupcakes with Chocolate Frosting

Prep: 40 min Bake: 25 min Cool: 30 min
(Photo on page 227)

1   package Betty Crocker SuperMoist yellow cake mix
1¼ cups water
¼   cup vegetable oil
3   eggs
¾   cup creamy peanut butter
1   tub Betty Crocker Rich & Creamy chocolate ready-to-spread frosting
¼   cup creamy peanut butter
⅓   cup chopped peanuts

1. Heat oven to 350°. Line 30 medium muffin cups, 2½ × 1¼ inches, with paper baking cups. Beat cake mix, water, oil, eggs and ¾ cup peanut butter in large bowl with electric mixer on low speed 30 seconds. Beat on medium speed 2 minutes, scraping bowl occasionally. Fill cups ⅔ full with batter.

2. Bake 20 to 25 minutes or until toothpick inserted in center comes out clean. Remove from pan to wire rack. Cool completely, about 30 minutes.

3. Stir together frosting and ¼ cup peanut butter in medium bowl. Frost cupcakes with frosting mixture. Sprinkle with peanuts; press lightly into frosting.

30 cupcakes.
1 Cupcake: Calories 235 (Calories from Fat 115); Fat 13g (Saturated 5g); Cholesterol 20mg; Sodium 170mg; Carbohydrate 25g (Dietary Fiber 1g); Protein 4g
% Daily Value: Vitamin A 0%; Vitamin C 0%; Calcium 2%; Iron 4%
Exchanges: 1 Starch, ½ Other Carbohydrate, 2½ Fat
Carbohydrate Choices: 1½

BETTY'S TIPS

⊛ **Substitution**
Betty Crocker Rich & Creamy cream cheese ready-to-spread frosting can be substituted for the chocolate frosting.

⊛ **Success Hint**
Using an ice cream scoop is an easy way to fill muffin cups. Use one that measures about ⅓ cup of batter.

⊛ **Variation**
If you don't want to chop peanuts, look for a chopped nut mix in the baking section of the supermarket. The package size is usually ½ cup and contains a mix of nuts including peanuts.

Easy Raspberry Brownie Wedges

Prep: 10 min Bake: 50 min Cool: 1 hr

3 cups raspberries

1 package (19.8 ounces) Betty Crocker fudge brownie mix

$^1/_2$ cup vegetable oil

2 eggs

$^1/_2$ cup whipping (heavy) cream

1 tablespoon sugar

Easy Raspberry Brownie Wedges

1. Heat oven to 350°. Spray pie plate, 9 × 1$^1/_4$ inches, with cooking spray.

2. Mash 1 cup of the raspberries, using fork. Stir mashed raspberries, brownie mix, oil and eggs in large bowl until blended. Stir in $^1/_2$ cup whole raspberries. Spread in pie plate.

3. Bake 45 to 50 minutes or until toothpick inserted 2 inches from side of pie plate comes out almost clean. Cool completely, at least 1 hour.

4. Beat whipping cream and sugar in chilled small bowl with electric mixer on high speed until soft peaks form. Serve brownie wedges with whipped cream and remaining 1$^1/_2$ cups raspberries.

12 servings.
1 Serving: Calories 535 (Calories from Fat 290); Fat 32g (Saturated 11g); Cholesterol 85mg; Sodium 30mg; Carbohydrate 63g (Dietary Fiber 5g); Protein 6g
% Daily Value: Vitamin A 4%; Vitamin C 12%; Calcium 4%; Iron 12%
Exchanges: 2 Starch, $^1/_2$ Fruit, 1$^1/_2$ Other Carbohydrate, 6 Fat
Carbohydrate Choices: 4

BETTY'S TIPS

⊛ **Time-Saver**
When time is at a premium, omit the whipping cream and sugar and top brownies with frozen (thawed) whipped topping or canned whipped cream topping.

⊛ **Do-Ahead**
Make the brownies ahead and cool completely, then wrap in foil until ready to use. For longer storage, freeze the brownies.

⊛ **Special Touch**
Delicious red raspberries work best in this dessert, but if you have golden raspberries, mix them with red raspberries for the garnish.

Betty Crocker
MAKES IT EASY

Cookies and Cream Bonbons

Prep: 25 min Bake: 10 min Cool: 21 min

1	package Betty Crocker SuperMoist devil's food cake mix
$^1/_4$	cup vegetable oil
2	eggs
18	foil-wrapped white chocolate candies with chocolate cookie bits (from 12-ounce bag), unwrapped
	White and Dark Chocolate Glazes (below)

1. Heat oven to 350°. Lightly grease cookie sheet with shortening, or spray with cooking spray. Mix cake mix, oil and eggs in large bowl with spoon until dough forms (some dry mix will remain). Cut each candy crosswise in half.

2. Shape one level measuring tablespoon of dough around each candy half, covering completely. Place 2 inches apart on cookie sheet.

3. Bake 7 to 10 minutes or until cookies begin to look dry and cracked on surface. Cool 1 minute; remove from cookie sheet to wire rack. Cool completely, about 20 minutes.

4. Make White and Dark Chocolate Glazes. Place each glaze in separate resealable plastic food-storage bags. Cut small tip from one corner of each bag. Drizzle glazes over cookies.

3 dozen cookies.

White and Dark Chocolate Glazes

1	ounce white baking bar (white chocolate) or vanilla-flavored candy coating
1	teaspoon vegetable oil
2	tablespoons semisweet chocolate chips

Microwave white baking bar and $^1/_2$ teaspoon oil in small microwavable bowl uncovered on High 20 to 30 seconds; stir until melted and smooth. In another small bowl, microwave chocolate chips and remaining $^1/_2$ teaspoon oil uncovered on High 20 to 30 seconds; stir until melted and smooth.

1 Cookie: Calories 110 (Calories from Fat 45); Fat 5g (Saturated 2g); Cholesterol 15mg; Sodium 140mg; Carbohydrate 15g (Dietary Fiber 1g); Protein 1g
% Daily Value: Vitamin A 0%; Vitamin C 0%; Calcium 2%; Iron 2%
Exchanges: $^1/_2$ Starch, $^1/_2$ Other Carbohydrate, 1 Fat
Carbohydrate Choices: 1

Cut candy crosswise in half.

Shape dough around candy half.

Cookies and Cream Bonbons

Snickerdoodles

Prep: 20 min Bake: 12 min

1 package Betty Crocker SuperMoist white cake mix

$1/4$ cup vegetable oil

2 eggs

2 tablespoons sugar

1 teaspoon ground cinnamon

1. Heat oven to 350°. Mix cake mix, oil and eggs in large bowl with spoon until dough forms (some dry mix will remain).

2. Shape dough into 1-inch balls. Mix sugar and cinnamon in small bowl. Roll balls in cinnamon-sugar mixture. Place about 2 inches apart on ungreased cookie sheet.

3. Bake 10 to 12 minutes or until set. Remove from cookie sheet to wire rack.

About 4 dozen cookies.
1 Cookie: Calories 60 (Calories from Fat 20); Fat 2g (Saturated 1g); Cholesterol 10mg; Sodium 80mg; Carbohydrate 9g (Dietary Fiber 0g); Protein 1g
% Daily Value: Vitamin A 0%; Vitamin C 0%; Calcium 0%; Iron 0%
Exchanges: $1/2$ Starch, $1/2$ Fat
Carbohydrate Choices: $1/2$

BETTY'S TIPS

⊛ **Substitution**
French vanilla cake mix is a great stand-in for the white cake mix.

⊛ **Variation**
For **Super Snickerdoodles,** shape dough into $1/2$-inch balls and place them 3 inches apart on the cookie sheet; bake 12 to 14 minutes. You'll get about 26 large cookies.

⊛ **Did You Know?**
This sweet little cookie with the whimsical name originated in 19th-century New England and has become an American classic. In this recipe, cake mix provides convenience to the traditional version, but the method of rolling the dough in sugar and cinnamon before baking has been kept.

Snickerdoodles

Dreamy Desserts

Cakes, Pies and More to Treat Your Friends and Family

Chocolate Silk Pecan Pie (page 255)

Peach and Raspberry Cobbler (page 268)

Tropical Fruit Dip for Cookies and Fruit

Prep: 15 min
(Photo on page x)

1	cup vanilla yogurt
1/4	cup flaked coconut, toasted if desired
1	can (8 ounces) crushed pineapple in juice, drained
2	tablespoons packed brown sugar
2	nectarines, sliced
16	strawberries
8	small bunches grapes
16	fudge-striped cookies

1. Mix yogurt, coconut, pineapple and brown sugar.

2. Serve dip immediately with fruit and cookies, or cover and refrigerate at least 1 hour.

8 servings.
1 Serving: Calories 235 (Calories from Fat 65); Fat 7g (Saturated 6g); Cholesterol 0mg; Sodium 100mg; Carbohydrate 40g (Dietary Fiber 3g); Protein 3g
% Daily Value: Vitamin A 2%; Vitamin C 32%; Calcium 6%; Iron 4%
Exchanges: 1 Starch, 2 Fruit, 1 Fat
Carbohydrate Choices: 2 1/2

BETTY'S TIPS

❁ **Variation**
If you like, substitute Yoplait Original Key Lime Pie yogurt for the vanilla yogurt. With this snack, you can have your fruit and cookies, too! Dunk any fruit or cookies you desire into this tasty, tropical dip.

Grilled Caramel Apples

Prep: 10 min Grill: 9 min
(Photo on page viii)

2	large apples
1/2	cup caramel topping

1. Heat coals or gas grill for direct heat. Fold four 18 × 12-inch pieces heavy-duty aluminum foil crosswise in half; spray with cooking spray. Cut apples in half; remove cores. Cut each half into 4 wedges.

2. Place 4 apple wedges in center of each piece of foil. Drizzle 2 tablespoons caramel topping over apple wedges on each piece of foil. Wrap foil securely around apples.

3. Grill foil packets, seam sides up, 5 to 6 inches from medium-low heat 8 to 9 minutes or until apples are crisp-tender. Open packets carefully to avoid steam; caramel will be hot. Serve immediately.

4 servings.
1 Serving: Calories 175 (Calories from Fat 0); Fat 0g (Saturated 0g); Cholesterol 0mg; Sodium 140mg; Carbohydrate 43g (Dietary Fiber 3g); Protein 1g
% Daily Value: Vitamin A 0%; Vitamin C 4%; Calcium 2%; Iron 2%
Exchanges: 1 Fruit, 2 Other Carbohydrate
Carbohydrate Choices: 3

BETTY'S TIPS

❁ **Success Hint**
Check out local varieties of late-summer apples at your farmers' market. Most vendors will let you taste a sample so you can choose your favorite. Be sure to ask for cooking apples, which work best for this recipe. Cortland, Golden Delicious and Granny Smith would be good choices available at the supermarket.

❁ **Special Touch**
Sprinkle a few chopped peanuts over the gooey caramel and apples.

Quick

Strawberries with Cheesecake Cream

Prep: 15 min Bake: 5 min

10   vanilla wafer cookies

2   teaspoons butter, melted

$^1/_2$ cup soft cream cheese (from 8-ounce tub)

6   tablespoons sugar

3   tablespoons milk

1   tablespoon orange juice

1   teaspoon orange-flavored liqueur, if desired

1   quart fresh strawberries, sliced (3 cups)

1. Heat oven to 350°. Place cookies in blender. Cover and blend on high speed until finely crushed. Mix cookie crumbs and butter in small bowl; spread on ungreased cookie sheet. Bake about 5 minutes or until golden brown.

2. Beat remaining ingredients except strawberries in large bowl with electric mixer on medium speed until smooth.

3. Divide strawberries among 4 large wine glasses or individual dessert dishes. Top each with about $^1/_4$ cup cream cheese mixture; sprinkle each with 2 tablespoons crumbs.

4 servings.
1 Serving: Calories 280 (Calories from Fat 110); Fat 12g (Saturated 6g); Cholesterol 30mg; Sodium 125mg; Carbohydrate 39g (Dietary Fiber 4g); Protein 4g
% Daily Value: Vitamin A 8%; Vitamin C 100%; Calcium 6%; Iron 6%
Exchanges: 1 Starch, 1$^1/_2$ Fruit, 2$^1/_2$ Fat
Carbohydrate Choices: 2$^1/_2$

BETTY'S TIPS

❂ **Substitution**
You can use raspberries or a combination of your favorite berries in this elegant dessert instead of just strawberries.

❂ **Success Hint**
Keep strawberries at their freshest by waiting to wash them gently until just before you hull them. As strawberries absorb water, they begin to lose flavor.

❂ **Did You Know?**
Liqueurs were originally used as an aid to digestion. Liqueurs are more frequently used in cooking today, especially in desserts. Orange-flavored liqueur may be found under several brand names.

Strawberries with Cheesecake Cream

Easy Orange-Cranberry Dessert

Prep: 15 min Refrigerate: 3 hr

1 package (3 ounces) vanilla pudding and pie filling mix (not instant)

2 cups milk

1 cup whipping (heavy) cream

1 tablespoon powdered sugar

1 package (10.65 ounces) frozen pound cake, thawed

1/4 cup orange-flavored liqueur or orange juice

3/4 cup frozen cranberry-orange sauce (from 12-ounce container), thawed

1 cup fresh raspberries

1 can (11 ounces) mandarin orange segments, drained

Additional fresh raspberries, if desired

1. Mix pudding mix and milk in 2-quart saucepan. Heat to boiling over medium heat, stirring constantly; remove from heat. Place plastic wrap directly on pudding. Refrigerate 2 hours or until completely cooled.

2. Beat whipping cream in chilled small bowl with electric mixer on high speed until soft peaks form. Add powdered sugar; beat until stiff peaks form. Fold 1/2 cup of the whipped cream into the pudding.

3. Cut pound cake into 1/2-inch slices; cut each slice crosswise in half. Arrange about one-third of the cake pieces in bottom of bowl with slanted side, or arrange one-half of the cake pieces in bottom of bowl with straight side. Sprinkle with 2 tablespoons of the liqueur. Spread about one-third or one-half of the cranberry-orange sauce over cake pieces. Top with half each of the raspberries and orange segments. Spoon 1 cup of the pudding mixture over fruit. Repeat layers with remaining cake, liqueur, cranberry-orange sauce, raspberries, orange segments and pudding mixture. Top with remaining whipped cream. Refrigerate 1 hour before serving. Garnish with additional raspberries.

12 servings.
1 Serving: Calories 280 (Calories from Fat 125); Fat 14g (Saturated 7g); Cholesterol 55mg; Sodium 100mg; Carbohydrate 24g (Dietary Fiber 2g); Protein 4g
% Daily Value: Vitamin A 8%; Vitamin C 24%; Calcium 8%; Iron 4%
Exchanges: 1 Starch, 1 Fruit, 3 Fat
Carbohydrate Choices: 1 1/2

BETTY'S TIPS

❀ **Success Hint**
Layered desserts, such as this holiday delight, can be prepared in any large pretty glass bowl. If the side is straight, divide the layers evenly. If the side is slanted, layer a little less in the narrower bottom of the bowl.

❀ **Time-Saver**
For quick preparation, use instant pudding mix prepared according to package directions, and use frozen (thawed) whipped topping in place of the whipped cream.

❀ **Do-Ahead**
This is a perfect make-ahead dessert because the flavors improve as it stands in the refrigerator for several hours.

Easy Orange-Cranberry Dessert

Fruit Tart

Prep: 25 min Bake: 18 min Cool: 30 min

1 package Betty Crocker SuperMoist lemon cake mix

$^1/_2$ cup butter or margarine, softened

1 egg

3 containers (6 ounces each) vanilla yogurt (2 cups)

1 package (4-serving size) vanilla instant pudding and pie filling mix

3 cups sliced fruits, berries and/or mandarin orange segments

3 tablespoons apricot preserves

1 cup fresh raspberries

1. Heat oven to 350°. Grease 12-inch pizza pan or bottom only of rectangular pan, 13 × 9 × 2 inches, with shortening, or spray with cooking spray.

2. Mix cake mix, butter and egg in large bowl with spoon until crumbly. Press on bottom of pan. Bake 15 to 18 minutes or until set. Cool completely, about 30 minutes.

3. Beat yogurt and pudding mix (dry) in medium bowl with electric mixer on medium speed until blended. Spoon over baked layer. Smooth surface with rubber spatula.

4. Arrange fruit on yogurt mixture. Heat preserves over medium heat until melted; brush over fruit. Mound raspberries in center. Serve immediately, or refrigerate up to 24 hours. Store covered in refrigerator.

12 servings.
1 Serving: Calories 370 (Calories from Fat 115); Fat 13g (Saturated 6g); Cholesterol 40mg; Sodium 500mg; Carbohydrate 59g (Dietary Fiber 2g); Protein 5g
% Daily Value: Vitamin A 6%; Vitamin C 44%; Calcium 12%; Iron 6%
Exchanges: 1 Starch, 1 Fruit, 2 Other Carbohydrate, 2$^1/_2$ Fat
Carbohydrate Choices: 4

BETTY'S TIPS

⊛ **Substitution**
In a hurry? A 21-ounce can of blueberry, cherry or apple pie filling can be substituted for the fruit, preserves and raspberries. Spoon pie filling to within 1 inch of edge of yogurt mixture.

⊛ **Success Hint**
To keep your berries from becoming soft and mushy, rinse and dry them just before you're ready to use them.

⊛ **Variation**
For a **Fresh Peach Tart,** use 1 package Betty Crocker SuperMoist spice cake mix instead of lemon, and top with sliced fresh peaches.

Fruit Tart

Pumpkin-Ginger Mousse Tart

Prep: 25 min Bake: 9 min Cool: 20 min Refrigerate: 2 hr

1 refrigerated pie crust (from 15-ounce package), softened as directed on package

1 teaspoon sugar

1 can (15 ounces) pumpkin (not pumpkin pie mix)

1 jar (7 ounces) marshmallow creme

$1/2$ teaspoon pumpkin pie spice

$1/4$ cup finely chopped crystallized ginger

1 container (8 ounces) frozen whipped topping, thawed

8 purchased gingerbread men cookies

1. Heat oven to 450°. Roll pie crust into 12-inch circle on lightly floured surface. Sprinkle with sugar; lightly roll sugar into crust. Place in 10$1/2$-inch tart pan with removable bottom. Gently press in bottom and up side of pan; trim excess crust. Prick bottom and side with fork. Bake 7 to 9 minutes or until lightly browned. Cool completely, about 20 minutes.

2. Beat pumpkin, marshmallow creme and pumpkin pie spice in large bowl with spoon until smooth. Fold in ginger and 2 cups of the whipped topping. Spoon into crust. Refrigerate about 2 hours or until firm. Remove side of pan. Garnish tart with remaining whipped topping and cookies.

8 servings.
1 Serving: Calories 360 (Calories from Fat 135); Fat 15g (Saturated 4g); Cholesterol 0mg; Sodium 250mg; Carbohydrate 53g (Dietary Fiber 3g); Protein 3g
% Daily Value: Vitamin A 100%; Vitamin C 4%; Calcium 2%; Iron 10%
Exchanges: 1 Starch, 2$1/2$ Other Carbohydrate, 3 Fat
Carbohydrate Choices: 3$1/2$

Pumpkin-Ginger Mousse Tart

BETTY'S TIPS

❁ **Substitution**
Gingersnap cookies can be used to garnish the tart if you don't have gingerbread men.

❁ **Success Hint**
Even when pie crust has been pricked, it sometimes forms bubbles while baking. Watch during baking, and prick any bubbles as they form.

❁ **Variation**
The filling for this tart also makes a wonderful dip for fresh pear and apple slices or gingersnaps.

Blueberry Almond Tart

Prep: 15 min Bake: 30 min

2	cups blueberries
$^1/_3$	cup sugar
$1^1/_2$	tablespoons cornstarch
2	tablespoons water
$^1/_4$	teaspoon almond extract
1	refrigerated pie crust (from 15-ounce package), at room temperature
$^1/_2$	cup sliced almonds
1	teaspoon coarse sugar

1. Heat oven to 400°. Mix blueberries, sugar, cornstarch, water and almond extract in large bowl.

2. Place pie crust on ungreased cookie sheet. Spread $^1/_4$ cup of the almonds over crust; lightly press into crust.

3. Spoon blueberry mixture onto center of crust to within 2 inches of edge of crust. Fold 2-inch edge of crust over blueberry mixture, crimping crust slightly. Sprinkle crust edge with coarse sugar.

4. Bake 25 to 30 minutes, sprinkling remaining $^1/_4$ cup almonds over blueberry mixture during last 5 minutes of baking, until crust is golden. Cool slightly.

Fold 2-inch edge of crust over blueberry mixture, crimping crust slightly.

6 servings.
1 Serving: Calories 240 (Calories from Fat 100); Fat 11g (Saturated 2g); Cholesterol 0mg; Sodium 140mg; Carbohydrate 32g (Dietary Fiber 3g); Protein 3g
% Daily Value: Vitamin A 0%; Vitamin C 10%; Calcium 2%; Iron 6%
Exchanges: 1 Starch, $^1/_2$ Fruit, $^1/_2$ Other Carbohydrate, 2 Fat
Carbohydrate Choices: 2

Blueberry Almond Tart

Low-Fat

Banana Split Ice Cream Sandwiches

Prep: 20 min Cook: 3 min Freeze: 1 hr

2	tablespoons butter or margarine
36	large marshmallows (8 ounces)
6	cups Cocoa Puffs® cereal
1	pint (2 cups) strawberry ice cream, slightly softened
1	medium banana, very thinly sliced

1. Line jelly roll pan, 15½ × 10½ × 1 inch, with aluminum foil. Spray foil with cooking spray.

2. Place butter in large microwavable bowl. Microwave uncovered on High about 30 seconds or until melted. Stir in marshmallows. Microwave on High 1 to 3 minutes, stirring every 30 seconds, until marshmallows are melted and smooth. Stir in cereal. Spoon cereal mixture into pan; spread evenly and firmly. Freeze 15 minutes.

3. Turn pan upside down onto cutting board; remove foil. Cut cereal mixture into 18 squares. Spoon about ¼ cup ice cream onto 9 of the squares; spread slightly. Place 4 banana slices on each. Top with remaining squares; press slightly. Freeze about 45 minutes or until firm.

4. Cut each sandwich crosswise in half. Wrap each in waxed paper. Freeze up to 1 week.

18 sandwiches
1 Sandwich: Calories 135 (Calories from Fat 25); Fat 3g (Saturated 2g); Cholesterol 10mg; Sodium 85mg; Carbohydrate 26g (Dietary Fiber 0g); Protein 1g
% Daily Value: Vitamin A 2%; Vitamin C 8%; Calcium 2%; Iron 8%
Diet Exchanges: ½ Starch, 1½ Fruit
Carbohydrate Choices: 2

Banana Split Ice Cream Sandwiches

Chocolate Silk Pecan Pie

Prep: 25 min Bake: 45 min Cool: 1 hr Refrigerate: 2 hr 30 min
(Photo on page 245)

1 refrigerated pie crust (from 15-ounce package), softened as directed on package

$1/3$ cup granulated sugar

$1/2$ cup dark corn syrup

3 tablespoons butter or margarine, melted

$1/8$ teaspoon salt, if desired

2 eggs

$1/2$ cup chopped pecans

1 cup hot milk

$1/2$ teaspoon vanilla extract

$1^1/3$ cups semisweet chocolate chips

1 cup whipping (heavy) cream

2 tablespoons powdered sugar

Chocolate curls, if desired

1. Prepare pie crust as directed on package for one-crust filled pie using 9-inch pie plate. Heat oven to 350°. Beat granulated sugar, corn syrup, butter, salt and eggs in small bowl with electric mixer on medium speed 1 minute. Stir in pecans. Pour into pie crust in pie plate. Bake 35 to 45 minutes or until center of pie is puffed and golden brown. Cool 1 hour.

2. While filled crust is cooling, place hot milk, $1/4$ teaspoon vanilla and the chocolate chips in blender or food processor; cover and blend on medium speed about 1 minute or until smooth. Refrigerate about 1 hour 30 minutes or until mixture is slightly thickened but not set. Gently stir; pour over cooled filling in pie crust. Refrigerate about 1 hour or until firm.

3. Beat whipping cream, powdered sugar and $1/4$ teaspoon vanilla in chilled small bowl on high speed until stiff peaks form. Spoon or pipe over filling. Garnish with chocolate curls. Store in refrigerator.

10 servings.
1 Serving: Calories 445 (Calories from Fat 250); Fat 28g (Saturated 13g); Cholesterol 80mg; Sodium 160mg; Carbohydrate 44g (Dietary Fiber 2g); Protein 5g
% Daily Value: Vitamin A 10%; Vitamin C 0%; Calcium 6%; Iron 8%
Exchanges: 2 Starch, 1 Other Carbohydrate, 5 Fat
Carbohydrate Choices: 3

BETTY'S TIPS

⚙ **Success Hint**
For quick chocolate curls, pull a vegetable peeler along a chunky bar of milk chocolate. Milk chocolate is softer than semisweet or bittersweet chocolate. Lift the curls onto the dessert with a toothpick.

⚙ **Do-Ahead**
Make this pie early in the day so it has time to set up, plus you'll eliminate last-minute preparation. The chocolate curls can also be made ahead and refrigerated in a single layer in a small container.

⚙ **Did You Know?**
Dark corn syrup has a caramel flavor and color, which gives it a darker color and stronger flavor. It works well with the chocolate in this pie.

Betty Crocker ON BASICS

Chocolate Cookie Crust

Prep: 10 min Bake: 10 min Cool: 30 min

$1\frac{1}{2}$ cups finely crushed chocolate wafer cookies (about 30 cookies)

$\frac{1}{3}$ cup butter or margarine, melted

1. Heat oven to 350°. Mix cookie crumbs and butter. Press mixture firmly against bottom and side of pie plate, 9 × $1\frac{1}{4}$ inches.

2. Bake about 10 minutes or until firm. Cool completely, about 30 minutes.

Press crumb mixture firmly against bottom and side of pie plate.

8 servings.
1 Serving: Calories 160 (Calories from Fat 100); Fat 11g (Saturated 6g); Cholesterol 20mg; Sodium 170mg; Carbohydrate 15g (Dietary Fiber 1g); Protein 1g.
% Daily Value: Vitamin A 6%; Vitamin C 0%; Calcium 0%; Iron 4%
Exchanges: 2 Bread; 2 Fat
Carbohydrate Choices: 1

Decadent Chocolate Ice Cream Pie

Prep: 20 min Freeze: 4 hr Stand: 20 min

Chocolate Cookie Crust (opposite page)
or 1 package (6 ounces) ready-to-use
chocolate-flavored pie crust

1 bar (7 ounces) chocolate with almonds
and toffee chips candy, chopped

2 bars (7 ounces each) white chocolate with
cookie crumbs candy, chopped

1 quart (4 cups) chocolate ice cream,
softened

$^1/_2$ cup hot fudge sauce, heated

1. Make Chocolate Cookie Crust.

2. Stir candies into ice cream in large bowl until
mixture is smooth. Spoon hot fudge sauce over
bottom of cookie crust (sauce is heated so it will
spread more easily). Spoon ice cream mixture into
crust. Cover and freeze at least 4 hours or
overnight.

3. Let pie stand at room temperature 15 to 20 minutes before serving.

8 servings.
1 Serving: Calories 760 (Calories from Fat 360); Fat 40g (Saturated
20g); Cholesterol 35mg; Sodium 330mg; Carbohydrate 90g
(Dietary Fiber 5g); Protein 10g
% Daily Value: Vitamin A 6%; Vitamin C 0%; Calcium 22%; Iron
14%
Exchanges: $3^1/_2$ Bread, 8 Fat
Carbohydrate Choices: 6

BETTY'S TIPS

✿ **Special Touch**
Drizzle each serving with additional warmed hot
fudge sauce.

✿ **Success Hint**
To soften ice cream, place in the refrigerator for 25
to 35 minutes.

Decadent Chocolate Ice Cream Pie

Piña Colada Ice Cream Pie

Prep: 20 min Freeze: 4 hr Stand: 15 min

½ cup canned cream of coconut (not coconut milk)

1 can (8 ounces) crushed pineapple in juice, drained

2 tablespoons light rum, if desired

5 cups vanilla ice cream, softened

1 package (9 ounces) ready-to-use graham cracker pie crust (10 inches in diameter)

1. Gently stir cream of coconut, pineapple and rum into ice cream in large bowl. Spoon into pie crust. Cover and freeze at least 4 hours or overnight.

2. Let pie stand at room temperature 10 to 15 minutes before serving.

8 servings.
1 Serving: Calories 395 (Calories from Fat 215); Fat 24g (Saturated 13g); Cholesterol 35mg; Sodium 160mg; Carbohydrate 41g (Dietary Fiber 1g); Protein 4g
% Daily Value: Vitamin A 6%; Vitamin C 2%; Calcium 12%; Iron 4%
Exchanges: 1½ Starch, 1½ Fruit, 4 Fat
Carbohydrate Choices: 3

BETTY'S TIPS

⊛ **Success Hint**
Make sure you use cream of coconut, not coconut milk. When frozen, the coconut milk creates a layer of ice crystals.

⊛ **Special Touch**
Sprinkle pie with toasted coconut. To toast coconut, cook ¾ cup of flaked coconut in a skillet over medium heat 3 to 4 minutes, stirring constantly, until coconut is light golden brown. Cool; store in airtight container.

Piña Colada Ice Cream Pie

S'Mores Ice Cream Sandwiches

Prep: 20 min Freeze: 2 hr

32 graham cracker squares

$^1/_2$ cup Betty Crocker Rich & Creamy chocolate ready-to-spread frosting

$^1/_2$ cup marshmallow creme

$^1/_2$ gallon brick-style chocolate ice cream

1. Arrange 16 of the graham crackers in bottom of ungreased jelly roll pan, $15^1/_2 \times 10^1/_2 \times 1$ inch. Spread frosting on top of each cracker. Spread marshmallow creme on one side of remaining crackers, marshmallow sides down, pressing lightly.

2. Cut ice cream crosswise into four $^3/_4$-inch thick slices. Cut each slice into fourths to make 16 pieces. (Freeze remaining ice cream for another use.) Place one ice cream piece on each cracker in pan. Top with remaining crackers, marshmallow sides down, pressing lightly.

3. Cover and freeze about 2 hours or until firm. Wrap each sandwich in aluminum foil or plastic wrap; store in freezer.

S'Mores Ice Cream Sandwiches

16 sandwiches.
1 Sandwich: Calories 260 (Calories from Fat 100); Fat 11g (Saturated 6g); Cholesterol 20mg; Sodium 130mg; Carbohydrate 37g (Dietary Fiber 1g); Protein 3g
% Daily Value: Vitamin A 6%; Vitamin C 0%; Calcium 8%; Iron 4%
Exchanges: 1 Starch, $1^1/_2$ Fruit, 2 Fat
Carbohydrate Choices: $2^1/_2$

BETTY'S TIPS

✪ **Success Hint**
If ice cream is too hard to cut, place it in the refrigerator for 20 to 30 minutes to soften.

✪ **Do-Ahead**
Kids of all ages will love this frozen version of a camping favorite. Keep the sandwiches in the freezer for up to 2 weeks.

White Silk Raspberry Tart

Prep: 30 min Refrigerate: 4 hr

- 20 creme-filled chocolate sandwich cookies, crushed (2 cups)
- 1/4 cup butter or margarine, melted
- 1 package (6 ounces) white baking bars (white chocolate), chopped
- 2 cups whipping (heavy) cream
- 1 teaspoon vanilla extract
- 1 package (8 ounces) cream cheese, softened
- 1 package (10 ounces) frozen raspberries in syrup, thawed
- 2 teaspoons cornstarch
- 1 cup fresh raspberries

1. Heat oven to 375°. Mix cookie crumbs and butter in medium bowl. Press in bottom and 1 inch up side of 9- or 10-inch springform pan. Bake 7 to 9 minutes or until set. Cool completely, about 30 minutes.

2. Meanwhile, heat white baking bars and 1/2 cup of the whipping cream in heavy 1-quart saucepan over low heat, stirring frequently, until chocolate is melted. Stir in vanilla. Cool to room temperature, about 15 minutes.

3. Beat cream cheese in large bowl with electric mixer on medium speed until smooth. Add white chocolate mixture. Beat on medium speed until creamy; set aside. Beat remaining 1 1/2 cups whipping cream in chilled large bowl on high speed until stiff peaks form. Fold half of the whipped cream into cream cheese mixture until blended. Fold in remaining whipped cream. Spoon into crust. Refrigerate 3 to 4 hours or until set.

4. Pour package of raspberries into small strainer set over 1-quart saucepan. Press raspberries through strainer with back of spoon to remove seeds; discard seeds. Stir cornstarch into raspberry puree. Heat to boiling over medium heat. Cool completely, about 20 minutes. Spoon fresh raspberries around edge of dessert. Remove side of pan. Cut tart into wedges. Drizzle raspberry sauce over individual servings.

White Silk Raspberry Tart

12 servings.
1 Serving: Calories 410 (Calories from Fat 280); Fat 31g (Saturated 18g); Cholesterol 80mg; Sodium 170mg; Carbohydrate 29g (Dietary Fiber 2g); Protein 4g
% Daily Value: Vitamin A 18%; Vitamin C 10%; Calcium 8%; Iron 4%
Exchanges: 1 Starch, 1 Other Carbohydrate, 6 Fat
Carbohydrate Choices: 2

BETTY'S TIPS

⊕ **Success Hint**
For attractive serving slices, wipe the knife with a damp paper towel between each cut.

⊕ **Time-Saver**
Cut the tart into wedges and keep in the refrigerator until you're ready for dessert. Drizzle the sauce over wedges just before serving.

⊕ **Do-Ahead**
This is a great make-ahead dessert for the holidays because it needs time to set before serving. The raspberry sauce can also be made the day before.

Sherbet and Melon

Prep: 15 min

1 medium honeydew melon

1 pint (2 cups) lemon sherbet

1½ cups fresh raspberries

6 tablespoons melon-flavored liqueur
or crème de menthe syrup

1. Cut melon lengthwise in half; remove seeds. Cut melon into ¼-inch slices; cut away rind. Cut slices in half.

2. For each serving, arrange 5 half-slices of melon in fan shape on serving plate. Place 1 scoop of sherbet at base of slices. Sprinkle with ¼ cup of the raspberries. Drizzle with 1 tablespoon liqueur.

6 servings.
1 Serving: Calories 200 (Calories from Fat 10); Fat 1g (Saturated 1g); Cholesterol 0mg; Sodium 45mg; Carbohydrate 45g (Dietary Fiber 4g); Protein 2g
% Daily Value: Vitamin A 4%; Vitamin C 100%; Calcium 4%; Iron 2%
Exchanges: 3 Fruit
Carbohydrate Choices: 3

BETTY'S TIPS

⊘ **Do-Ahead**
Prepare melon slices ahead. Place on flat plate, cover and refrigerate until serving time.

⊘ **Special Touch**
Garnish each plate with a fresh mint sprig.

Sherbet and Melon

Butter Pecan Cantaloupe Wedges

Prep: 10 min

1 large cantaloupe
1 pint (2 cups) butter pecan ice cream
1 cup real maple syrup
8 pecan halves

1. Cut cantaloupe in half; remove seeds. Cut each half into 8 wedges. Remove peel from each wedge.

2. For each serving, arrange 2 cantaloupe wedges in shallow bowl. Top with $1/4$-cup scoop of ice cream. Drizzle with about 2 tablespoons maple syrup. Top with pecan half.

8 servings.
1 Serving: Calories 225 (Calories from Fat 45); Fat 5g (Saturated 2g); Cholesterol 15mg; Sodium 40mg; Carbohydrate 43g (Dietary Fiber 1g); Protein 2g
% Daily Value: Vitamin A 56%; Vitamin C 72%; Calcium 8%; Iron 4%
Exchanges: 1 Starch, 2 Fruit, 1 Fat
Carbohydrate Choices: 3

Berry Angel Delight

Prep: 15 min Chill: 4 hr

1 cup whipping (heavy) cream
2 tablespoons sugar
2 cups Yoplait Custard Style vanilla yogurt
1 round angel food cake (8 inches in diameter), cut into 1-inch pieces
1 cup fresh blueberries
1 cup quartered fresh strawberries
1 cup fresh raspberries

1. Beat whipping cream and sugar in chilled medium bowl with electric mixer on high speed until stiff peaks form. Fold in yogurt.

2. Place cake pieces in large bowl; fold in yogurt mixture. Gently mix berries together in medium bowl.

3. Spoon half of the cake mixture into 9-inch spring-form pan; press firmly in pan with rubber spatula. Top with half of the berries. Repeat with remaining cake mixture; press with spatula. Top with berries. Cover and refrigerate at least 4 hours or overnight.

4. Run metal spatula carefully along side of dessert to loosen; remove side of pan. Cut dessert into wedges.

10 to 12 servings.
1 Serving: Calories 320 (Calories from Fat 70); Fat 8g (Saturated 5g); Cholesterol 30mg; Sodium 480mg; Carbohydrate 55g (Dietary Fiber 2g); Protein 7g
% Daily Value: Vitamin A 6%; Vitamin C 24%; Calcium 10%; Iron 4%
Exchanges: 2 Starch, $1/2$ Fruit, $1/2$ Fat
Carbohydrate Choices: $3^{1}/_{2}$

BETTY'S TIPS

✿ **Variation**
Any combination of fresh berries will work well in this refreshing dessert.

✿ **Special Touch**
Just before serving, lightly dust fruit with powdered sugar sprinkled through a small strainer. Garnish with fresh fruit and mint.

Berry Angel Delight

Butter Pecan Cantaloupe Wedges

Chocolate Strawberry Shortcakes

Prep: 15 min Stand: 30 min Bake: 16 min

3 cups sliced strawberries

$^1/_3$ cup sugar

$2^1/_4$ cups Original Bisquick mix

$^1/_2$ cup miniature semisweet chocolate chips

$^1/_4$ cup butter or margarine, melted

$^1/_2$ cup milk

3 tablespoons sugar

Sweetened Chocolate Whipped Cream (right)

1. Mix strawberries and $^1/_3$ cup sugar; let stand at least 30 minutes.

2. Heat oven to 400°. Mix remaining ingredients except Sweetened Chocolate Whipped Cream until dough forms. Drop dough by 6 spoonfuls onto ungreased cookie sheet.

3. Bake 15 to 16 minutes or until deep golden brown. Split warm shortcakes; fill with strawberries and Sweetened Chocolate Whipped Cream.

6 servings.

Sweetened Chocolate Whipped Cream

1 cup whipping (heavy) cream

$^1/_2$ cup powdered sugar

$^1/_4$ cup baking cocoa

1 teaspoon vanilla extract

Beat all ingredients in chilled small bowl with electric mixer on low speed about 1 minute or until well combined. Beat on high speed 1 to 2 minutes or until soft peaks form.

1 Serving: Calories 595 (Calories from Fat 290); Fat 32g (Saturated 17g); Cholesterol 65mg; Sodium 720mg; Carbohydrate 71g (Dietary Fiber 4g); Protein 6g
% Daily Value: Vitamin A 16%; Vitamin C 78%; Calcium 14%; Iron 14%
Exchanges: 2 Starch, 3 Fruit, $5^1/_2$ Fat
Carbohydrate Choices: 5

BETTY'S TIPS

⊕ **Do-Ahead**

Mix the strawberries and sugar; cover and refrigerate. Bake shortcakes ahead, and store in an airtight container. The whipped cream can be prepared 3 hours ahead, covered and refrigerated.

⊕ **Special Touch**

Decoratively drizzle chocolate sauce over serving plates. Garnish with whole strawberries.

Chocolate Strawberry Shortcakes

Berry Brownie Parfaits

Prep: 10 min Chill: 40 min

1 package (4-serving size) white chocolate instant pudding and pie filling mix

1½ cups milk

½ teaspoon rum extract

1 cup frozen (thawed) whipped topping

4 brownies (2½-inch square)

1 cup fresh raspberries

1. Beat pudding mix, milk and rum extract in medium bowl 2 minutes, using wire whisk. Refrigerate 10 minutes. Fold in whipped topping.

2. Cut each brownie into 12 squares. For each serving, spoon about 2 tablespoons pudding mixture into 6- to 10-inch parfait glass. Top with 4 brownie pieces and 4 raspberries; press lightly. Repeat layers. Top each with 2 tablespoons pudding mixture. Refrigerate 30 minutes. Garnish with remaining raspberries.

6 servings.
1 Serving: Calories 345 (Calories from Fat 135); Fat 15g (Saturated 5g); Cholesterol 35mg; Sodium 350mg; Carbohydrate 48g (Dietary Fiber 3g); Protein 3g
% Daily Value: Vitamin A 10%; Vitamin C 4%; Calcium 10%; Iron 6%
Exchanges: 2 Starch, 1 Fruit, 3 Fat
Carbohydrate Choices: 3

Berry Brownie Parfaits

Peach Bread Pudding with Raspberry Sauce

Peach Bread Pudding with Raspberry Sauce

Prep: 20 min Stand: 15 min Bake: 40 min

$^1/_2$ loaf (1-pound size) French bread, cut into 1-inch cubes (about 8 cups)

1 cup frozen sliced peaches, thawed and cut into 1-inch pieces

2 cups half-and-half

3 eggs

1 cup sugar

$^1/_4$ teaspoon almond extract

$^1/_4$ cup butter or margarine, melted
Raspberry Sauce (below)

1. Heat oven to 350°. Spray rectangular baking dish, 11 × 7 × 1$^1/_2$ inches, with cooking spray. Place bread cubes and peaches in baking dish; toss to mix.

2. Beat half-and-half, eggs, sugar and almond extract in large bowl with electric mixer on low speed until well blended. Pour over bread and peaches. Let stand about 15 minutes or until absorbed by bread; mix once to coat all bread cubes. Pour melted butter over top.

3. Bake uncovered 30 to 40 minutes or until set and light golden brown. Meanwhile, make Raspberry Sauce; serve over warm bread pudding.

8 servings.

Raspberry Sauce

2 packages (10 ounces each) frozen raspberries in syrup, thawed

$^1/_4$ cup sugar

2 teaspoons cornstarch

Pour 1 package of raspberries into strainer set over 2-quart saucepan. Press raspberries through strainer with back of spoon to remove seeds; discard seeds. Pour second package of raspberries into strainer. Drain raspberries into saucepan, leaving berries whole. Set whole berries aside. Mix sugar and corn-starch into raspberry purée with wire whisk. Cook over medium-low heat, stirring occasionally, until mixture boils and thickens. Remove from heat; stir in whole raspberries.

1 Serving: Calories 545 (Calories from Fat 155); Fat 17g (Saturated 9g); Cholesterol 115mg; Sodium 420mg; Carbohydrate 88g (Dietary Fiber 5g); Protein 10g
% Daily Value: Vitamin A 16%; Vitamin C 34%; Calcium 12%; Iron 14%
Exchanges: 3 Starch, 1 Fruit, 2 Other Carbohydrate, 2$^1/_2$ Fat
Carbohydrate Choices: 6

BETTY'S TIPS

❀ **Substitution**
Well-drained canned peaches can be used in place of the frozen peaches.

❀ **Special Touch**
A garnish of fresh mint adds a touch of color and a burst of flavor to this warm, homey dessert.

❀ **Did You Know?**
Bread pudding is a great way to use leftover bread. Most loaves of French bread are too large for families to use all at once. Use the day-old bread for this yummy dessert.

Peach and Raspberry Cobbler

Prep: 20 min Bake: 30 min
(Photo on page 245)

2¹/₂ cups sliced fresh peaches

2 cups fresh raspberries

¹/₂ cup granulated sugar

1 tablespoon cornstarch

1 teaspoon ground nutmeg

2 cups Original Bisquick mix

¹/₂ cup milk

3 tablespoons butter or margarine, melted

2 tablespoons packed brown sugar

1. Heat oven to 375°. Lightly butter bottom and side of deep-dish pie plate, 9 × 1¹/₂ inches.

2. Mix peaches, raspberries, granulated sugar, cornstarch and nutmeg in large bowl. Let stand 10 minutes. Spoon into pie plate.

3. Stir together remaining ingredients in same bowl until dough forms. Drop dough by spoonfuls onto fruit mixture. Bake 25 to 30 minutes or until fruit is bubbly and topping is deep golden brown and thoroughly baked.

8 servings.
1 Serving: Calories 270 (Calories from Fat 80); Fat 9g (Saturated 4g); Cholesterol 15mg; Sodium 0mg; Carbohydrate 46g (Dietary Fiber 4g); Protein 3g
% Daily Value: Vitamin A 6%; Vitamin C 8%; Calcium 8%; Iron 6%
Exchanges: 1 Starch, 2 Fruit, 1¹/₂ Fat
Carbohydrate Choices: 3

BETTY'S TIPS

☺ **Substitution**
Frozen sliced peaches and raspberries, thawed, can be used instead of fresh.

☺ **Serve-With**
Top this summertime favorite with frozen yogurt or ice cream.

☺ **Special Touch**
Sprinkle coarse decorating sugar over the top of the cobbler dough just before baking.

Quick & Low Fat

Razzle-Dazzle Berry Shortcake

Prep: 10 min

1¹/₂ cups raspberry pie filling (from 21-ounce can)

1 cup sliced fresh strawberries

³/₄ cup fresh blueberries

6 slices (3 × 2¹/₂ inches) angel food or pound cake (about ³/₄ inch thick)

Whipped cream topping (from 7-ounce can)

1. Mix pie filling, strawberries and blueberries in medium bowl.

2. Cut each cake slice diagonally in half to make 2 triangles. Arrange 2 triangles on each of 6 serving plates. Top with fruit mixture and whipped cream.

6 servings.
1 Serving: Calories 155 (Calories from Fat 10); Fat 1g (Saturated 0g); Cholesterol 0mg; Sodium 140mg; Carbohydrate 34g (Dietary Fiber 2g); Protein 2g
% Daily Value: Vitamin A 0%; Vitamin C 32%; Calcium 0%; Iron 2%
Exchanges: 1 Starch, 1 Fruit
Carbohydrate Choices: 2

Razzle-Dazzle Berry Shortcake

Two-Berry Crisp with Pecan Streusel Topping

Prep: 15 min Bake: 40 min

$^3/_4$ cup quick-cooking oats

$^1/_2$ cup Gold Medal all-purpose flour

$^1/_2$ cup packed brown sugar

$^1/_2$ cup butter or margarine, cut into pieces

$^1/_4$ cup chopped pecans

1 can (21 ounces) blueberry pie filling

2 cups frozen unsweetened raspberries

3 tablespoons granulated sugar

1 tablespoon Gold Medal all-purpose flour

1. Heat oven to 400°. Spray bottom and sides of square baking dish, 8 X 8 X 2 inches, with cooking spray. Mix oats, $^1/_2$ cup flour and brown sugar in large bowl. Cut in butter, using pastry blender or crisscrossing 2 knives, until crumbly. Stir in pecans.

2. Mix remaining ingredients in large bowl. Spread in baking dish. Sprinkle oat mixture over top.

3. Bake 30 to 40 minutes or until fruit mixture is bubbly and topping is golden brown.

6 servings.
1 Serving: Calories 460 (Calories from Fat 180); Fat 20g (Saturated 10g); Cholesterol 40mg; Sodium 110mg; Carbohydrate 74g (Dietary Fiber 8g); Protein 4g
% Daily Value: Vitamin A 12%; Vitamin C 18%; Calcium 4%; Iron 12%
Exchanges: 1 Starch, 2 Fruit, 2 Other Carbohydrates, 3 Fat
Carbohydrate Choices: 5

BETTY'S TIPS

⊛ **Substitution**
If you like, use another flavor of fruit pie filling for the blueberry. Try raspberry, cherry, blackberry, strawberry or peach for a different twist.

⊛ **Special Touch**
Top crisp squares with whipped cream and a few chopped pecans, or serve scoops of vanilla ice cream on the side of the warm crisp.

⊛ **Did You Know?**
Pecans are often associated with the South and its cuisine. These nuts have a rich, buttery flavor. Pecans can be purchased unshelled whole, in halves or chopped. To save time, purchase chopped pecans for this recipe.

Two-Berry Crisp with Pecan Streusel Topping

Betty Crocker
ON CAKES

Make-and-Bake Basics

Looking for a "recipe" to create a picture-perfect cake? Start with a generous amount of cake-baking tips, stir in easy directions and add a dash of love.

PICK THE PAN

▶ Use the pan size called for in the recipe. To assure easy pan removal, make sure to follow recipe instructions for greasing and flouring pans, as well as special instructions for using waxed paper or parchment paper.

▶ Shiny metal aluminum pans are best because they reflect heat away from the cake and produce a tender, light brown crust.

▶ If you use dark nonstick or glass baking pans, follow the manufacturer's directions, which may call for reducing the temperature by 25°. These pans absorb heat so cakes will bake and brown faster.

▶ For the best volume when making cupcakes, use paper baking cups.

THE GREAT BAKE

▶ Be sure to follow the recipe directions for each recipe rather than following the package directions. Many of the recipes call for additional ingredients, which can change how the cake bakes.

▶ Bake cakes on the rack in the center of the oven, unless the recipe tells you otherwise.

▶ Check for doneness as directed in each recipe. If a bake range is for 35 to 40 minutes, don't open the oven before 35 minutes, or your cake could fall. Use a toothpick to test for doneness in the center of the cake. If it comes out clean, the cake is done.

▶ Cool cakes on a wire rack away from drafts (see Removing Cake Layers at right) for the length of time the recipe recommends.

Lemon Mousse Cake (page 272)

REMOVING CAKE LAYERS

1 After removing cakes from the oven, cool them in the pan on a wire cooling rack for 10 to 15 minutes.

2 Run a dinner knife around the side of the pan to loosen the cake. Cover a rack with a towel. Place wire rack, towel side down, on top of cake layer; turn rack and pan upside down together. Remove pan.

3 Place a second wire rack, top side down, on bottom of cake layer; turn over both racks so the layer is right side up. Remove towel and top wire rack. Repeat with remaining layer(s). Let layers cool completely on racks.

FROSTING A LAYER CAKE

1 Place 4 strips of waxed paper around the edge of a large plate. The waxed paper will protect the plate as you frost and can be removed later. Brush any loose crumbs from the cooled cake. Place one layer, rounded side down, on the plate (unless directed otherwise in the recipe).

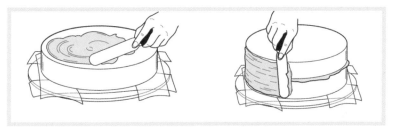

2 Spread about ⅓ cup creamy frosting (or ½ cup fluffy frosting) over the top of the first layer to within ¼ inch of the edge.

3 Place second layer, rounded side up, on top of first layer so that the 2 flat sides are together with frosting in between. Coat side of cake with a very thin layer of frosting to seal in crumbs.

4 Frost the side of the cake in swirls, making a rim about ¼-inch high above the top of the cake. Spread the remaining frosting on top, just to the built-up rim.

Raspberry-Fudge Fantasy Torte (page 282)

Lemon Mousse Cake

Prep: 25 min Bake: 32 min Cool: 1 hr 10 min
(Photo on page 270)

 1 package Betty Crocker SuperMoist white cake mix
 1¼ cups water
 ⅓ cup vegetable oil
 3 egg whites
 2 cups whipping (heavy) cream
 ¼ cup powdered sugar
 1 jar (10 ounces) lemon curd
 2 teaspoons grated lemon peel

1. Heat oven to 350°. Grease bottoms only of 2 round pans, 8 × 1½ or 9 × 1½ inches, with shortening or spray with cooking spray.

2. Beat cake mix, water, oil and egg whites in large bowl with electric mixer on low speed 30 seconds. Beat on medium speed 2 minutes, scraping bowl occasionally. Pour into pans.

3. Bake 8-inch rounds 27 to 32 minutes, 9-inch rounds 23 to 28 minutes, or until toothpick inserted in center comes out clean and center springs back when lightly touched in center. Cool 10 minutes. Run knife around side of pans to loosen cakes; remove from pans to wire rack. Cool completely, about 1 hour.

4. Beat whipping cream and powdered sugar in chilled medium bowl with electric mixer on high speed until stiff peaks form. Fold in lemon curd and lemon peel. Place 1 cake layer, rounded side down, on serving plate. Spread with 1 cup of the lemon mixture to within ¼ inch to edge. Top with second layer. Frost side and top of cake with remaining lemon mixture. Store loosely covered in refrigerator.

12 to 16 servings.
1 Serving: Calories 445 (Calories from Fat 205); Fat 23g (Saturated 10g); Cholesterol 45mg; Sodium 340mg; Carbohydrate 55g (Dietary Fiber 10g); Protein 4g
% Daily Value: Vitamin A 8%; Vitamin C 2%; Calcium 8%; Iron 4%
Exchanges: 1 Starch, 2½ Other Carbohydrate, 5 Fat
Carbohydrate Choices: 3½

BETTY'S TIPS

◎ **Substitution**
If you can't find lemon curd in the jams and jellies section of your supermarket, use ¾ cup canned lemon pie filling instead. The only difference is that the mousse will be slightly softer.

◎ **Success Hint**
Top this luscious cake with thin slices of lemon and fresh raspberries.

◎ **Did You Know?**
Lemon curd is a rich, tart custard made with sugar, lemon juice, lemon peel, butter and eggs. Although you can make it from scratch, it's much easier to pick up a jar in the jams and jellies section of the supermarket.

Strawberry-Amaretto Cake

Prep: 35 min Bake: 37 min Cool: 1 hr 10 min

1 cup slivered almonds
1 package Betty Crocker SuperMoist white cake mix
³/₄ cup water
¹/₂ cup amaretto liqueur
¹/₃ cup vegetable oil
3 egg whites
  Amaretto Cream (below)
1 cup thinly sliced fresh strawberries
6 large fresh strawberries, cut in half

1. Heat oven to 350°. Grease bottoms and sides of 2 round pans, 8 × 1¹/₂ or 9 × 1¹/₂ inches, with shortening; lightly flour. Place almonds in food processor or blender. Cover and process until almonds are finely ground.

2. Beat cake mix, almonds, water, liqueur, oil and egg whites in large bowl with electric mixer on low speed 30 seconds. Beat on medium speed 2 minutes, scraping bowl occasionally. Pour into pans.

3. Bake 8-inch rounds 30 to 37 minutes, 9-inch rounds 25 to 30 minutes, or until toothpick inserted in center comes out clean. Cool 10 minutes. Run sharp knife around side of pans to loosen cakes; remove from pans to wire rack. Cool completely, about 1 hour.

4. Place 1 layer on cake plate. Spread with ¹/₂ cup Amaretto Cream; arrange sliced strawberries evenly on top. Top with second layer. Frost side and top of cake with remaining Amaretto Cream. Garnish with strawberry halves just before serving. Store loosely covered in refrigerator.

12 to 16 servings.

Amaretto Cream

1¹/₂ cups whipping (heavy) cream
¹/₄ cup granulated or powdered sugar
¹/₄ cup amaretto liqueur

Beat all ingredients in chilled large bowl with electric mixer on high speed until soft peaks form.

Strawberry-Amaretto Cake

1 Serving: Calories 455 (Calories from Fat 240); Fat 27g (Saturated 8g); Cholesterol 35mg; Sodium 330mg; Carbohydrate 48g (Dietary Fiber 2g); Protein 5g
% Daily Value: Vitamin A 6%; Vitamin C 10%; Calcium 10%; Iron 6%
Exchanges: 2 Starch, 1 Other Carbohydrate, 5 Fat
Carbohydrate Choices: 3

BETTY'S TIPS

⊗ **Substitution**
Instead of the amaretto liqueur, you can use 1 tablespoon almond extract plus enough water to equal ¹/₂ cup to use in the cake batter. For the Amaretto Cream, substitute 1 teaspoon almond extract plus ¹/₄ cup whipping (heavy) cream for the amaretto liqueur.

⊗ **Success Hint**
A food processor makes quick work of grinding the almonds. For even grinding, scrape the sides and bottom of the food processor bowl occasionally. Some of the juice from the strawberry halves will soak into the frosting, so add the strawberry garnish just before serving.

Betty Crocker
MAKES IT EASY

Butterfly Cake

Prep: 30 min Bake: 40 min Cool: 45 min Freeze: 1 hr

1 package Betty Crocker SuperMoist yellow cake mix

1 1/4 cups water

1/3 cup vegetable oil

3 eggs

1 tub Betty Crocker Rich & Creamy vanilla ready-to-spread frosting

1 candy stick (8 to 10 inches long)

Food color (in desired colors)

Betty Crocker decorating gel (from 0.68-ounce tube) in any color

Decorating sugar crystals (any color)

8 jelly beans

Small round candy decorations

1. Heat oven to 350°. Grease bottom and side of 1 round pan, 8 × 1 1/2 or 9 × 1 1/2 inches, with shortening; lightly flour.

2. Beat cake mix, water, oil and eggs in large bowl with electric mixer on low speed 30 seconds. Beat on medium speed 2 minutes, scraping bowl occasionally. Pour half of the batter into pan.*

3. Bake 35 to 40 minutes or until toothpick inserted in center comes out clean. Cool cake 15 minutes; remove from pan to wire rack. Cool completely, about 30 minutes. Freeze cake 1 hour or until firm.

4. Cut cake crosswise in half; cut each half into 1/3 and 2/3 pieces (as shown in diagram). Place cake pieces on platter or foil-covered cardboard to form butterfly. Gently separate cake pieces to form wings.

5. Reserve 1/2 cup frosting. Frost cake pieces with remaining frosting. Place candy stick between cake pieces for butterfly body. Stir food color into reserved frosting until well blended. Spread over cake in desired pattern on wings. Outline wing patterns with gel. Sprinkle with sugar crystals. Place jelly beans on corners of wings. Decorate butterfly with candy decorations.

*Use remaining batter for cupcakes. Line 12 muffin cups with paper baking cups. Divide batter evenly among cups. Bake at 350° for 20 to 30 minutes or until toothpick inserted in center comes out clean. Remove from pan to wire rack; cool completely. Frost and decorate as desired.

12 servings.
1 Serving: Calories 445 (Calories from Fat 180); Fat 20g (Saturated 9g); Cholesterol 55mg; Sodium 320mg; Carbohydrate 63g (Dietary Fiber 0g); Protein 3g
% Daily Value: Vitamin A 2%; Vitamin C 0%; Calcium 6%; Iron 4%
Exchanges: 1 Starch, 3 Other Carbohydrate, 4 Fat
Carbohydrate Choices: 4

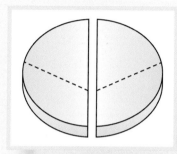

Cut cake crosswise in half; cut each half into ⅓ and ⅔ pieces.

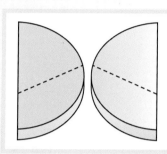

Place cake pieces on platter to form butterfly.

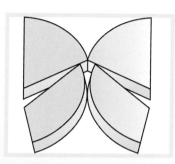

Separate cake pieces to form wings.

Butterfly Cake

Caramel-Pecan Brownie Cake

Prep: 40 min Bake: 1 hr 10 min Cool: 30 min Refrigerate: 2 hr 15 min

21 ounces caramels (about 75 caramels) from two 14-ounce bags

³/₄ cup evaporated milk

1 package (19.8 ounces) Betty Crocker fudge brownie mix

¹/₄ cup water

¹/₂ cup vegetable oil

3 eggs

1¹/₂ cups semisweet chocolate chips

1 cup finely chopped pecans

1 teaspoon vegetable oil

1. Heat oven to 350°. Wrap outside of 9-inch springform pan with heavy-duty aluminum foil. Spray inside of pan with cooking spray. Heat caramels and milk in 2-quart saucepan over low heat about 15 minutes, stirring frequently, until caramels are melted and smooth; remove from heat.

2. Stir brownie mix, water, ¹/₂ cup oil and eggs in large bowl until well blended. Stir in 1 cup chocolate chips and ¹/₂ cup pecans. Pour into pan.

3. Gently and evenly drizzle ³/₄ cup caramel sauce over batter; gently swirl caramel sauce through batter with knife. (Cover and refrigerate remaining caramel sauce to serve with cake.) Bake 1 hour to 1 hour 10 minutes or until top springs back when touched lightly in center.

4. Melt remaining ¹/₂ cup chocolate chips and 1 teaspoon oil in 1-quart saucepan over low heat, stirring constantly, until smooth. Drizzle over warm cake. Sprinkle with remaining ¹/₂ cup pecans. Cool 30 minutes. Run knife around side of pan to loosen cake. Refrigerate about 2 hours 15 minutes or until chocolate is set.

5. Remove side of pan. Microwave remaining caramel sauce on High 1 to 2 minutes or until warm. Cut cake into wedges. Drizzle each serving with about 1 tablespoon caramel sauce.

16 servings.
1 Serving: Calories 710 (Calories from Fat 325); Fat 36g (Saturated 13g); Cholesterol 60mg; Sodium 140mg; Carbohydrate 89g (Dietary Fiber 4g); Protein 8g
% Daily Value: Vitamin A 2%; Vitamin C 0%; Calcium 12%; Iron 12%
Exchanges: 3 Starch, 3 Other Carbohydrate, 6¹/₂ Fat
Carbohydrate Choices: 6

BETTY'S TIPS

◎ Success Hint

Be sure to taste-test nuts before you use them. Nuts can become rancid quickly, so it's best to store them in an airtight container in the freezer where they will keep longer.

◎ Special Touch

For a truly decadent dessert, serve slices of this rich cake with vanilla ice cream or whipped cream.

◎ Did You Know?

Evaporated milk is milk that has had 60 percent of the water removed. It is sold in cans and should not be confused with sweetened condensed milk, which is mixed with sugar.

Caramel-Pecan Brownie Cake

Maple-Pecan Cake

Prep: 30 min Bake: 50 min Cool: 2 hr 10 min

1 package Betty Crocker SuperMoist yellow cake mix
1 cup water
$^1/_3$ cup butter or margarine, softened
3 eggs
$^1/_2$ cup maple-flavored syrup
$^1/_2$ cup chopped pecans, toasted
   Cream Cheese Frosting (right)

1. Heat oven to 350°. Grease 12-cup bundt cake pan with shortening; lightly flour. Beat all ingredients except Cream Cheese Frosting in large bowl with electric mixer on low speed 30 seconds. Beat on medium speed 2 minutes. Pour into pan.

2. Bake 40 to 50 minutes or until toothpick inserted in center comes out clean. Cool 10 minutes; remove from pan to wire rack. Cool completely, about 2 hours.

3. Frost cake with Cream Cheese Frosting.

16 servings.

Cream Cheese Frosting

1$^1/_2$ cups powdered sugar
3 tablespoons butter or margarine, softened
1$^1/_2$ ounces cream cheese (half of 3-ounce package), softened
3 to 4 tablespoons maple-flavored syrup

Beat powdered sugar, butter, cream cheese and 3 tablespoons of the syrup in large bowl with electric mixer on low speed. Beat in enough of the remaining syrup to make a smooth, soft frosting that will drip down side of cake.

1 Serving: Calories 330 (Calories from Fat 125); Fat 14g (Saturated 6g); Cholesterol 60mg; Sodium 300mg; Carbohydrate 48g (Dietary Fiber 1g); Protein 3g
% Daily Value: Vitamin A 6%; Vitamin C 0%; Calcium 4%; Iron 4%
Exchanges: 1 Starch, 2 Other Carbohydrates, 3 Fat
Carbohydrate Choices: 3

BETTY'S TIPS

☺ **Substitution**
Instead of making the scratch frosting recipe, mix a 16-ounce tub of Betty Crocker Rich & Creamy cream cheese ready-to-spread frosting with 4 to 5 tablespoons of maple-flavored syrup.

☺ **Variation**
You can serve this rich cake without the frosting and instead just drizzle with the maple syrup.

Maple-Pecan Cake

Chocolate Lover's Dream Cake

Prep: 20 min Bake: 1 hr 5 min Cool: 2 hr 10 min

1 package Betty Crocker SuperMoist butter recipe chocolate cake mix

$1/2$ cup chocolate milk

$1/3$ cup butter or margarine, melted

3 eggs

1 container (16 ounces) sour cream

1 package (4-serving size) chocolate fudge instant pudding and pie filling mix

1 bag (12 ounces) semisweet chocolate chips (2 cups)

Rich Chocolate Glaze (below)

1. Heat oven to 350°. Generously grease 12-cup bundt cake pan with shortening; lightly flour.

2. Mix cake mix, chocolate milk, butter, eggs, sour cream and pudding mix (dry) in large bowl with spoon until well blended (batter will be very thick). Stir in chocolate chips. Spoon into pan.

3. Bake 55 to 65 minutes or until top springs back when touched lightly in center. Cool in pan 10 minutes. Turn pan upside down onto wire rack or heatproof serving plate; remove pan. Cool completely, about 2 hours. Drizzle Rich Chocolate Glaze over cake. Store loosely covered at room temperature.

16 servings.

Rich Chocolate Glaze

$3/4$ cup semisweet chocolate chips

3 tablespoons butter or margarine

3 tablespoons light corn syrup

$1^1/2$ teaspoons water

Heat all ingredients in 1-quart saucepan over low heat, stirring frequently, until chocolate chips are melted and mixture is smooth.

1 Serving: Calories 460 (Calories from Fat 225); Fat 35g (Saturated 13g); Cholesterol 75mg; Sodium 450mg; Carbohydrate 54g (Dietary Fiber 3g); Protein 5g
% Daily Value: Vitamin A 10%; Vitamin C 0%; Calcium 10%; Iron 12%
Exchanges: 2 Starch, $1^1/2$ Other Carbohydrate, $4^1/2$ Fat
Carbohydrate Choices: $3^1/2$

Chocolate Lover's Dream Cake

BETTY'S TIPS

✿ **Success Hint**
You don't want to lose even a drop of this divine batter, so measure the volume of your bundt cake pan using water to make sure it holds 12 cups. If the pan is smaller than 12 cups, the batter will overflow during baking.

✿ **Serve-With**
Topped with a scoop of vanilla ice cream, this extra-moist, chocolate-loaded cake is a dessert lover's dream.

✿ **Variation**
For a mild chocolate flavor, use milk chocolate chips instead of semisweet chocolate chips.

Caramel-Carrot Cake

Prep: 10 min Bake: 33 min Cool: 15 min Refrigerate: 2 hr

1 package Betty Crocker SuperMoist carrot cake
1 cup water
⅓ cup butter or margarine, melted
3 eggs
1 jar (16 to 17.5 ounces) caramel or butterscotch topping
1 tub Betty Crocker Rich & Creamy vanilla ready-to-spread frosting

1. Heat oven to 350°. Grease bottom only of rectangular pan, 13 × 9 × 2 inches, with shortening, or spray bottom with cooking spray.

2. Beat cake mix, water, butter and eggs in large bowl with electric mixer on low speed 30 seconds. Beat on medium speed 2 minutes. Pour into pan.

3. Bake 27 to 33 minutes or until toothpick inserted in center comes out clean. Cool 15 minutes. Poke top of warm cake every ½ inch with handle of wooden spoon, wiping handle occasionally to reduce sticking. Reserve ½ cup caramel topping. Drizzle remaining caramel topping evenly over top of cake; let stand about 15 minutes or until caramel topping has been absorbed into cake. Run knife around side of pan to loosen cake. Cover and refrigerate about 2 hours or until chilled.

4. Set aside 2 tablespoons of the reserved ½ cup caramel topping. Stir remaining topping into frosting; spread over top of cake. Drizzle with reserved 2 tablespoons caramel topping. Store covered in refrigerator.

15 servings.
1 Serving: Calories 445 (Calories from Fat 130); Fat 15g (Saturated 9g); Cholesterol 55mg; Sodium 430mg; Carbohydrate 76g (Dietary Fiber 1g); Protein 3g
% Daily Value: Vitamin A 4%; Vitamin C 0%; Calcium 6%; Iron 2%
Exchanges: 1 Starch, 4 Other Carbohydrate, 3 Fat
Carbohydrate Choices: 5

BETTY'S TIPS

✪ **Substitution**
Forget the frosting! You can use an 8-ounce container of frozen whipped topping, thawed, instead.

✪ **Success Hint**
Some caramel toppings are thicker and stickier than others. If the type you purchased is too thick to pour, warm it in the microwave just until it can be poured.

✪ **Serve-With**
This ooey-gooey, very rich cake needs to be accompanied by only a glass of milk or a cup of steaming coffee.

Caramel-Carrot Cake

Deep Dark Mocha Torte

Prep: 50 min Bake: 39 min Cool: 1 hr 10 min

1 package Betty Crocker SuperMoist chocolate fudge cake mix

1⅓ cups water

½ cup vegetable oil

3 eggs

⅓ cup granulated sugar

⅓ cup rum

1¼ teaspoons instant espresso coffee (dry)

Mascarpone Filling (right)

Chocolate Ganache (right)

1. Heat oven to 350°. Grease bottoms only of 2 round pans, 8 × 1½ or 9 × 1½ inches, with shortening; lightly flour.

2. Beat cake mix, water, oil and eggs in large bowl with electric mixer on low speed 30 seconds. Beat on medium speed 2 minutes, scraping bowl occasionally. Pour into pans.

3. Bake 8-inch rounds 34 to 39 minutes, 9-inch rounds 29 to 34 minutes, or until toothpick inserted in center comes out clean. Cool 10 minutes. Run knife around side of pans to loosen cakes; remove from pans to wire rack. Cool completely, about 1 hour.

4. Meanwhile, stir sugar, rum and coffee (dry) in 1-quart saucepan until coffee is dissolved. Heat to boiling, stirring occasionally; remove from heat. Cool completely. Make Mascarpone Filling and Chocolate Ganache.

5. Cut each cake layer horizontally to make 2 layers. (To cut, mark side of cake with toothpicks and cut with long, thin serrated knife.) Brush about 1 tablespoon of the rum mixture over cut side of each layer; let stand 1 minute to soak into cake. Fill each layer with about ⅔ cup Mascarpone Filling. Frost side and top of cake with Chocolate Ganache. Store loosely covered in refrigerator.

12 to 16 servings.

Mascarpone Filling

2 tubs (8 ounces each) mascarpone cheese

1 cup powdered sugar

1 teaspoon vanilla extract

Beat all ingredients in medium bowl with electric mixer on low speed just until blended.

Chocolate Ganache

1½ cups semisweet chocolate chips

6 tablespoons butter (do not use margarine)

⅓ cup whipping (heavy) cream

Heat all ingredients in 1-quart saucepan over low heat, stirring frequently, until chips are melted and mixture is smooth. Refrigerate about 30 minutes, stirring occasionally, until slightly thickened.

1 Serving: Calories 665 (Calories from Fat 380); Fat 42g (Saturated 19g); Cholesterol 120mg; Sodium 560mg; Carbohydrate 64g (Dietary Fiber 30g); Protein 8g
% Daily Value: Vitamin A 18%; Vitamin C 0%; Calcium 10%; Iron 14%
Exchanges: 3 Starch, 1 Other Carbohydrate, 8 Fat
Carbohydrate Choices: 4

BETTY'S TIPS

✪ **Substitution**
Instead of the rum, you can use 1 tablespoon rum extract plus enough water to measure ⅓ cup. The mild, delicate flavor of mascarpone really has no match. But if you can't find it, softened cream cheese makes a good substitute.

✪ **Success Hint**
If the cake has been refrigerated, let it stand at room temperature for 30 minutes, so it will be easier to cut.

✪ **Special Touch**
Dress up the top of this decadently dark chocolate cake with dollops of whipped cream and chocolate-covered espresso beans.

Deep Dark Mocha Torte

Raspberry-Fudge Fantasy Torte

Prep: 35 min Bake: 40 min Cool: 1 hr 15 min
(Photo on page 271)

1	package Betty Crocker SuperMoist chocolate fudge cake mix
$1^1/_3$	cups water
$^1/_2$	cup butter or margarine, softened
3	eggs
$^2/_3$	cup miniature semisweet chocolate chips
3	cups whipping (heavy) cream
$^1/_3$	cup powdered sugar
$1^1/_2$	cups fresh raspberries
$^1/_3$	cup seedless raspberry preserves
$1^1/_2$	cups miniature semisweet chocolate chips

1. Heat oven to 350°. Grease bottoms and sides of 2 round pans, 8 × $1^1/_2$ or 9 × $1^1/_2$ inches, with shortening; lightly flour.

2. Beat cake mix, water, butter and eggs in large bowl with electric mixer on low speed 1 minute, scraping bowl constantly. Stir in $^2/_3$ cup chocolate chips; pour into pans.

3. Bake 8-inch rounds 35 to 40 minutes, 9-inch rounds 30 to 35 minutes, or until toothpick inserted in center comes out clean. Cool 15 minutes. Run knife around sides of pans to loosen cakes; remove from pans to wire rack. Cool completely, about 1 hour.

4. Beat whipping cream and powdered sugar in chilled large bowl with electric mixer on high speed until soft peaks form. Gently stir together 1 cup of the raspberries and the preserves in medium bowl; fold in $1^1/_2$ cups of the whipped cream.

5. Cut each cake layer horizontally to make 2 layers. (To cut, mark side of cake with toothpicks and cut with long, thin serrated knife.) Place 1 layer, cut side up, on serving plate; spread with about $^3/_4$ cup raspberry-cream mixture. Repeat with second and third layers. Top with remaining layer. Frost side and top of cake with remaining whipped cream. Arrange remaining $^1/_2$ cup raspberries over top of cake. Press $1^1/_2$ cups chocolate chips into side of cake. Store loosely covered in refrigerator.

12 to 16 servings.
1 Serving: Calories 660 (Calories from Fat 370); Fat 41g (Saturated 23g); Cholesterol 140mg; Sodium 480mg; Carbohydrate 66g (Dietary Fiber 4g); Protein 6g
% Daily Value: Vitamin A 20%; Vitamin C 8%; Calcium 12%; Iron 14%
Exchanges: 2 Starch, 2 Other Carbohydrate, $8^1/_2$ Fat
Carbohydrate Choices: 4

BETTY'S TIPS

✿ **Success Hint**
Raspberries are delicate little gems. Be sure to look for brightly colored and plump berries with no signs of mold. You can store raspberries, in a single layer if possible, in the refrigerator up to 3 days. To prevent them from becoming mushy, rinse lightly just before using. Wait to add the raspberries to the top until just before serving. If you place them on the frosting too soon, some of their color may "bleed" into the frosting.

✿ **Variation**
Try an almond-flavored frosting and filling. Simply add 1 teaspoon almond extract to the whipping cream and powdered sugar before beating in step 4.

helpful **nutrition** and **cooking** information

nutrition guidelines

We provide nutrition information for each recipe that includes calories, fat, cholesterol, sodium, carbohydrate, fiber and protein. Individual food choices can be based on this information.

Recommended intake for a daily diet of 2,000 calories as set by the Food and Drug Administration

Total Fat	Less than 65g
Saturated Fat	Less than 20g
Cholesterol	Less than 300mg
Sodium	Less than 2,400mg
Total Carbohydrate	300g
Dietary Fiber	25g

criteria used for calculating nutrition information

- The first ingredient was used wherever a choice is given (such as ⅓ cup sour cream or plain yogurt).
- The first ingredient amount was used wherever a range is given (such as 3- to 3½–pound cut-up broiler-fryer chicken).
- The first serving number was used wherever a range is given (such as 4 to 6 servings).
- "If desired" ingredients and recipe variations were not included (such as sprinkle with brown sugar, if desired).
- Only the amount of a marinade or frying oil that is estimated to be absorbed by the food during preparation or cooking was calculated.

ingredients used in recipe testing and nutrition calculations

- Ingredients used for testing represent those that the majority of consumers use in their homes: large eggs, 2% milk, 80%-lean ground beef, canned ready-to-use chicken broth and vegetable oil spread containing not less than 65 percent fat.

- Fat-free, low-fat or low-sodium products were not used, unless otherwise indicated.

- Solid vegetable shortening (not butter, margarine, nonstick cooking sprays or vegetable oil spread because they can cause sticking problems) was used to grease pans, unless otherwise indicated.

equipment used in recipe testing

We use equipment for testing that the majority of consumers use in their homes. If a specific piece of equipment (such as a wire whisk) is necessary for recipe success, it is listed in the recipe.

- Cookware and bakeware without nonstick coatings were used, unless otherwise indicated.

- No dark-colored, black or insulated bakeware was used.

- When a pan is specified in a recipe, a metal pan was used; a baking dish or pie plate means ovenproof glass was used.

- An electric hand mixer was used for mixing only when mixer speeds are specified in the recipe directions. When a mixer speed is not given, a spoon or fork was used.

cooking terms glossary

Beat: Mix ingredients vigorously with spoon, fork, wire whisk, hand beater or electric mixer until smooth and uniform.

Boil: Heat liquid until bubbles rise continuously and break on the surface and steam is given off. For rolling boil, the bubbles form rapidly.

Chop: Cut into coarse or fine irregular pieces with a knife, food chopper, blender or food processor.

Cube: Cut into squares ½ inch or larger.

Dice: Cut into squares smaller than ½ inch.

Grate: Cut into tiny particles using small rough holes of grater (citrus peel or chocolate).

Grease: Rub the inside surface of a pan with shortening, using pastry brush, piece of waxed paper or paper towel, to prevent food from sticking during baking (as for some casseroles).

Julienne: Cut into thin, matchlike strips, using knife or food processor (vegetables, fruits, meats).

Mix: Combine ingredients in any way that distributes them evenly.

Sauté: Cook foods in hot oil or margarine over medium-high heat with frequent tossing and turning motion.

Shred: Cut into long thin pieces by rubbing food across the holes of a shredder, as for cheese, or by using a knife to slice very thinly, as for cabbage.

Simmer: Cook in liquid just below the boiling point on top of the stove; usually after reducing heat from a boil. Bubbles will rise slowly and break just below the surface.

Stir: Mix ingredients until uniform consistency. Stir once in a while for stirring occasionally, often for stirring frequently and continuously for stirring constantly.

Toss: Tumble ingredients (such as green salad) lightly with a lifting motion, usually to coat evenly or mix with another food.

metric conversion chart

Volume

U.S. Units	Canadian Metric	Australian Metric
¼ teaspoon	1 mL	1 ml
½ teaspoon	2 mL	2 ml
1 teaspoon	5 mL	5 ml
1 tablespoon	15 mL	20 ml
¼ cup	50 mL	60 ml
⅓ cup	75 mL	80 ml
½ cup	125 mL	125 ml
⅔ cup	150 mL	170 ml
¾ cup	175 mL	190 ml
1 cup	250 mL	250 ml
1 quart	1 liter	1 liter
1½ quarts	1.5 liters	1.5 liters
2 quarts	2 liters	2 liters
2½ quarts	2.5 liters	2.5 liters
3 quarts	3 liters	3 liters
4 quarts	4 liters	4 liters

Weight

U.S. Units	Canadian Metric	Australian Metric
1 ounce	30 grams	30 grams
2 ounces	55 grams	60 grams
3 ounces	85 grams	90 grams
4 ounces (¼ pound)	115 grams	125 grams
8 ounces (½ pound)	225 grams	225 grams
16 ounces (1 pound)	455 grams	500 grams
1 pound	455 grams	½ kilogram

Measurements

Inches	Centimeters
1	2.5
2	5.0
3	7.5
4	10.0
5	12.5
6	15.0
7	17.5
8	20.5
9	23.0
10	25.5
11	28.0
12	30.5
13	33.0

Temperatures

Fahrenheit	Celsius
32°	0°
212°	100°
250°	120°
275°	140°
300°	150°
325°	160°
350°	180°
375°	190°
400°	200°
425°	220°
450°	230°
475°	240°
500°	260°

Note: The recipes in this cookbook have not been developed or tested using metric measures. When converting recipes to metric, some variations in quality may be noted.

Index

Note: <u>Underscored</u> page references indicate boxed text or sidebars. **Boldfaced** page references indicate photographs.

S